Understanding the Older Consumer
The grey market

Barrie Gunter

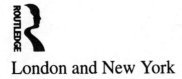

London and New York

First published 1998 by Routledge
2 Park Square, Milton Park, Abingdon, Oxon, OX14 4RN

Simultaneously published in the USA and Canada
by Routledge
270 Madison Ave, New York NY 10016

Transferred to Digital Printing 2006

Typeset in Times by Keystroke, Jacaranda Lodge, Wolverhampton

British Library Cataloguing in Publication Data
A catalogue record for this book is available from the British Library

Library of Congress Cataloging in Publication Data
A catalogue record for this book has been requested

ISBN 0–415–18643–9 (hbk)
ISBN 0–415–18644–7 (pbk)

Contents

Tables

Understanding the Older Consumer

Demographic trends in Western industrialised nations show an increasing proportion of people over 50 who are also an active consumer group. They have more money to enjoy themselves due to more widespread occupational pensions and freedom from the financial burdens of mortgages and child rearing, whilst better medical care, diet and fitness mean that they are physically capable of more youthful behaviour than earlier generations. With the growth in early retirement or semi-retirement, the 'grey market' also has more time to devote to non-working pursuits.

Long stigmatised by unfavourable stereotypes and a lack of informed knowledge, this population subgroup must be understood better by marketers and advertisers wishing to manufacture, distribute and sell products to this important market segment. *Understanding the Older Consumer* examines the demographic and psychographic characteristics of the market, the consumer-related behaviours of the over-50s and how to market and research this consumer category. It shows it to be a complex group with varied psychological characteristics, patterns and interests. Older consumers have different financial circumstances, consumer tastes and key motivations. They show varying reactions to marketing and advertising messages.

In a world of increasing competitiveness between products and services, *Understanding the Older Consumer* provides a valuable tool for those wishing to develop marketing campaigns and retail services that more comprehensively represent the needs and wishes of this group.

Barrie Gunter is a psychologist and Professor of Journalism at the University of Sheffield. He has written over 30 books on various media, marketing and management topics and conducted his own widespread research on media and advertising issues.

International Series in Social Psychology
Edited by W. Peter Robinson
University of Bristol, UK

This series provides a showcase of original contributions of the highest quality, as well as thorough reviews of existing theories suitable for advanced students and researchers. Many will be useful as course texts for higher level study; applied topics are well represented and social psychology is defined broadly to include other psychological areas like social development, or the social psychology of abnormal behaviour. A reflection of contemporary social psychology, the series is a rich source of information for dissertations, new research projects and seminars.

Recent books in this series:

Adjustment of Adolescents
Cross-cultural similarities and differences
Ruth Scott and W.A. Scott

Adolescence from Crisis to Coping
A thirteen nation study
Janice Gibson-Cline

Changing European Identities
Social psychological analyses of social change
Glynis M. Breakwell and Evanthia Lyons

Children as Consumers
A psychological analysis of the young people's market
Barrie Gunter and Adrian Furnham

Making Sense of Television
The psychology of audience interpretation (2nd edition)
Sonia Livingstone

Social Groups and Identities
Exploring the legacy of Henri Tajfel
Edited by W. Peter Robinson

Stereotypes During the Decline and Fall of Communism
György Hunyady

1 The importance of the older consumer

Changing demographic profiles in modern industrialised countries mean that increasing proportions of their populations will fall into older age bands, above the age of 50. While older people are often stigmatised with negative stereotypes regarding their physical and mental capacities, they represent a segment of the population which has increasing economic significance. For long ignored by marketers, older consumers cannot be dismissed as a politically and socially insignificant homogeneous group with negligible spending power. Instead, traditional concepts of ageing need to be rethought as the over-50s evolve into an increasingly dynamic consumer group.

This book will examine the phenomenon of the 'grey market', the segment of the population aged 50 and over and its consumer-related activities. It will adopt a mainly psychological approach to its analysis, although drawing occasionally on sociological and anthropological theory or research in reviewing evidence on older consumers' lifestyles, leisure and media-related activities and consumption. It will explore what is known about the way this age-band has been represented in the media, and how the image of this demographic group is changing. It will also examine how people over 50 respond to marketing and advertising messages and are influenced by such messages in their consumerism.

THEORIES OF AGEING

Before beginning this review, it may be helpful, in setting the scene, to examine some of the established theories about ageing. These theories reflect different conceptions about what it is to grow old and what might be expected of those who do in terms of the way they conduct themselves and live their lives. Key theories include disengagement theory, activity theory, development theory, continuity theory, exchange theory and labelling theory.

Disengagement theory represents one of the earliest theoretical perspectives which postulated that ageing involves a gradual withdrawal or disengagement of the individual from certain social roles in order to clear the way for other, younger people to come through. Such withdrawal in its ultimate form is regarded as a period of preparation for death. The individual plays fewer social roles and experiences a deterioration in both the quality and quantity of their relationships. Disengagement therefore implies a triple loss for the individual: a loss of roles, a restriction of social contacts and relationships, and a reduced commitment to social mores and values. Central to this theory is the assumption that both the individual and the wider society benefit from the process. Withdrawal for the individual may mean a release from social pressures which stress productivity, competition and continued achievement. For society, the withdrawal of older members provides openings for younger individuals to take over the roles which need to be filled.

There is little sound empirical evidence to support the opinion that the withdrawal of older people from the workforce and other social roles is necessarily and invariably for the good of the social system. Such a step may result in the removal of some of the most knowledgeable and experienced members of society. Some writers have argued that disengagement theory was used to avoid confronting and dealing with issues surrounding ageing and the problems that older people may pose for society (Blau 1973). It forms a justification for social policies which segregate older people and treat them separately from other less advantaged groups (Estes, Swan and Gerard 1982).

In contrast to the notion of disengagement is *activity theory*, which proposes that successful ageing is to be obtained through preserving, for as long as possible, the attitudes and activities of middle age (Havighurst 1963). While some changes in activities are to be expected with age, whether these occur in a person's professional life, social life or private life, it is important to remain active in other ways. Maintaining an outlook on life which is distinctly middle-aged rather than old aged, an individual can sustain a higher level of personal morale and general satisfaction with life. The maintenance of social networks can play a key part in achieving this objective. Although this theory reflects an outlook on growing older which can be found increasingly, especially among the more affluent older persons, it does not explain what happens to those who fail to sustain a middle-aged outlook.

Holding on to an earlier life stage for as long as possible may be one strategy for not growing old too soon, but for some writers, successful adaptation at each stage of life depends upon what happened during earlier life stages. *Development theory* represents a perspective which regards life as a continuous process of development, from birth until death. Perhaps the best developed theory of this type is Erikson's (1950), who describes life as being composed of eight phases: early infancy, late infancy, early childhood, late childhood, adolescence, late adolescence, the productive years and later life. At each phase, individuals must acquire certain understanding and competencies which will equip them to cope effectively with the next phase. Old age is a time when the individual takes stock of his or her life and must come to terms with what has or has not been achieved during their life and with the changing circumstances which accompany retirement and the inevitable losses of people close to them. How a person adapts to this final stage of life is dependent on developmental processes which occurred during earlier life phases. If the individual has treated each new life stage as offering a challenge, this attitude is likely to prevail into later life. Such an attitude can be expected to keep an older person more 'youthful' in many respects.

A similar view of life development is offered by *continuity theory*, which regards ageing as a process of continuing development. However, there is a growing tendency among people as they get older to try harder to maintain stability in their lives. New challenges may be relished, but most of all, according to this theory, individuals strive to preserve activities, tastes and a preferred lifestyle acquired over time. Retirement is regarded as a problem period for the individual who must come to terms with occupational role loss and the direction and goals which accompany that role. Disengagement is not seen as the most desirable reaction to this state of affairs. Instead, individuals need to become active in other ways. Finding new interests and goals lies at the centre of healthy and positive adjustment to this later stage of life.

The importance, in older age, of maintaining a social network and a body of activity which continue to give life purpose represented a core part of activity theory. This view that a person must strive to remain integrated as fully as possible with groups and events in the social environment, even when retired from working life, is elaborated upon more fully in *exchange theory* (Mauss 1954; Simmons 1945). Under exchange theory, however, as ageing takes place social interaction may decrease, or it becomes more selective and more targeted. In the pursuit of goals, whether professional or social, individuals seek out relationships which will be useful to them. Where the costs incurred by an individual in establishing or maintaining a relationship outweigh the benefits, the individual will gradually invest less and less time and effort in it. Where one individual values the rewards to be gained from a relationship more than another, there is an imbalance in terms of exchanged benefits. Power derives from this imbalance, whereby the individual who values the relationship less achieves a stronger position. For older people, this imbalance of power in interpersonal relationships may become more prevalent, gradually causing their interactions with others to diminish (Dowd 1980). For effective adaptation and coping during later stages of life, it is clearly necessary to maintain sufficient balance in a network of satisfying relationships, to avoid a significant diminution in the individual's perceived personal social 'power'.

Finally, another conception of ageing derives from *labelling theory* which posits that old age is socially defined and often labelled as a 'deviant' condition. Older people thus become stigmatised in a way which places them potentially at a disadvantage across a wide range of social relationships and interactions. Older people may be more susceptible than other age-groups to negative stereotyping which labels them as worn-out, over-the-hill, ineffectual, dependent and therefore socially (and perhaps politically) insignificant. Not only are such labels used by younger people, but they may become conditioned into the self-perceptions of older people. If older people become convinced of their own inadequacies, they may in turn live up (or perhaps 'down') to them (Kuypers and Bengtson 1973). This model of negative labelling can be turned on its head, however, to produce a strategy for inculcating a more positive view of older age both among the age-group itself and among people in general. This can be achieved by recognising that a person's status does not (or should not) depend simply upon their economic position or the type of occupation they have. Improvements could be made in the services offered to older people and to the environmental conditions in which many of the poorer older persons live. The self-confidence and self-determination of older people could be boosted by presenting more positive images of ageing and by providing opportunities for this age segment to establish new life goals and the means to have a greater say in the management of their lives.

AGEING AND CONSUMERISM

Contrary to popular belief, older consumers are not mainly poor consumers. Indeed, on average, they are no more likely to be poor than their younger counterparts. In the United States in 1984, 14.7 per cent of people aged under 65 were at or beneath the poverty level, while for those aged 65 or over the comparable percentage was 12.4 per cent (Burnett 1991). Discretionary buying power among the over-50s was greater than among the under-50s (French and Fox 1985; Linden 1986). This spending power derives significantly from reduced expenses on child-rearing, paying off home or car loans, and the maturation of insurance policies (Allan 1984; Gelb 1978). By the mid-1980s, for example, around three-quarters of individuals aged 65 or over owned their own homes and among these, well over four-fifths had no mortgage to repay (Lazer and Shaw 1987). Not only do older consumers have greater spending power than other age-defined market segments, they are more willing to spend than ever before (Petre 1986).

Older consumers of today are not sedentary and retiring individuals who have withdrawn from the mainstream of a previously active lifestyle. They are involved and far younger in their outlook and activities than were their pre-decessors two generations ago. They are not the helpless, infirm dependants of our society; their members include heads of state, government leaders, chairmen of major corporations, and other people of stature, affluence and influence. The myth of poor health permeating the older consumers' market should now be dispelled. Although some individuals do suffer physical limitations, these are neither as serious nor as widespread as many popular stereotypes would imply. Most older people tend to describe their health as good or excellent when asked to compare it with others of their own age (Schewe 1985). While negative stereotypes of older people are generally misleading and untrue, they do acknowledge that, in many ways, people in later years have been regarded as comprising a specific sub-culture (Rose and Peterson 1965). This outcome is thought to be the almost inevitable consequence of any group whose members interact more often with individuals of their own kind than with anyone else. The sub-culture view, however, fails to reflect the fact that older people comprise a highly diverse group. In some cases, older people maintain considerable prestige and power in areas such as politics, law or business. Additionally, though poverty is common in old age, by no means all of those who can be included as members of the 'grey market' are poor (Falkingham and Victor 1991; Walker 1980).

Stages of life and consumption

A person's age is a poor indicator of their capacity and worth as an individual. To tag a person with the label 'old' because they have reached a certain chronological age, whether it is 60, 70 or 80, has little meaning. 'Ages', representing stages of life, may have more relevance in the consumer context, and are becoming increasing preferred as an impartial classifier of individuals, as this book will show. The onset of older age is marked most significantly not by a sudden decline into senility, but by the end of paid work or the completion of family-raising (although the last point is not always true). These activities constitute the 'Second Age', following the 'First Age' of childhood and socialisation. Earlier retirement and improved health have resulted in increasing, and now substantial, numbers of people who have entered the 'Third Age' of independent and still active life beyond work and familial tasks, which may continue for a long period prior to the 'Fourth Age' of decline, dependence and death.

The onset of the Third Age can vary from one individual to the next. For some it may begin at 50, while for others it may not start until the age of 70 or even later. Thus, chronological age alone does not mean inactivity or that a person is 'old'. For some interests and activities, such as voting, cultural affairs, the arts, fine foods, luxury cruises and five-star hotels, the older age-groups are among the most important participants.

The older consumers' market is among the least intensively researched and understood of market segments. Disagreement exists about both the age brackets that comprise this market and the terms used to describe them. Sometimes a classification of 65 and over is used, since that often marks the age of retirement. Sometimes a classification of 60 and over is adopted, indicating the decline in physical and mental skills. At other times, a classification of 55 and over is used because that represents consumers who have entered the pre-retirement years. Increasingly, however, early retirement may mean entry into a 'Third Age' as young as 50. The grey market can therefore be taken to mean those individuals aged 50 and over, who may be in the retirement or pre-retirement phase of their lives. A variety of terms have been used to describe consumers in this age-group, such as older consumers, oldsters, senior citizens, the elderly, old-agers, geriatric population, retirees, and maturities. Many of these terms are either patronising or simply inappropriate given the nature of many people in this section of the population, and particularly those at the younger end of this age spectrum. For the purposes of this book, reference will be made to 'older consumers' since that seems best to fit what these people are.

Some of the marketing misconceptions held about the grey market were succinctly listed by Loudon and Della Bitta (1993):

1 Older consumers are all the same. (Actually this is not a monolithic market at all, but rather one comprised of numerous segments.)
2 They think of themselves as old. ('Older age' is typically 15 years older than they are, and doesn't begin until well past 70.)
3 They aren't an important consumer segment. (Those 50 and over possess almost half of all American discretionary income and account for almost one-third of spending on refrigerators, floor coverings, new cars, jewelry, and groceries.)
4 They won't try something new. (A survey for Golding and Company found that in the preceding 12 months 45 per cent had tried a new brand of cereal and 30 per cent had tried a new canned soup and soft drinks brand.)
5 They have impaired mental faculties. (Only about five per cent have serious mental impairment. Moreover, intelligence tests reveal little change from age 51 to 80.)
6 They are in poor health. (Most are not incapacitated and will remain healthy until their last years.)
7 They keep to themselves. (Many are sexually active, are involved as volunteers, and are taking on new responsibilities.)
8 They aren't physically active. (A recent Gallup poll revealed half of those 65 and over regularly engage in exercise.)

(1993: 156)

The significance of the older consumer stems from the fact that there has been a growth in the market potential of the 'grey' population. This has occurred because of increased numbers of people in this age bracket, an upward shift in income and wealth, and enhanced expectations of older people. Increasing 'grey' income has been emerging from occupational pensions, asset holding, capital gains on property, and windfalls (Johnson 1990). Better health has resulted in a more active older population who wish to maximise the enjoyment they derive from their free time.

With their children having left home, and their mortgages paid off, empty nesters in modern western societies may have plenty of disposable income, particularly before retirement. For many years, this fact went unnoticed by marketing and advertising people whose eyes were fixed firmly on the under-35s and under-44s. Now that many older people are inheriting property from their parents and average life expectancy is increasing, the over-50s can no longer be ignored.

THE DEMOGRAPHIC SHIFT

To appreciate the importance of changes in the number of older people, it is important to grasp the magnitude of the demographic restructuring now under way in the developed economies. The high birth rates of the post-war baby-boom, followed by the very low fertility, or 'baby-bust', of the 1970s and 1980s, has produced populations that are ageing and, in many countries, declining in size.

In 1990, 32 million people in 20 million households in the USA were aged 65 or over, representing 13 per cent of the total population of the country. Each census during the twentieth century has indicated that the elderly make up an increasingly larger share of the population generally. If current trends continue, those 65 or over will account for 22 per cent of the US population by 2030.

Johnson and Falkingham (1992) explain the context in which the demographic transition characterising the population developments in most western countries has occurred:

1   An initial stage with high levels of fertility and mortality and low population growth rates. The population has a 'youthful' age profile with a high proportion of young people and relatively few older persons.
2   Mortality rates begin to fall in the second stage while fertility levels remain at a high level. Thus, the natural rate of population growth rises and so too does the size of the population. If the improvement in mortality is concentrated at younger ages the population structure may become younger at this stage.
3   Now fertility rates also begin to decline. The rate of population growth starts to trail off and the proportion of the population who are elderly begins to increase.
4   Fertility and mortality reach equilibrium. Population growth is again low and could be approaching zero. The age structure of the population stabilises with a relatively high proportion of elderly people.

(1992: 22)

Expectation of life at birth is an important indicator. Mortality levels have fallen since the middle of the nineteenth century. People born in 1991 in Britain could expect to live 20 years longer on average than those who were born in 1901. This is largely down to lower infant mortality rates. Looking at the British population since the beginning of the twentieth century, the size of the elderly population has risen in absolute terms by over 400 per cent – from 2.2 million in 1900 to approximately 10.5 million in 1991. Over the same period, the proportion of children aged under 16 years in the British population has fallen from 35 per cent to 20 per cent.

The populations of western industrialised societies have thus been growing steadily older. In 1790 the median age in America was 16. In 1990 it was 33. By the middle of the next century it will be over 40, or maybe even 50. The trend in other developed countries is much the same. The median age in England and Wales in 1901 was 24 years, by 1931 it had risen to just over 30 years, and in 1981 it was nearly 35 years. By the end of the first decade of the next century it is projected to rise further to around 40 (Johnson and Falkingham 1992).

Such shifts in the age composition of the population are being experienced by countries all around the world. In most other developed countries, the proportion of the population aged 65 and over has increased dramatically since the beginning of the twentieth century (Scott and Johnson 1988). Indeed, in many developed countries the percentage of older persons has more than doubled. The United Nations has indicated that any population with more than 7 per cent of the people in it aged over 65 is an 'aged population'. One analysis found that by the late 1980s, 14 advanced countries qualified for this label (Scott and Johnson 1988).

If being middle-aged or older becomes the norm rather than the exception, the definition of 'old' will have to be revisited. The standard retirement ages of 60 or 65 are no longer widely regarded as a watershed for declining health and energy. The widespread silent assumption that 'old' means 'decrepit' will have to be abandoned or at least moved up the age scale by a couple of decades. Affluent older consumers will become an irresistible market for everything from cars to credit cards, all customised to suit their target group's tastes.

THE WORKING POPULATION

Analysis of working population data (for the 15–64 age band) in six leading OECD countries, with the size of this population in 1990 set equal to 100, has revealed an important trend (see Table 1.1). Since the Second World War all these countries have experienced an increase in their working population, but in the decades to come this trend will be interrupted or reversed.

In the United States, population growth will slow down and then stop in 25 years time; in France and Britain the working population is already stagnant and will begin to decline within a couple of decades. In Japan, Germany and Italy the number of workers is already falling, and the decline is gathering pace.

Over the next 50 years, the working population of the European Community is projected to fall by 20 per cent to 45 million people. For the first time in over 200 years the potential European market will be shrinking, and success may in future be measured in terms of the lowest rate of market contraction rather than the highest rate of market growth. This trend is illustrated in Table 1.2 which shows the changing age profile of the labour force in Britain (Office for National Statistics 1996). The numbers in the 16 to 24 age-group are projected to decline over the next few years compared with ten or even five years ago. Meanwhile, numbers in the 45 to 59 and 60 to 64 age-ranges will show a marked increase.

Table 1.1 Index of working age (15–64) population

Country	1950	1980	1990	2000	2010	2020	2030	2040	2050
France	75.1	94.0	**100**	101.7	104.4	100.0	94.9	90.5	88.5
Germany	79.1	96.5	**100**	95.0	88.6	80.7	68.2	61.2	58.2
Italy	79.0	94.3	**100**	97.9	95.5	90.0	81.0	72.8	69.6
Japan	57.6	91.3	**100**	99.2	94.1	90.8	88.6	83.2	81.7
UK	90.7	96.4	**100**	99.9	101.5	101.1	97.4	95.7	95.2
US	60.3	91.9	**100**	108.1	116.0	115.8	113.5	115.7	118.0

Source: Labour Force Survey, Office for National Statistics 1996

Table 1.2 Age profile of the British labour force

		Age-groups				All
	16–24	25–44	45–59	60–64	65+	aged 16+
			Millions			
Estimates						
1984	6,214	12,201	7,077	1,252	429	27,172
1986	6,326	12,788	6,968	1,083	402	27,566
1991	5,684	14,256	7,311	1,102	462	28,815
1992	5,224	14,192	7,596	1,069	501	28,582
1993	4,941	14,258	7,742	1,070	443	28,454
1994	4,710	14,301	7,922	1,051	437	28,421
Projections						
1996	4,404	14,609	8,227	1,049	429	28,717
2001	4,313	14,893	8,748	1,105	409	29,469
2003	4,519	14,609	9,252	1,295	416	30,092

Source: Labour Force Survey, Office for National Statistics 1996

In the shorter term, through the 1990s, changes in the overall size of the European market will be less important than awareness of changes in the number of people in different age-groups. This is because the age structure of Britain and Europe is changing sharply. Attention has tended to focus on the bottom end of the age spectrum because of the decline by 25 per cent (from 800,000 to 600,000) in the number of 16-year-olds in Britain between 1987 and 1993. However, numbers in other age-groups are changing too, and these changes present both market problems and market opportunities. The population of the EC will be virtually stagnant throughout the 1990s (though numbers will be falling in Belgium, Germany and Italy). But within this general picture there are dramatic age-group variations.

The teenager (15–19) and young adult (20–24) populations will fall by 22 per cent and 26 per cent respectively, but this does not mean that there will be a simple shift in demand from the young to the old. The booming teenager and young adult markets of the 1960s/1970s is a thing of the past: the new growth area will be people in late middle age, the 'grey' population, who have hitherto largely been ignored or deliberately avoided in marketing campaigns.

The term 'late middle age' is vague because there is no consensus about how this older population should be defined in age terms, or what it should be called. 'Older person', 'senior citizens', 'pensioners' are all inappropriate because, aside from the pejorative overtones, they refer primarily or exclusively to people over pension age, and much of the most significant population change will affect age-groups under pension age, but over 50. Another reason for using a deliberately vague term to describe this population is to incorporate the very different patterns of age restructuring now taking place in European Community countries, and which are, therefore, of direct relevance to anyone with an eye on pan-European marketing opportunities.

National patterns of ageing and old age vary greatly. Findings reported by Victor (1994) indicated that people in Sweden had a higher life expectancy than those in any other European country; almost every fifth Swede (18 per cent) was found to be 65 or over. The German-speaking countries also showed a profile of high expectancy. They constituted the largest market of older consumers in Europe: about 15 million people aged over 65, most of them relatively well off and in good health, and with active lifestyles. The UK, France and Italy also had high age expectancies.

The majority of older people are less of a strain on the medical system than most people believe. Medical costs do not rise in proportion to the number of years people live. For most, it is only the very last year of life that entails the high medical costs, and each individual generally has only one such year. Dividing people into those in their 50s, 60s and 70+, the next decade in Europe will see an increase of 20 per cent in the number of people in their 50s in the UK. In Germany, this age-group was projected to decline by 5 per cent. France, Germany and Italy, will, however, experience substantial increases in the number of people over 70. By the end of the century, one in five of the UK population will be over 60 years of age. They will therefore number 12 out of 59 million, with about 7.5 million falling into the 60 to 75 range and 4.5 million being over 75 years. Placed within the context of a largely static overall European population, the expansion of any age-group must be perceived as providing a new market opportunity.

LONGER LIFE AND ITS LUXURIES

In the world's rich countries, when you retire at 65 you can expect to live, on average, for another 15 or 20 years. A hundred years ago you would, on average, have been already dead. The late twentieth century has brought to many the ultimate gift: the luxury of ageing. Like any other luxury, ageing is expensive. Governments are fretting about the cost already; but they know that worse is to come. Over the next 30 or 40 years, the demographic changes of longer lives and fewer births will force most countries to rethink in fundamental ways their arrangements for paying for and looking after older people.

In 1990, 18 per cent of people in OECD countries were aged over 60. By 2030 that figure will have risen to over 30 per cent. The share of the 'oldest old' (those over 80), now around 3 per cent, is set to double. The vast majority of these older people will be consumers, not producers. Thanks to state transfers, being old in developed countries mostly no longer means being poor. The old people will expect decent pensions to live on; they will make heavy demands on medical services; and some will need expensive nursing care.

Mass survival to a ripe old age will not be confined to rich countries. Most developing countries, whose populations are now much younger than the developed world's, are starting to age fast. In Latin America and most of Asia, the share of over-60s is set to double between now and 2030, to 14 per cent. In China, it will increase from less than 10 per cent now to around 22 per cent in 2030, thanks partly to the government's stringent population-control measures. Only Africa is likely to remain exuberantly young right through to the middle of the next century, though AIDS may reduce population growth in some countries.

In poor countries, old people usually work on until frailty or ill health force them to stop. Most of them have no means of support or care other than, with luck, their families. But as countries become richer, more people are covered by formal retirement schemes; worldwide, about 40 per cent of the labour force are members of formal schemes of any kind, whereas in high-income countries nearly all workers and their dependants are included.

The position in rich countries

In many countries, older people are still too small in number, and for the most part too politically passive, to act as an effective pressure group for long-term policies to further their own interests. But that is changing as their numbers increase, and they learn to flex their political muscles.

America offers a foretaste of things to come. The American Association of Retired Persons (AARP), set up in 1958, is a highly effective lobbying organisation employing some 1,700 people, including 15 full-time lobbyists in Washington. With 33 million members, it can afford a lot for its $8-a-year subscription: insurance services, credit cards, discounts, low-price prescription medicines, motoring plans, advice of all kinds, even a training programme to help hard-up over-55s find jobs. Other, smaller organisations – such as the Seniors Coalition – are competing for the grey market.

In other rich countries they are not as lively – yet; in Japan, older men are too busy working on beyond retirement age to spend time politicking. In Europe most people retire early, but still show little interest in joining pressure groups. Organisations such as Age Concern in Britain have more of a charitable image, providing help and information for older people, although they do campaign on issues such as old-age poverty.

According to a Europe-wide poll, over three-quarters of the European Union's pensioners think their governments do not do enough for older people; 22 per cent feel so strongly that they would join a political party formed to further their interests. Prominent among these interests are pensions, health care, long-term care and (for those who are still working, or would like to be) jobs.

Capacity to consume

The capacity to consume depends critically upon disposable rather than gross income. Some households may exhibit significantly higher total incomes than others, but may have less spending power than households with smaller total incomes if their basic outgoings and expenses account for a substantial proportion of that income. Thus, upon retiring, individuals would normally expect to experience a drop in basic income. However, those who are able to more than compensate for this through a marked reduction in such expenses as mortgages, raising children, and certain other home-related bills, could witness their disposable income actually increase.

Among people aged 50 and over, a wide-ranging spread of gross and disposable income levels may be found. The 'grey market' does not comprise a homogeneous mass of individuals. Among the characteristics in terms of which they can be differentiated is their capacity to consume. The tenor of this book is that older consumers represent a significant market which has, to date, largely been under-estimated, inadequately catered for or simply ignored in many marketing circles. The growth in size of this population segment and increased spending power to be found among certain sections of it, mean that for many kinds of products and services the over-50s represent a significant buying force.

The increasing market potential and spending propensity of the older, better-off sector, however, does not mean that the over-50s age-group is a universally affluent market segment. As with other age-groups, a considerable degree of poverty can be found among older people. By the early 1990s, for example, just over one in five (21 per cent) of people in Britain were over pension age, and comprised nearly three out of ten of those living on incomes on or below the income support level, the official standard of poverty (Walker 1993). In 1989, just under one-third of pensioners were living on incomes at or below the poverty line compared with less than one-fifth (17 per cent) of those under pension age. Not only does poverty affect a substantial proportion of older people, but when it does it is likely to be an enduring experience. For many years, a substantial number of long-term supplementary benefit claimants have been found among pensioners (Walker 1993).

On the basis of this sort of evidence, therefore, some writers have challenged the view that pensioners generally are better off these days (Walker 1993). Some may well be, but others are not. Whether they are or not depends upon the sources of income available to them. Even so, in a general sense members of the grey market, including those of retirement age, have been found to be better off today than they were 30 years ago, despite the fact that some of them remain on relatively low incomes. One analysis by the Department of Health and Social Security's Economic Advisers' office showed that between 1951 and 1984/95 pensioners' share of total disposable income in Britain (i.e. total income from earnings, savings, investment, pensions and other social security benefits) increased from 7 per cent to 15 per cent (DHSS 1985). The reasons for this improvement appeared to be twofold. First, there was a growth in the overall number of pensioners during this period, and second, there was an improvement in the disposable income of this age-group relative to non-pensioners. The latter change was accounted for by a slowing down in the growth of real disposable income among those below pension age caused mainly by the reduction of numbers in full-time employment, and also by the increased value of basic pensions relative to average earnings.

Further independent assessments confirmed the rising income trend among older people. One analysis reported that 45 per cent of married pensioners were in the bottom fifth in terms of net income in 1971, and this figure had fallen to 28 per cent in 1982. For single pensioners, the shift was even more dramatic; 43 per cent were among the poorest in 1971 compared with 22 per cent in 1982 (Bradshaw and O'Higgins 1984). These recent improvements in the relative incomes of retired people should not, according to some commentators, be interpreted to mean that all older people are better off (Walker 1993). The state pension declined in real value during the 1980s, after improving in earlier years. Some compensation can be found for this income loss among this demographic category as a function of the growing prevalence of occupational pensions, but many pensioners do not receive such income. By 1987, for example, 60 per cent of employed men and 35 per cent of employed women were in occupational schemes (an average overall of 49 per cent of employed people), compared with 43 per cent of men and 21 per cent of women (35 per cent overall) in 1956 (Johnson and Falkingham 1992).

Care must be taken over too readily accepting the validity of any assessment of the relative affluence or poverty of this group which can depend on the benchmark against which comparisons are made. In the case of state pensioners, for instance, such comparisons were once benchmarked against the average income position of people in full-time employment. After 1980, however, pensions were no longer linked to average earnings, but to the income position of other groups in poverty. On this basis, the position of pensioners could more easily be made to look favourable, when in real terms, state pensioners, along with other poverty groups, have become worse off (Walker 1993). Although state pensions have not increased significantly in value compared with average earnings, they have improved relative to other social security benefits, especially unemployment benefit.

Despite these caveats, there is clear evidence emerging to support the view that older people are better off. Indeed, for some older people, there has been a marked increase in wealth – giving rise to market segment concept of the 'Woopie', the well-off older person. As predicted by Titmuss (1955), distinct groups seem to have become well established at different ends of the income distribution, one of which is very well off, and the other much less so. This difference in income reflects income inequalities among different sections of the grey market, and particularly that section aged over the statutory retirement age. Underlying this growing inequality is the differential rate of increases in the various components of older people's incomes. For example, social security benefits rose by just 14 per cent in real terms between 1979 and 1988, compared with a 99 per cent increase for occupational pensions.

Occupational status not only determines salary level during working life, which itself can affect the capacity of the individual to save and accumulate wealth over time, which may then be enjoyed in later life, but may also affect the kind of pensionable income received once the individual enters retirement. Individuals who are dependent primarily on state benefits may have experienced some improvement in income over the years, but remain fixed at a low income level. Those whose working lives have afforded them opportunities to enter private welfare schemes in the form of occupational pensions may experience a standard of living which does not depart significantly from that they enjoyed while still working. Around half of the retired population in Britain today enjoy the benefits of occupational pensions. This index-related benefit means a secure income for life designed to keep pace with inflation and largely sustain the post-deductions income level enjoyed by the individual while in full-time employment. When coupled with reduced living expenses, this may leave even the retired person almost as well off as when they were working, and with more time to enjoy their disposable income.

Marketing opportunities

The extent of new market opportunities will depend not just on the numbers of people involved, but on the resources of this older population. There are various indicators which point to a grey population of increased affluence in the years ahead. If resources are defined in terms of income and wealth, free time, and good health, then it seems likely that the over-50s will witness an expansion in all three resource areas in the 1990s and beyond, continuing trends that are well established.

Taking income and wealth first, in Britain as in other European countries and North America, there has, in the last decade, been an upward shift in the age distribution of economic power. On almost any economic measure available, the young, particularly young people with families, have faced a deterioration in economic prospects through the 1980s; while the old have experienced an improvement. In all West European countries, the proportion of pensioners living in poverty has declined since the late 1970s, while the proportion of families with children living in poverty has increased.

For some years, in the United Kingdom, it has been generally acknowledged that the older population are better off than they have been before. The 1985 green paper on social security reform which first proposed the abolition of SERPS (Stated Earnings-Related Pension Scheme) as a result of fear of its rising cost due to the ageing of the population, also concluded that 'many pensioners are now as well off as workers with families' (DHSS 1985: 11).

The image of later life is changing, with many more of those individuals of retirement age enjoying a certain degree of affluence. People are retiring with higher incomes, large occupational pensions and, more than ever before, are likely to own assets in the form of their own home. The growth in services aimed specifically at older people such as package holidays, financial services, and private sheltered housing developments, are taken as indicative of the greater purchasing power and, therefore, affluence of older people.

It was noted in *Social Trends* in the mid-1980s that pensioners' share of the total personal disposable income in Britain had risen from 7 per cent in 1951 to 15 per cent in 1984/85, while the retired population had increased from 13.5 per cent to 18 per cent of the total population over the same period (Central Statistical Office 1986). This improvement was explained in terms of a rise in the real value of the state pension and a relative improvement in the position of a retired person's disposable income, which stood at around 70 per cent of a non-retired person's in 1985/86 compared with about 40 per cent in 1951.

This does not mean that all older people are high spenders and they are certainly not a homogeneous population. Pensioners over 75 are still poor relations to the working population, but pensioners aged 65 to 75 in Britain now have a per capita income slightly above the national average, and those aged 50 to 64 have a per capita income 20 per cent higher than the national average. This is particularly significant in Britain because it is the 50 to 60 age-group that will experience the greatest expansion in size in the 1990s; and this will make marketing to people in their 50s much more lucrative in Britain than in Italy or Germany, where this age-group will be stagnant or declining in size over the next decade.

These income improvements of older people are likely to be maintained or improved on in years to come, because an increasing proportion of their income is derived from occupational pensions: both the coverage of occupational pensions, and the value of pension payments, are rising for each generation of newly-retired people. Older people are also the major asset-holders in modern societies, so they have been direct beneficiaries of the high real interest rates earned on savings in recent years, and the large capital gains seen in the equities market.

Many older people have also enjoyed enormous capital gains on their houses; two-thirds of people aged 50 to 60 in Britain and over half of those over 65 now own their own property, and of these almost all owner-occupiers over 65, and over half those aged 50 to 65 own their property outright. No other age-group has so much net wealth. In addition to their own wealth, income-rich and asset-rich people in their 50s are also the recipients of substantial windfall gains. Just as they have paid off their mortgage and freed themselves of financial responsibility for their children, they are likely to inherit from their parents – the average age of inheritance is around 55 these days.

As well as having larger financial resources, more of the grey population now enjoy the resource of free time. People over pension age, almost by definition, have an abundance of free time, but increasingly this is the case for people in their 50s as well, and this is largely a matter of choice. During the mid-1970s, nine out of ten men aged 55 to 64 in Britain were in some form of employment, but by the beginning of the 1990s this figure had fallen to little over five out of ten. Similar trends in the labour force participation of older men have become apparent in all the countries of Western Europe and North America; although it is clear that some of these people have been pushed out of employment because of personal ill-health or macro-economic downturns, in many cases early retirement has been a response to the high levels of net wealth owned by this age-group.

The consequences of this are both clear and striking. A person who opts for early retirement at some time in their 50s with a generous occupational pension, substantial savings and a house that is owned outright, will experience as many years of well-financed, healthy retirement as their grandchildren will spend in full-time education.

The expectations of older people are changing. Age-groups comprise different generations of people passing through them. These different generations come equipped with different values and outlooks. There are different expectations of what old age means. For many people currently over the age of 70 or 75, retirement never held out particularly bright prospects because they entered retirement relatively poor, with few assets or pension rights, and consumption patterns tailored to many decades of tight budgeting. People now entering their 50s have enjoyed substantial economic growth, and generally have accumulated sufficient assets over their life cycle to allow them to pursue an active consumption path. They are not going to want to scale down their expectations as they enter their 60s and nor, given their financial resources, will they have to.

DEFINING THE OLDER CONSUMER

On the evidence presented in this chapter, it is clear that older consumers these days represent a market segment with enough significance in terms of their purchasing power that it should not be ignored by marketers. The reasons for this emergent market segment are manifold. Older people are not, as a rule, spending money to the same extent as younger people on raising children, acquiring and establishing homes, or consuming considerable amounts of foodstuffs. They may have smaller incomes, but for many there is a larger percentage of discretionary income than ever before.

In the United States, the majority of older people own their own homes, and most of these are free of mortgage (Davis 1980; Linden 1986). In general, they spend less money on housing that do younger people. Rena Bartos, writing in the *Harvard Business Review* (1980), identified the older market as starting at age 49, which does not coincide with the gerontologists' concept of where old age begins (60+). This gives a certain advantage in profiling 'older' consumer spending patterns. Most people are still working and probably earning their largest incomes from age 50 until retirement.

In devising any sensible marketing strategy for reaching older consumers, however, it would be a mistake to treat them as a single homogeneous market (Gelb 1982; Towle and Martin 1976). The term 'elderly' or older consumer should be regarded as a global label for a collection of distinctive subgroups. These subgroups can be differentiated in terms of age, life stage, financial status, values and lifestyle, and a variety of other characteristics related to consumer behaviour. The United States census, for example, divides the 55 and over group into four age segments: the olders, 55 to 64; the elders, 65 to 74; the aged, 75 to 84; and the very old, 85 and over (US Bureau of the Census 1982).

Regardless of the classification used, and this issue will be examined more closely in the next chapter, two points are evident. First, the older consumers' market is not homogeneous, but is composed of several segments that are vastly different in their market and purchase behaviour (US Bureau of the Census 1984; Gelb 1982; Eckstein 1992). In fact, there is evidence of considerable differentiation between aged-defined and other demographically-defined bands within the older consumer market. Second, current members of the older consumers' market differ in terms of outlook, attitudes, values and self-perceptions, as well as their financial means, from their predecessors of even a generation ago (Allan 1984; Greco 1984; Lazer 1986). Their attitudes, outlooks and lifestyles are far more youthful (Siegel and Davidson 1984). They are actively involved in the leisure and recreational pursuits of far younger people. Their attitudes are those of younger, vigorous consumers rather than of old, retired senior citizens. Also, as a market, they have the wealth to indulge themselves and enjoy a much more luxurious lifestyle than did their cohorts of previous generations.

Some descriptive data suggest that the consumer behaviour of the older consumer differs from that of other age-groups and consistently changes. Research in the United States in the 1960s and 1970s showed that the older consumer spent up to 66 per cent of their total expenditures on food and housing (Berger 1985). Proportionately more money was spent on medical care and household operations, whereas expenditures for household furnishings, transportation, clothing, personal care and vacations tended to decrease with age (Dodge 1958). The older consumer was generally found to be wiser about spending their money, they were more price conscious and demanded more warranties and guarantees than did younger consumers (*Media Decisions* 1977; Phillips and Sternthal 1977). It has also been observed that the older consumer's information processing skills are likely to be different from those of younger consumers (Phillips and Sternthal 1977).

As people in the older consumer market grow older, they tend to interact rather differently with various sources of consumer information. In particular, there appears to be a marked increase in exposure to newspapers and television, especially once people get beyond 60 years of age (Real, Anderson and Harrington 1980), which declines after the age of 70. Interestingly, the criteria for media use preference also seem to change with age. Starting at about age 60, older people use the mass media for information rather than entertainment purposes (Bernhardt and Kinnear 1976; Phillips and Sternthal 1977; Schramm 1969). In Chapter 4, we will take a closer look at the older consumer's use of media as an aspect of leisure. Another important feature of media use is the influence the media might have upon public conceptions of older consumers. According to the way older people are featured in different types of media content, such as television programmes or any form of media advertising, particular images of the older person will be promulgated which might impact upon how older consumers see themselves as well as how they are perceived by others. In Chapter 5, evidence is examined on the way the older consumer is portrayed and the impact that such media images can have. Then, in Chapter 6, attention is turned to advertising as an information source for older consumers and a variety of factors are reviewed relating to the media of presentation, advertising message format and content, and consumer information processing capabilities, which all play a part in mediating the effectiveness and utility of advertising within the mature market. Before turning to these issues, however, it is important to understand more about the character of the mature market itself. Older consumers are not a homogeneous group. They comprise a diverse range of individuals who can be distinguished in terms of demographic features, consumption habits, and the kinds of lifestyles and values to which they adhere. The next two chapters examine some of the key defining characteristics of the older consumer.

2 Demographics and consumption patterns

The over-50s are becoming increasingly important to marketers and advertisers. Statistics alone underscore the growing appeal of this market. The number of people in this age bracket is expanding and they are becoming wealthier with more disposable income. Older consumers typically have greater discretionary income than their younger counterparts, who are considered to be a 'more attractive' market by many businesses. In fact, discretionary income coupled with a greater youthfulness among members of the grey market who are healthier and more active than any previous generation, makes this market segment an extremely attractive proposition for many commodity and service advertisers.

Many businesses have become firmly entrenched in this market, while others are developing new products and services as well as adapting marketing strategies to make their offerings more appealing to older customers. But there is considerable debate among advertisers and academics about how best to take advantage of these new marketing opportunities. Moreover, there is a very real problem in determining how to reach older consumers. With respect to media strategy, a critical consideration is that media usage by older consumers, as a group, is low compared with other demographic groups. As for creative strategy, a paramount question is whether it is more appropriate to view older consumers as constituting one market or several market segments. The issue of whether the older consumer comprises one fairly homogeneous market or several heterogeneous segments, has received increased attention from marketers in recent years. More and more, a segmentation approach is recommended, though there are differences in opinion on the most meaningful basis for segmentation.

In this chapter, we focus on demographic characteristics as segmentation variables. A study of the demography of this age-group provides marketers with the means to understand older consumers as a generational cohort and to compare them, in terms of objective identifiers, with other age-groups. Demography is only one type of classifier. Gerontologists have found that older people can be differentiated in terms of the social roles they occupy, while social psychologists have provided valuable insights into how older individuals can be distinguished according to their attitudes, values, personality profiles and lifestyles they enjoy. The marketing of products and services to older consumers can benefit from an understanding of systems of older consumer segmentation which derive from each of these approaches.

Demographic segmentation can proceed by dividing older consumers according to age, gender, socio-economic class, level of education, marital status, or a combination of these and other such factors. In some studies, these variables have been used singly, while elsewhere they may be examined conjointly. Some researchers (e.g. Vishvabharanthy and Rink 1984) have suggested combining age breakdowns with other characteristics such as income, education or personality. Still others (e.g. Keane 1985) have recommended the use of lifestyle or psychographic variables in order to achieve a better understanding of the diversity of sub-segments among the older consumer. Lifestyle and psychographic segmentation of the older consumer market will be examined in more detail in Chapter 3.

One review of more than 30 separate studies of segmenting the older market identified five critical segmentation variables: (1) discretionary income; (2) health; (3) activity level; (4) discretionary time; and (5) response to other people. Income levels ranged from the poor to the super-affluent; health from poor to excellent; activity level from limited to engaged in work, recreation and social activities; discretionary time from non-involved to committed to activities; and response to other people ranged from sociable to seeking separation (Bone 1991).

A further distinguishing feature relates not to how old people actually are, but to how old they perceive themselves to be. In this regard, there are differences between age-groups. Young adults, between 20 and 24 years old, often wish to be older than their chronological age, whereas those who are between 25 and 29 years are more likely to be satisfied with their real age. Once people get older, however, there is an increased likelihood that they will express an 'ideal age' that is younger than their actual age (Lepisto 1989). Among older people, age perceptions may be at least as important as real age in determining behaviour. There is some evidence that, among older consumers, the younger their 'perceived age', the more likely they are to be satisfied with their lives (Sherman, Schiffman and Dillon 1988). Life satisfaction may be affected less by real age than by the age people feel.

Age perceptions themselves may not be uni-dimensional, but occur in a number of different forms. Barak and Schiffman (1981) distinguished between four different categories or types of perceived age: (1) 'feel-age', representing how old a person feels; (2) 'look-age', representing how old a person looks; (3) 'do-age', representing how involved a person is in activities favoured by members of a specific age-group; and (4) 'interest-age', representing how similar a person's interests are to those of members of a specific age-group. Individuals in their 50s, 60s, 70s and 80s were generally more likely to consider themselves 'younger' than their chronological age in all of these respects. There were marked differences between older age-groups in the percentages who said they felt their age, looked their age, and shared the same interests as the rest of their age-group. The percentages who claimed to feel and look their age increased from just over 50 per cent among individuals in their 50s to around 70 per cent among individuals in their 80s. Shared interests with their own age-group were reported by around two-thirds of individuals in their 50s, by over 70 per cent of those in their 60s and 70s, and by over 80 per cent of those in their 80s. More work needs to be done on whether these types of perceived age differ in their ability to predict consumer-related behaviour.

The significance of segmentation

The very real possibility that there may be distinct segments within the older consumer market has important implications for advertisers hoping to reach all or some portion of this market. Research findings that provide some additional insights into the viability of taking a segmentation approach come from three areas: gerontology, marketing and communications.

Much of the empirical work in gerontology has led to the identification of different types of people comprising the older age segments. The profiles of these different types tend to be rooted in the manner in which people adjust or adapt to advancing age, and often the descriptions of the different types are similar to personality profiles. While there is considerable agreement in the gerontological literature that there are different types of adjustment patterns among the older consumer, no clear inference that these different types constitute distinct market segments can be drawn.

Academics and practitioners in marketing have been more directly concerned with answering the question as to whether the older-aged consumer group can be meaningfully segmented. Although research from this perspective has been limited, it has so far provided promising evidence that there is sufficient hetero-geneity among older consumers to justify a segmentation approach.

'AGE' AS A SEGMENTING VARIABLE

One way in which older consumers can be segmented is by their actual age. The population of consumers subsumed under the label of 'the grey market' comprise a broad age-group which itself changes in composition over time. The effective age-range of individuals in statutory retirement is approximately 35 to 40 years. This is such a wide age-span that the same researchers have recommended dividing them into two sub-categories of 'young elderly' aged 60/65 to 74 years and the 'old elderly' aged 75 and above. This convention is now widely recog-nised, reflecting the importance of distinguishing the separate needs and characteristics of the young elderly and old elderly due to the heterogeneity of the age bracket they together cover (Taylor and Ford 1983; Evandrou and Victor 1989).

In this book, the consumer group being examined extends beyond the 60-plus age range and it will consider the character and behaviour of those people in what might be broadly termed 'late middle age'. These individuals, aged 50 and over, may have taken early retirement, or may still be an active part of the workforce (as indeed may some of those aged 60 to 65).

Lazer (1986), for example, suggested looking at the 'mature market' as comprising four different age-groups: 55 to 64, 65 to 74, 75 to 84, and over 85. This view has been supported elsewhere, with the observation that older consumers as a group are more diverse in interests, opinions and activities than other segments of the adult population. A parallel distinction between market segments, by age groupings, distinguished between the 'young-old' (aged 65–74 years), the 'old' (75–84 years) and 'old-old' (85+ years). Members of the 'young-old' segment were regarded as tending to have both health and money and therefore represented a potentially profitable market for a number of commodities and services, such as holidays and travel. In contrast, the 'old-old' were in an age category that is likely to require various specialised housing and medical services (Riche 1986).

Age and health have been combined with activity levels to classify older people. Pol, May and Hartranft (1992) identified eight stages of ageing for non-institutionalised people aged 50 and older. The eight stages were in five-year increments until age 84. Thereafter one category was formed for those 85 and older. The first stages (50–54 and 55–59) showed relatively few differences in male : female ratio, health status, and work status. As the population reached 60, a significant percentage retired and the chances of being widowed nearly doubled. Throughout their 60s, most of those surveyed were in good to excellent health and fewer were working. At age 70, just over one in ten were living below the poverty line, just one in ten were working, and increasing numbers of women were surviving their spouses and living alone. Half of those over 85 lived alone.

The 65 plus market

Although consumers at this age are no longer likely to be bringing home monthly salary payments, they have incomes that allow most of them to consume beyond the bare necessities. Because there has always been a mythology about the poor elderly, it has been easy to assume that there was no money to be spent by the retired, and therefore there was no attempt to market to them.

What do they purchase? They purchase more drugs and health-care products than the general population. Specifically, asthma remedies, laxatives, sleeping tablets, vitamins and denture cleaners are purchased in greater quantity. They purchase personal care items in significant quantity, but much less so than does the 55 to 64 age-group. They spend more on foods to be consumed at home than do younger groups. They are larger consumers of coffee. This older market also spends more on home fuel and on household supplies than do younger groups, who spend less time at home. They do not spend money on away-from-home purchases such as eating out, movies, theatres, or on petrol for the car. They are still a significant market for new cars and for travel, however, especially scheduled tours by plane and boat cruises.

A *Marketing Week* (Sturges 1990) survey of people in the United Kingdom aged between 50 and 80 years found that shopping habits seemed to be determined by whether or not the shopper had access to a car. Nearly half of all the respondents went grocery shopping once a week and a quarter shopped daily. One in six shopped once a month or less, and one-third of the men interviewed did not go shopping at all.

The younger people interviewed tended to be the least frequent shoppers and were most likely to make major supermarket shopping trips just once or twice a month by car. The large majority of over-70s shopped every day and they usually walked or took a bus. However, they were still more likely to visit a local supermarket than a corner shop, where the prices were perceived to be higher and the premises not so clean. The less mobile respondents were reliant on public transport or lifts from friends and family, and this restricted their freedom or choice of shop.

The older consumers' market has generally come to be seen as a heterogeneous rather than a uniform group in terms of consumer and media-related habits and attitudes. Marketers and advertisers have increasingly recognised the need to deal with this age-group's diversity. Demographic and psychographic or lifestyle segmentation have been used to help advertisers and marketing professionals to improve their understanding of the older consumer.

The continued growth of the older consumers' market has spawned a rush by marketers to develop products and services that will meet the needs of this expanding segment. In addition to segmentation of this market segment by age, other demographic factors have been found to provide useful divisions which are linked to different consumption patterns. Some of these segmentation factors are examined in the remaining sections of this chapter.

FAMILY AND HOUSEHOLD COMPOSITION

Marketers need to know the types of residences older people live in and the structure of their households because these can represent significant factors in shaping consumerism. While a small proportion of the older consumer market are institutionalised, the great majority live in their own homes. Since the 1960s significant changes have occurred in life cycle stages, reflected in changes in kinds of living arrangements which prevail among older people. Changes to fertility, marriage and mortality rates have given rise to changes in the life cycle of individuals and these changes may, in turn, have contributed to the decline of inter-generational households and the rise of one-person households. Some people may relocate on retirement to quieter, cleaner, safer situations or to locations offering a better climate.

A falling age of marriage and lowered average age at which the last child is born during the 1960s and 1970s, combined with a closer spacing of surviving children as a result of lower infant mortality rates, have all led to a shortening of the duration of the nuclear family. With increasing life expectancy this has led to a lengthening of the 'empty nest' phase of the life cycle, when a couple may find themselves living alone (Grundy 1991).

In the United Kingdom, three-quarters of men aged over 65, but only one-third of women, are married. Half the women over 65 are widowed, a tenth are single, and a small but growing percentage are divorced or separated. Around one-third of women have had no children. The great majority of older people live either alone or with their spouse. Few, only around 4 to 5 per cent, live in institutional settings, with most living in their own house. Living alone may be the mark of independence as well as of isolation. In fact, worries about loneliness fall well behind health, financial and mobility anxieties in the minds of older people, and are no more and no less than those of the 35 to 64 age-group (Midwinter 1991).

GENDER DIFFERENCES

Gender differences in the older consumers' roles regarding decision-making in relation to consumer behaviour have been reported. Specifically, findings suggest that the female becomes more dominant in decision-making, especially upon the retirement of her husband (Neugarten 1964). This dominance appears to be reflected in their perceptions of roles regarding consumer-related decisions. One study found female respondents to hold less egalitarian perceptions regarding consumer decision-making (Smith *et al.* 1982).

SOCIO-ECONOMIC SEGMENTATION

Socio-economic status, as determined by educational level and/or current or former occupation, is another variable that seems to affect the consumer behaviour of the older consumer. Smith *et al.* (1982) found higher socio-economic status to be associated with more positive perceptions of the older consumer and with a greater range of brand preferences.

Schreiber and Boyd (1980) found that occupation and social class influence various media use patterns. Older persons in upper status jobs were more likely to report that print media had more influence on their consumer decisions than did television. Some occupational effects on television viewing habits of the older consumer also emerged: professionals, clinical workers and proprietors watched fewer hours of television each day than those in 'less skilled' occupations.

Income and education were found to affect the older person's interaction with print media. Those of higher income and of higher education were more likely to spend time reading newspapers than lower income and education groups (Harris and Associates 1975). Similarly, book and magazine reading remained relatively high across life-span for those with better education and higher income (Schramm 1969; Harris and Associates 1975).

Schreiber and Boyd (1980) found education to be related to choices of most influential advertising medium in consumer decision-making. As educational level increased, respondents were increasingly likely to choose magazines as the most influential advertising medium. Among older consumers with a low educational level, television was chosen nearly as often as newspapers. The selection of television as most influential source appeared to decline as education increased. The same study found education to be negatively related to the amount of television viewing.

FINANCIALLY DIFFERENTIATING OLDER CONSUMERS

We have already noted that older consumers cannot be considered as a homogeneous market. There are significant differences among them in terms of various demographic attributes which are important in understanding how they behave. Another way in which the older consumer may be differentiated is in terms of expenditure capability (Abrams 1990). Economic segmentation can enable marketers to classify older consumers in terms of their spending and saving activities. It may also be used to examine the extent to which older consumers represent a tax burden on younger generations by demanding social services.

One of the attractions of the older market is the discretionary income they are purported to have (Kelly 1992). Yet, there is significant variation in wealth in the mature market, ranging from the 'pension elite' (Longino 1988) to those living at or below the poverty line. The structure of the older person's household, its income stream, and spending patterns are important clues to the marketer who is designing a new product line, or devising a new pricing strategy or promotional campaign.

In the United States, older Americans have generally lower incomes (40 per cent of the income earned by 45–54 year olds), but they also have fewer expenses and smaller households to maintain. Many have completed mortgage payments and sent their children to college, and thus have more discretionary income than younger age-groups (Longino and Crown 1991). Mature consumers also have a higher propensity to save than younger people (Lazer and Shaw 1987).

Global figures about household disposable income are provided for the United Kingdom by the annual Family Expenditure Survey. However, this survey masks considerable inequalities of gross weekly income with the older section of the population. These inequalities are in part related to age. For instance, households where the head is aged between 55 and 59 tend to have a higher gross weekly income than households in which the head is aged 75 or over. Such inequalities are reduced to some extent by direct taxation paid by the more affluent older person, by additional investment and other factors not taken into account by the Family Expenditure Survey analysis.

Figures reported by Abrams (1990) from the 1987 Family Expenditure Survey served to reveal some of the differences which did exist. Here, a comparison of younger affluent older persons' households (those where the head was aged 50 to 64) with older and impoverished older persons' households (head aged 75 or over) showed two particular differences between them. First, the younger households outnumbered the older households by more than two to one; they constituted nearly half of all older consumer households and nearly one in four of all UK households. Second, there was a gap of 23 years between the average age of heads of younger affluent older consumer households and the average age of heads of the impoverished older consumer households.

In economic terms, the life course of the average younger affluent heads of household was very different compared with older heads of household. Younger people had missed the First World War and the depressions of the early and mid-1920s which left such a lasting impression on older people. By the time the 'young' older consumer had started school in 1935, the Great Depression had given way to economic boom. When World War Two broke out in 1939 those who lived in militarily vulnerable areas (for the most part urban and industrial working class) were sent off by the authorities to safe and often rural parts of the country and a diet which, in terms of nutritional values, was usually better than their pre-war diet.

When the war ended in 1945 and they returned to their parental homes, most had finished their schooling and found themselves in a labour market where the supply of manpower was so tight that the gap between their teenage wages and those of their parents contracted very sharply; unemployment levels among those in insured occupations hovered around 2 per cent.

By the time they married in the 1950s and became parents, the Welfare State was providing them, among other groups, with maternity benefits and child allowances. Currently, of all those in employment, at least 70 per cent can look forward to enjoying various sources of income when they retire: 'in 1986 . . . 70 per cent of newly retired pensioners had an occupational pension . . . and 80 per cent . . . were receiving investment income' (Economic Report, Treasury, October 1989).

As noted earlier, though, direct taxation and other factors operated to reduce the inequality of gross incomes among the older consumer, so the inequality of household expenditure is not quite so substantial. In 1987, while the gross weekly income of the average 'younger' older consumer was at least three times greater than that of the average older consumer household, the difference in household expenditure between the two groups was little more than two to one; and when total household expenditure was turned into expenditure per head, it was barely 1.5 to one (see Table 2.1).

Figures for 1987 showed that the total weekly expenditure of the average 'older' older consumer household was no more than 43 per cent of the average 'younger' older consumer household. This gap was not identical for all items in the household budget, however. The reasons for some variations are obvious; for example, in households where the expenditure by the oldest of the older consumers was below 43 per cent.

By 1995, the difference in weekly expenditure of the oldest older consumer group and the youngest older consumer group had widened, with the former spending 40 per cent of the average amount spent by the latter. Indeed, the 50 to 64-year-olds were the second highest spenders on average per week of any age-group (£315.80). Only the 30 to 49-year-olds spent more (£356 per week).

Table 2.1 Average weekly household expenditure patterns: 1987 and 1995

	50–64 (a) £	65–74 (b) £	75+ (c) £	(c) as % of (a) %
1987				
Housing	32.36	26.95	22.55	70
Fuel, light and power	11.24	9.45	8.45	75
Food	38.37	25.96	18.93	49
Alcohol and tobacco	15.75	7.84	3.81	24
Clothing and footwear	13.69	7.21	3.42	25
Household goods	13.56	8.86	4.63	34
Household services	8.48	6.18	5.12	60
Personal goods and services	7.85	4.95	3.67	47
Motoring, fares and travel	33.10	17.78	7.54	23
Leisure goods and services	31.79	15.13	9.97	31
Miscellaneous	0.58	—	0.13	22
Total	**206.71**	**130.31**	**88.20**	**43**
Per head	87.85	75.08	62.78	71
1995				
Housing	41.01	24.85	19.04	46
Fuel, light and power	14.42	11.59	10.23	71
Food	55.26	37.68	27.59	50
Alcohol and tobacco	20.00	10.56	5.50	28
Clothing and footwear	18.30	8.69	6.36	35
Household goods	26.84	16.09	9.58	36
Household services	15.52	10.47	10.69	69
Personal goods and services	12.33	8.19	5.64	46
Motoring, fares and travel	51.38	25.85	11.86	23
Leisure goods and services	58.00	29.18	20.49	35
Miscellaneous	2.33	1.07	0.26	11
Total	**315.80**	**185.21**	**127.23**	**40**
Per head	142.51	111.04	90.88	64

Sources: Family Expenditure Surveys 1987 and 1995

The gap between the youngest and oldest members of the 'grey market' was not identical for all items in the household budget. Both in the 1980s and 1990s there was a marked range of variation in the household expenditure patterns of people in the 50 to 64, 65 to 74 and 75+ age brackets. In the 1980s and 1990s, younger 'grey market' members spent significantly more on housing expenses each week, although the gap has widened in recent years. The biggest difference between these subgroups of older consumers, which has persisted over time, is the level of expenditure on motoring, travel and fares. This clearly reflects the greater activity level of younger 'grey market' members, many of whom are still in employment and have to travel to work each day. Few of the most elderly householders have driving licences – in some cases because they never learned to drive and in others because they surrendered their licences when the normal defects of old age (poor eyesight, poor hearing, slow physical response to stimuli, forgetfulness) made safe driving impossible, and low expenditure on fares is made possible by the fact that for people over 60 the cost of travel is heavily subsidised. The oldest of the older consumers spent significantly less than the youngest on alcohol and tobacco, and on clothing and footwear.

In the mid-1980s in Britain, there were marked differences between the younger and older ends of the older consumer age spectrum in expenditure on leisure goods and services. A notably higher percentage of household expenditure went in this direction among the 'young' older consumers (aged 50 to 64). This general pattern remained true in the mid-1990s, although the gap between age-groups has reduced by around 50 per cent (see Table 2.2).

From a marketing standpoint, there are two aspects of the older market to be remembered; older consumers are older than the rest of the population and they are highly polarised as far as wealth is concerned. Thus, for example, older people may have more leisure time but they may also have less mobility. They are easier to reach via television, but need to be addressed in a different way from the young. These, and many similar points, require a different approach from sellers of goods and services if they are to meet the needs of older consumers effectively.

There is a problem in any tendency to treat older consumers as a single market and to use averages of wealth or purchasing as meaningful indicators. In fact, polarisation of wealth is higher among the old than in any other age-group. For most marketers the question is how to target the third or so of old people who have the resources to buy the product on offer. Targeting is always a problem and no method is perfect, but the high polarisation of wealth among older people makes it more necessary to try.

Banks (1990) examined the financial needs of the over-55s by looking at their financial behaviour and in particular the ways they managed their money.

Table 2.2 Household expenditure on specified items as a percentage of total expenditure: 1987 and 1995

	1987			1995		
	50–64	*65–74*	*75+*	*50–64*	*65–74*	*75+*
Housing	15.7	26.0	25.6	13.0	13.4	15.0
Fuel and power	5.4	9.1	9.6	4.6	6.3	8.0
Food	21.6	25.0	21.5	17.6	20.3	21.7
Alcohol and tobacco	7.6	7.6	4.3	6.3	5.7	4.3
Clothing and footwear	6.6	6.9	3.9	5.8	4.7	5.0
Household goods	6.6	8.5	5.2	8.5	8.7	7.5
Household services	4.1	6.0	5.8	4.9	5.7	8.4
Personal goods/services	3.8	4.8	4.2	3.9	4.4	4.4
Motoring/fares/travel	16.0	17.1	8.5	16.2	13.9	9.3
Leisure goods/services	15.4	14.6	11.3	18.3	16.3	16.1
Miscellaneous	0.3	—	0.1	0.7	0.6	0.2

Sources: Family Expenditure Surveys 1987 and 1995

This involved an analysis of the kinds of financial 'products' they held. The data to which he referred were obtained from surveys by NOP and Research International in the United Kingdom. NOP's Financial Research Survey (FRS) collects information on a continuous basis about the financial habits of the adult UK population. The FRS questionnaire is split into a number of sections, each of which deals with a range of products, such as savings and investments, building society accounts, general insurance, life assurance, medium-term credit, credit and charge card holding, and direct investment in equities.

Banks indexed the holdings of each financial product among the over-55s. This was accomplished by relating the proportion of the total holdings of each product to the penetration of a given age-group in the adult population. Tables 2.3 and 2.4 relate to the over-55s, and Tables 2.5 and 2.6 to the 45 to 54-year-old population. The higher the index, the more that given age-group holds a particular 'product'; the lower the figure, the less likely they are to use that financial instrument.

Table 2.3 Financial 'products' the over-55s are more likely to hold

Product	Index
Any National Savings Certificate	1.97
Building Society Term Share	1.78
Building Society Extra Interest	1.41
Whole Life	1.27
Unit Trust	1.27
Any National Savings Bond	1.22
Bank High Interest	1.19
Stocks and Shares	1.16
Building Society High Interest	1.13
Premium Bonds	1.13

Note: Where the average index score across all adult age groups (18+) equals 100, index scores indicate extent to which over-55s are more likely to hold each product
Source: Banks 1990

Table 2.4 Financial 'products' the over-55s are less likely to hold

Product	Index
Any Building Society Loan	0.18
Cash Card	0.22
Bank Loan	0.24
Any Hire Purchase	0.27
Any Finance House Loan	0.27
Mortgage Protection	0.36
Charge/Gold Card	0.45
Medical Insurance	0.64
Term Insurance	0.67
Any Credit Card	0.73

Note: Where the average index score across all adults (18+) equals 100, index scores indicate the extent to which over-55s are less likely to hold each product
Source: Banks 1990

Table 2.5 Financial 'products' 45–54s are more likely to hold

Product	Index
Mortgage Protection	1.60
Unit Trusts	1.57
Charge/Gold Card	1.53
Stocks and Shares	1.50
Building Society Subscription	1.43
Medical Insurance	1.33
Bank High Interest	1.29
Building Society Seven Day	1.29
Building Society Extra Interest	1.29
Building Society High Interest	1.21

Note: Where the average index score across all adult age groups (18+) equals 100, index scores indicate the extent to which 45–54s are more likely to hold each financial product
Source: Banks 1990

Table 2.6 Financial 'products' 45–54s are less likely to hold

Product	Index
Cash Card	0.64
Direct Finance House Loan	0.80
Any National Savings Bond	0.86

Note: Where the average index score across all adult age groups equals 100, index scores indicate the extent to which 45–54s are less likely to hold each financial product
Source: Banks 1990

These indices highlight some very interesting patterns. Patterns of behaviour in this group are fairly consistent – saving instruments such as building society term share, building society extra interest, whole life policies and unit trusts are particularly prevalent. National Savings Certificates head the list.

At a lower level, National Savings Bonds and bank interest accounts are also very well represented among the over-55s. The last two financial products in Table 2.3 confirm that the over-55s represent a particularly thrifty segment of the adult population – building society high interest accounts and premium bonds being relatively well represented.

At the other end of the spectrum, it is also possible to examine those areas the over-55s tend to avoid (the smaller the index, the less likelihood of the over-55s actually holding a given product). The over-55s clearly have a marked aversion to a wide range of credit facilities, in addition to having a relatively low propensity to hold cash cards. Mortgage is far less of an issue to the over-55s than to the other age-groups. Charge cards, gold cards, or indeed any credit cards are less well represented among this age-group – medical insurance and term assurance sharing a similar profile. It is also clear from these behaviour patterns that the over-55s were seen as being fairly risk averse – excess money tended to be held in interest-bearing accounts or government securities. They also tended to be far less interested than other age-groups in loan facilities of various types.

When the financial behaviour of the 45 to 54-year-old population was examined, a very different picture emerged. Unlike the over-55s, this age-group had a relatively high propensity to hold mortgage protection policies and was significantly more associated with the use of unit trusts, and charge and gold card products. Savings and investment vehicles still featured strongly, although direct investment in stocks and shares featured at a higher level than the (risk free) building society interest bearing accounts.

Given the number of 45 to 54-year-olds, this segment is also relatively more associated with the purchase of medical insurance and a range of bank and building society interest-bearing accounts. Those financial products that the 45 to 54-year-old segment is less likely to hold provides a less clear picture. The fact that only three products – cash cards, direct finance house loans, and National Savings Bonds – emerged, implies that this age-group tended in general to be more financially active than the over-55s.

What does emerge from this analysis is a suggestion that if such behaviour patterns were to persist, then the needs of the over-55s are likely to change markedly over the coming years. A wider range of financial services is being used by people who will subsequently fall into the older age category, and the individuals themselves seem to be less risk averse than the previous generation of mature consumer.

AGEING AND CONSUMPTION

Population ageing will affect the structure and ultimately the level of demand within each economy. Consumption projections are usually made by applying population projections to current age-specific expenditure patterns, but this procedure may not produce valid results. The expenditure patterns of today's elderly population are a consequence of the age of these individuals, of their lifetime socio-economic experience and of the socio-economic conditions now current in their country and place of residence.

The relatively low level of old age income and the limited variability in expenditure patterns among many older people today may be a consequence more of lifetime employment and saving opportunities than of age itself. Future changes in both the mean and variance of real income and wealth for the older consumer population, together with possible changes in labour force participation and in morbidity, could easily alter current demand patterns.

Studies in the USA and France (Musgrove 1982; Serow 1984; Ekert-Jaffe 1989) suggest that, once household expenditure patterns are standardised for differences in income and household composition, age alone has very little impact on the overall structure of consumer demand. Even when the analysis is subdivided into over 100 different consumption sectors, few types of consumption expenditure appear to be closely related to age.

A changing age structure among consumers, however, may require non-marginal adjustment by producers in order to adapt to changing demand preferences within particular consumption sectors. Marketing opportunities will derive from monitoring certain quite localised and age-specific consumption patterns associated with particular age cohorts as they move through different life stages. The consumer boom of the 1980s was driven by the baby-boom generation of yuppies, the high earners in their 20s and 30s. They were the target of advertisers and image makers who created the new icons of modern life – the filofax, sailboard, portable phone – but because of their cohort size and spending power, this broad age-group was also the centre of rather more mundane sales efforts for cars, soap powders and margarines. Over the next decade, the purchasing power of the 20 to 40 age-group, in countries such as the USA, will fade away as it shrinks by 10 per cent from 81 million to 74 million people. Meanwhile, the numbers of Americans in their 40s and 50s will rise by over a third, from 56 million to 75 million and marketing strategies will be forced, simply by weight of numbers, to give increased recognition to this older age-group. Baby-boomers may not change all their consumption habits as they get older, but the kinds of marketing messages which appeal to them may not be the same as ones which were effective on them when they were younger.

Woopies

Well-off older people, or 'Woopies' are usually defined as those individuals whose incomes place them in the top 20 per cent of the total individual income distribution in Britain. They represent a subgroup within the grey market which has particularly strong spending power. An analysis of the distinguishing characteristics of this group has indicated that, compared with all retired people aged 65 years or over, Woopies are more likely to be owner-occupiers of their home (90% versus 48%), more likely to own their home outright (79% versus 44%), more likely to have an occupational pension (60% versus 38%) and asset income (92% versus 55%), and more likely to own a car (83% versus 38%). Woopies were generally likely to have more access to consumer durables such as a video (16% versus 7%) and dishwasher (17% versus 2%) than were other retired people (Johnson and Falkingham 1992). Only 4 per cent of Woopies resided in a household with more than one other person, and they were more likely to be aged under 75 (68 per cent versus 51 per cent) than other retired people. Among the principal defining characteristics of Woopies were that they tended to have been employed in a non-manual job, had an occupational pension and had access to other non-state sources of income (Falkingham and Victor 1991).

DIFFERENTIATION BY CONSUMER BEHAVIOUR

As we have already seen, the general idea that all old people are poor is outmoded. At the same time, though, there are wide discrepancies among people aged over 50 in how much they can afford to spend on different items. According to Buck (1990) the over-55s are 'unquestionably the richest sector of the population in terms of actual wealth owned, and clearly the old are vital to financial markets, particularly for savings' (p. 21). An analysis of consumer behaviour patterns for the UK has revealed, however, the purchase levels among the over-50s may be important to a number of product and service sectors.

Older people have been found to be significant spenders in a number of categories, particularly food, and there are some product areas where they are *very* important. Research conducted by Audits of Great Britain has shown that the repertoire (number of different brands bought) of older housewives was only a little lower than that of younger housewives. The belief that older people are set in their ways in terms of brand loyalty is not true according to this market research evidence (Buck 1990).

Shopping behaviour

Most of the research on older consumers' shopping patterns has been conducted in an exploratory manner with limited samples. Many research findings must therefore be interpreted with caution. There are a number of helpful insights, however, from a few larger scale studies. Here, analyses of the shopping orientations of older consumers and the significance for them of various store attributes has begun to provide a better understanding of their shopping patterns.

One national study in the United States which examined store choice for apparel, found that older consumers generally based their patronage decisions on the same factors as their younger counterparts (Lumpkin, Greenberg and Goldstucker 1985). Older consumers (65+ years) in the sample exhibited a number of functional and recreational reasons for shopping. While older consumers enjoyed shopping as an activity, they tended not to shop around as much as younger consumers for the items they wished to buy. Even so, older consumers displayed confidence in knowing what they wanted from the shopping experience and were attuned to brand and store reputations. Consumers at this end of the age spectrum often looked for the reassurance that could be provided by warranties and money-back guarantees more than did younger consumers.

Another study of older shoppers indicated that there were sub-segments who could be identified by unique shopping orientations (Lumpkin 1985). Older consumers are active shoppers and men and women are significantly more likely than younger consumers to shop together and to make joint buying decisions for everything from everyday convenience goods to expensive durables (Tongren 1988). They tend to shop more often than younger consumers in department stores, but less often in discount stores, perhaps because of factors related to shopping enjoyment. Part of the enjoyment of shopping for the older consumer can be found in the recreational and social justification involved, although some research also indicates that they shop less and enjoy their shopping less than do younger age-groups.

Older consumers generally tend to enjoy shopping, but they particularly like to shop where they are known by the store personnel. Significantly though, while they may enjoy talking to and being recognised by shop assistants, they do not always value their opinions. This has been found to be true particularly in the context of clothes shopping (Lumpkin and Greenberg 1982).

While retail store shopping is the most frequently used mode of purchase by older consumers, relative to mail order, door-to-door sales, or telephone order, a great deal of anxiety and alienation can be experienced (Barnes and Peters 1982). Older consumers shop near their residences since many lack transportation. A lack of convenient transportation may mean that some older consumers shop less frequently than they would like to. In addition, substantial store loyalty has been exhibited by older consumers, especially with regard to low cost items or products about which the store owner may give advice (such as drugs and medicines). Store loyalty disappears as unit value for an item increases and frequency of purchase decreases (such as when shopping for appliances). Greater store loyalty, however, is exhibited by older consumers at higher income and age levels.

Quality merchandise, attractive prices and store reputation are important to the older shopper (Lumpkin *et al.* 1985). The significance of different aspects of a retail outlet may also be closely linked to whether the older shopper is self-reliant in terms of getting to the shops, or dependent on help from others. Dependent shoppers have a tendency to attach more significance to the physical aspects of stores (Lumpkin and Hunt 1989). In particular, this often means that they look for stores that are comfortable to move around in and offer a more personalised sales service.

Independence and self-reliance can be determined to a marked degree also by income and health of the older consumer. The better-off older consumer in a good state of health is more likely to be in the market for recreational and leisure-oriented products and services (Zimmer and Chappell 1996). Older consumers who can get around under their own steam, have also been found to be more frequent patrons of fast-food restaurants (Morris, Schneider and Macey 1995).

Some top retail stores and important retail institutions such as shopping centres and supermarkets have features that make them quite attractive to older shoppers. The generally favourable prices and the safe, comfortable atmosphere of these stores contribute to their appeal. At the same time, however, other features of these places inhibit older consumers and prevent them from taking advantage of the stores. First, they are generally located away from older neighbourhoods where many of the aged and poor live. Moreover, the right merchandise assortment to satisfy the needs of the older consumer frequently cannot be found. For these and other reasons, such retail institutions have not adequately met the needs of older consumers (Lambert 1979). There is evidence that retailers do not fully understand these needs and place greater emphasis on profit-related factors, while convenience and product-related aspects of service are desired by the older consumer (Lumpkin and Hunt 1989). A survey by Johnson and Johnson identified four broad suggestions older people had for retailers trying to reach this market: (1) make shopping easier; (2) make them feel important; (3) make shopping more interesting; and (4) help them obtain good value for their money (*Chain Store Age Executive* 1988).

Not all service organisations have ignored the older consumer. Some have been attuned to the needs of this market and have taken the trouble to find out what represents good value to this body of consumers. Certain large retail food chains in America have been particularly sensitive to the needs of older consumers. For instance, Kroger, the large mid-western supermarket chain, promoted a Senior Citizens Club that offered anyone over 59 years of age and on a fixed income a special shopping programme designed to cut food costs. Many of the major fast-food chains have sponsored various promotional programmes designed to attract the business of older consumers (Schiffman and Kanuck 1991).

Product purchase patterns

More attention by marketers and service providers to the tastes and needs of older consumers is vital if full advantage is to be taken of the potential buying power of this market segment. In terms of their general shopping behaviour, research has generally indicated that older consumers are more apt to pay cash for their purchases, use coupons giving money off, avoid using credit cards for instalment payments, prepare shopping lists, and engage in comparison shopping (Ross 1982).

Significant marketing potential appears to be available to those who provide the proper kinds of products to meet with the needs of the older consumer (Ostroff 1989). Some have ventured into this market to sell specially designed products more attuned to the older consumer's needs. Coca Cola moved into the wine, coffee, tea and orange juice markets during the 1980s to capture older consumer markets who were less interested in their coke brands. A number of cosmetics firms have identified needs to market special brands of hair care products for consumers aged over 50. In the services sector, a number of airlines and hotel chains have introduced discount schemes for older travellers.

Older consumers appear to place great importance on manufacturers' brand names. They tend to buy fewer private labels and demand guarantees and warranties more often than do average consumers. Because many over-65 shoppers are on fixed or low incomes, however, there is a trend toward increased acceptance of private labels and generic items among this shopper group. There is also an impression that older buyers are generally less inclined to try new products, especially those that involve adopting new technologies (Gilly and Zeithaml 1985). One study, however, found that the group aged 65 and over was more inclined than the middle-aged, 55 to 64-year-olds, to say that they buy products for the fun of it or just to try them once. It was also found that there is little self-initiated experimenting; instead, new product and service acceptance often comes as a response to a recommendation by others (Howard 1967). All this has important promotional implications for the marketer, and it means that messages must be well planned to take advantage of this word-of-mouth communication. Elsewhere, evidence has emerged that older consumers exhibit a strong interest in generic products. Given the apparent high brand loyalty of this group, manufacturers and retailers who properly serve them can expect to retain loyal, dependable customers (Fox, Roscoe and Feigenbaum 1984).

Consumer satisfaction and complaint behaviour

Older consumers have voiced specific concerns about the retail services which are offered to them as a group. It is important that marketers become more aware of the special needs associated with this market segment. Its members have concerns in particular about discount offers, money-back guarantees, courteous service, help when shopping, clear packaging and labelling, and rest facilities (Lambert 1979). Older consumers do not like waiting in long check-out queues, are choosy about when they do and do not want help from sales assistants, and object to patronising labels which imply negative stereotypes about their age-group (see Shoemaker 1978; Sciglimpaglia and Schaninger 1981). Failure to get the above mentioned aspects of customer service and retail environment right may lead to strong feelings of dissatisfaction among older shoppers.

Product labelling is a particularly sensitive issue. Older consumers exhibit a variety of responses to age-related segmentation labels on product packaging. These labels refer to various contextual elements of product promotions in which brands are marketed as being especially designed for 'senior citizens'. Research has indicated that older consumers may not wish to be identified and treated as a separate market segment on the basis of age (French and Fox 1985; Underhill and Cadwell 1983). Studies on this topic have found that older consumers respond less favourably to products that highlight the potential user's older age in advertising (Greco 1989) and resist participation in programmes that use 'golden years', 'retirement', or 'senior citizens' as key words in their promotions (Moschis 1991).

The reactions of older consumers in this context, however, have not been consistent, a finding which itself further serves to reflect the fact that this is not a homogeneous market segment. Most work on how older consumers respond to ageist labels has focused on the use of the phrase 'senior citizens'. Results have been mixed, with some studies suggesting that older consumers appear to favour such labels particularly when associated with special discount prices for their age-group (Lambert 1979; Mason and Bearden 1978b), while other research has indicated a more negative response (Lumpkin *et al.* 1985).

One explanation for these differences can be found in the age of older consumers. The over-65s do not seem to mind being singled out for special marketing or sales treatment or being called 'senior citizens', since this label seems to coincide fairly well with their self-image or the way they believe they are regarded by others. The under-55s, in contrast, object to being labelled as 'old', regardless of the terminology used. One social psychological theory, known as labelling theory, offers an explanation for this resistance to 'old' labels among certain sections of the older consumer segment. People tend to reject labels which do not comply with self-perceptions, particularly when they regard those labels as carrying negative connotations which they find personally hard to accept of themselves. Further, any labels which carry social stigma and threaten their social status in the eyes of others are likely to be rejected (see Tepper 1994). Recent research has confirmed in the marketing context that older consumers aged 50–54 years are less likely to use a discount-promoted product when age-related labelling has been used than are consumers aged over 65 years. For consumers aged 55 to 64 years, mixed reactions tended to occur which depended upon whether they held perceptions of themselves which were more consistent with their younger or older counterparts. The dissonance between discounted product usage and self-perceptions when age-related labelling was used was resolved once older consumers had begun to redefine their self-image to be more in line with the image of a 'senior citizen', an image which they no longer felt uncomfortable about (Tepper 1994).

Older consumers have been found to be less likely to complain about products and services than the consumer population as a whole (Bearden and Mason 1979; Bernhardt 1981). While they may be as likely to experience dissatisfaction with commodities as younger consumers, they are less likely to attribute the problem to the vendor or to take the matter up with the manufacturer or service provider. This finding is in contrast to the expectation that older consumers would be more confident and able to communicate lack of satisfaction as a result of their greater experience as consumers (Wall, Dickey and Talarzyk 1977). A number of explanations have been offered for this behaviour.

One view is that older consumers scale down their aspirations or expectations with regard to various types of commodity. Thus, older consumers are more ready to express satisfaction with goods than would other consumers even though the goods may not always meet their expectations (Pfaff and Blivice 1977). Several studies have indicated the greater likelihood of product satisfaction among older consumers (Handy 1977; Mason and Hunt 1973; Westbrook 1977).

Other psychological variables such as social integration, personal trust and the attribution of responsibility may be useful in explaining why older people appear to complain less. Valle and Lawther (1979) found evidence that older consumers who complain after an unsatisfactory buying experience tend to be highest in interpersonal mistrust and expect truthfulness from others. Older consumers' emphasis on trust may derive from being socialised in an era when shopping was conducted on a more personal basis and interpersonal judgements could be relied upon to assess honesty (Koeske and Srivastava 1977).

La Forge (1989) used the theory of learned helplessness and the notion of uncontrollability to explain older consumers' complaint behaviour. Learned helplessness theory posits that people will become passive or give up trying if they routinely meet with failure. They consider the situation beyond their control, even if circumstances change. La Forge offered strategies to change feelings of uncontrollability to increase satisfaction. Other reasons for not taking action included the older person's lack of familiarity with in-store sources of product or service information, consumer rights and regulations concerning product standards and the obligations of sales outlets, and store management policies. He argued that increased consumer education on store policies, product warranties and exchange privileges would improve the relationship between retailers and older consumers.

Even older consumers do not react in the same way with regard to all kinds of commodity purchase. One American study found that dissatisfaction may surface more readily for some products than for others. Older consumers have been found to express dissatisfaction more often for things such as cars, car repair, grocery items, appliance repair and mail order services than for other products and services. Older consumers here were classified as individuals aged 65 and over, however. This group exhibited markedly higher percentages of consumers who were dissatisfied, compared with consumers in general, for appliance repair (40.8% versus 23.7%), grocery items (33.2% versus 19.6%), cars (32.5% versus 14.9%), washer/dryers (27.9% versus 11.2%), and vacuum cleaners (24% versus 12.8%). Satisfaction levels tend to be highest for lamps, cosmetics, tools, blankets and sheets, radio sets, books and records, and tyres. With these products, over 90 per cent of older consumers expressed satisfaction, and satisfaction levels were very similar to those for consumers as a whole (Bernhardt 1981). Clearly it is not the case that older consumers never complain or show an equal disinclination to complain across all types of product or service. Furthermore, other evidence has emerged that distinct sub-segments of the mature market can be identified in terms of propensity to complain that are linked to a mixture of demographic and attitudinal factors. Allen *et al.* (1992) characterised older consumer segments in terms of their different preferences for businesses in terms of the way they handled customer complaints. A sample of older consumers evaluated 17 possible corporate responses to customer complaints and judged how likely it was that they would be satisfied with the response given. Four distinct groups were identified – Assentors, Credibles, Suspectors and Agnostics. Suspectors were more likely to be college educated and were more likely generally to complain about unsatisfactory commodities. Assentors were in a higher income bracket and were generally likely to be satisfied with vendor responses to complaints. Credibles would be satisfied with a written or verbal response from a represen- tative of the retailer provided that person was of sufficient seniority. The agnostics were sceptical individuals and prone to complain about all kinds of things, and were generally difficult to satisfy. This study found, in contrast to earlier research, that many older consumers do complain when they receive poor quality merchandise. However, a prompt and courteous attempt to resolve their complaint by someone in a position of authority is generally acceptable.

This chapter has shown that the grey market comprises a heterogeneous mix of people who can be distinguished in terms of their age, gender, education, financial circumstances and consumer behaviour patterns. An examination of each of these characteristics can reveal a range of significant and subtle differences among members of the mature market in terms of their consumerism. This sort of information should be of value to advertisers, marketers, retailers and others involved in the provision or promotion and distribution of products and services to older consumers. This is a market segment which has been growing in number and wealth, and will continue to do so over the next few decades. It would be a mistake to conceive of this market as comprising a single type of consumer, with common sets of interests, tastes, values and spending power. While great discrepancies in financial circumstances can be found among members of the mature market, most have generally enjoyed improved circumstances in the western world. The next chapter will further confirm the rich and varied nature of this market in terms of the diverse lifestyles and psychological types it embraces.

3 Lifestyles, life stages and consumption

The over-50s represent a growing and increasingly affluent section of society. The last chapter revealed, however, that they also comprise a heterogeneous group who can be subdivided further in terms of finer age-bands and a variety of other demographic and financial variables. Any advertising or marketing campaigns targeted at this age-group therefore would be ill-advised to assume that all individuals who fall within this segment of the population will be equally receptive to the same messages.

This fact needs to be underlined because the strategy adopted to 'sell' to the over-50s by marketers has involved attaching yuppie-style labels to them in an attempt to convince advertising and marketing people that this is a fashionable group at which to target their products, services and promotional appeals. Labels abound such as 'grey panthers', 'woopies' (well-off older people), 'jollies' (jet-setting oldsters with lots of loot), and 'glams' (greying leisured affluent middle-aged). Terms such as 'empty-nesters' and 'September people' come from America where 'grey power' began.

Other behavioural and psychological types have been coined from empirical research into the activity patterns, interests, attitudes, beliefs and values exhibited and verbalised by older people. Such 'psychographic' profiling can yield classifications of the older population which shed light on consumer motives and reactions which cannot be revealed by demographic and financial analyses alone. In this chapter, we take a look at the psychological characteristics of the older consumer.

LIFE STAGE SEGMENTATION

The diversity of the older consumers' market presents marketers with a great challenge. The effort and resources which are currently poured into marketing to youth will have to be redirected, and more sophisticated research and marketing techniques are going to be required if the potential of the mature market is to be realised. Profiling the 50-plus market, and identifying distinct patterns of purchasing behaviour, attitudes and lifestyle is the obvious starting point. The over-50s are not a homogeneous group, and marketing strategies which place members of this age-group into the same pigeon hole are likely to miss out.

One early form of segmentation which went beyond standard demographic and purely economic divisions of consumer markets focused upon the life stage which different individuals had reached. Life cycle is, of course, linked to the age of a person, but stages of life, as defined by an individual's current situation, do not map precisely on to age-bands. What this means is that while two individuals may share the same age and pass through the same life stages, one may do so at a different pace from the other.

Geodemographics have provided one way of classifying the over-50s. In the United Kingdom, the latest census (1992) provided invaluable information about this group. CMDS Marketing Services used census-based geodemographics to identify two groups, which were called the 'thriving greys' and 'senior citizens'. The thriving greys, as defined in this work, were aged 50 upwards, fairly prosperous, likely to own their own home, and had an active lifestyle. They represented the second most affluent group of British adults, and made up 11 per cent of the population. The senior citizens were more elderly, retired and less affluent. They had more passive recreational pursuits and many were older women living alone.

Family life cycle

The idea of 'family life cycle', which was first advocated in the mid-1960s, for example, was designed to provide a more sophisticated segmentation of consumers than age alone. This framework of segmentation focused upon such attributes as whether individuals were married; had children who were resident at home, or who had grown up and moved away; or had divorced or become widowed, and so on (Wells and Gubar 1966). Many marketing researchers felt that this kind of household life cycle concept represented a useful tool for capturing the large systematic components of consumer behaviour. There has been far from universal agreement among them, however, as to how to define the life cycle.

The basics of the life cycle approach to the study of the family were outlined by Hill and Rodgers (1964). Their framework presumed that certain events in the family significantly alter role relationships among family members, often launching a new stage. Examples of such precipitating events were the birth of the first child, departure of the last child from the household, dissolution of the marriage, death of a spouse, and retirement of the principal wage earner.

These and other events, such as changing jobs or moving to a new location to live, have been classified as direct life status changes because they are unique to the type of change, they are experienced by practically all households undergoing that change, and the nature and timing of such events are relatively predictable. These status-changing events are thought to produce a series of predictable stages that are associated with systematic patterns of expenditure by consumers (Andreason 1984).

The limitation of these initial models of family life cycle was that they were grounded in the episodic stages of life change which characterised traditional family structures. The Wells and Gubar (1966) model, for instance, excluded most non-family households (e.g. people who choose to remain single through middle and even older age) as well as all non-traditional family households (e.g. never married single parents or never married co-habiting couples). Thus, more recent models have begun to incorporate these 'non-traditional' types of household. Among the most widely discussed models are those developed by Stampfl (1978), Murphy and Staples (1979) and Gilly and Enis (1982). Whereas Stampfl and Murphy and Staples incorporated the idea of progression through a traditional life cycle path (i.e. via distinct stages), Gilly and Enis simply denoted household composition at given points in time, creating a set of life cycle categories. Moreover, because of the belief that the presence or absence of children is an important determinant of life cycle stage and that age 35 is important for women as a key milestone regarding childbearing, Gilly and Enis (1982) based category membership on the age of the wife rather than the age of the household.

Stampfl (1978) outlined seven major life cycle stages: childhood; adolescence; early singlehood; mature single; newly married couples (young, no children); full nest; and empty nest. The full nest and empty nest stages were each sub-divided into four further sub-categories. In the case of full nest, these were: (i) youngest child under six; (ii) youngest child six or over; (iii) older married couples with dependent children; and (iv) single parenthood. The empty nest period subsumed: (i) older married couples, no children at home, head in labour force; (ii) older married couples, no children at home, head retired; (iii) older solitary survivor in labour force; and (iv) solitary survivor, retired.

The empty nest stages represent the older consumer categories being considered in this book. Among the category (i) empty nesters, Stampfl identified growing preoccupation with travel, recreation, home improvements and hobby-related purchases. There is also an emphasis placed on home security and saving for retirement among this group. Category (ii) generally experience a drop in income, but still want to keep their own home and maintain a reasonable lifestyle. They are older and become bigger consumers of medical care products. They have more time for leisure and spend more time and money on leisure pursuits. Category (iii) individuals are faced with a life alone following the death of a spouse, but still have money to spend and indulge in hobby-related purchases. They also devote attention to younger members of their family and represent a market for gift-buying, especially for grandchildren. Category (iv) are also faced with having to take independent decisions in the absence of a spouse, but they have less income and mobility, and a limited range of product needs.

The Murphy and Staples (1979) family life cycle model bears a striking resemblance to that of Stampfl, although it focuses upon adult categories and makes distinctions based on age, marital status, and presence or absence of children. It allows for the fact that marital status can change regardless of age. It thus includes young single and older unmarried categories; young, middle-aged and older married with or without children; and young and middle-aged divorced with or without children.

For Gill and Enis (1982) life stage categories are defined principally according to two dimensions: size of household and age of head of household. A threefold age division (under 35 years, 35–64 years, and over 64 years) is crossed over with a fourfold household size division (one adult household, two adult household, two adults plus children, and one adult plus children). Together these two dimensions yielded 13 different life stage groupings which included young, middle-aged and old single people, young, middle-aged and old people with no dependent children; young, middle-aged and older couples with children; and young, middle-aged and older single parents.

Consumer researchers have suggested that life cycle can be meaningfully related to consumption and spending (McCleod and Ellis 1982; Douthill and Fedyk 1988, 1990). Life cycle measures have also been found to differentiate significantly between individuals in terms of consumer-related attitudes, leisure activities, food and beverage consumption, ownership of various household items and use of services (Schaninger and Danko 1993).

Retirement

The life stage of 'retirement' has been suggested as a segmentation variable (Burnett 1989). To be effective, however, marketers must have a more thorough understanding of retirement status than whether or not an individual is gainfully employed on a full-time basis. They must understand the role of retirement and the psychological adjustment made to cope with the role. A successful retirement is anticipated and planned for, resulting in greater satisfaction at this stage of life.

Retirement status is a significant predictor of activity level and certain consumer behaviours. Burnett (1989) found that many newly retired men increased their participation in activities such as exercise, shopping and entertaining. Activity level was moderated by age, income level and state of health. Those individuals in poor health or with limited economic means were likely to drop activities such as returning an unsatisfactory product or joining a club.

BEHAVIOURAL SEGMENTATION

Behavioural segmentation differentiates between consumers in terms of their patterns of consumer-related behaviour. This approach focuses on psychological and product orientations of consumers. This form of segmentation can be carried out on the basis of three different types of criteria: (1) product buying patterns; (2) benefits derived from products; and (3) psychological classification of consumers. The latter deals with broad-based measures of patterns of behaviour connected with different lifestyles, and is not restricted just to a consideration of behaviour. In addition, consumers may be distinguished in terms of the values and beliefs which may underpin their consumer activities. These characteristics are examined, in the context of the older consumer, in a separate section later on in this chapter.

With product usage segmentation, consumers are classified in terms of whether they ever buy certain products and, if so, how often they buy them. Even finer distinctions than those based upon product orientations can be achieved within product categories by examining the particular brands that consumers prefer within a product range. The usefulness of such an analysis is that, by pinpointing specific product buying and brand preference patterns, it can yield information of value to marketers wishing to reach specific target markets by distinguishing fairly precisely the types of people at whom marketing messages for particular products should be targeted (Gunter and Furnham 1992).

Product benefit analysis goes beyond simply identifying how often particular products or brands are purchased to uncover the benefits consumers perceive they get from products. Knowing that one brand is bought more often than another may reveal little about the reasons for success or failure in a particular product market (Haley 1968, 1984a, 1984b). A product benefit assessment can indicate what needs or expectations of consumers are being met by a product, and the extent to which one brand is believed to meet those needs or expectations better than another. Such information can be very important in the context of producing a marketing campaign designed to change or enhance a product's or brand's image.

Applying the benefit segmentation method to older consumers, French and Fox (1985) reported distinct patterns of adjustment characterised by varying levels of success in adapting to retirement living (see also Reichard, Livson and Peterson 1962). A classification system outlining nine separate approaches to ageing was produced with which to segment older consumer markets (see Table 3.1).

French and Fox (1985) questioned 200 gerontologists about the relative sizes of the nine groups of older consumers. Analysis of the gerontologists' ratings of the adjustment patterns suggested that two patterns underlay the characteristics of each group. The first factor was the extent to which old age is viewed as another stage of life to be experienced and enjoyed. The second factor is the degree of insecurity and dependence associated with the adjustment pattern.

Two of the groups were deemed to have adjusted well to retirement, the *Reorganiser* and *Focused* groups, and these accounted for about 40 per cent of older consumers. The individuals in these two groups behaved similarly and had similar outlooks to the point that they formed a cluster or segment. The Reorganisers and Focused were socially active, were willing to try new things, were independent, and possessed a positive image of themselves in the sense of self-respect.

The next largest segment contained the two groups – *Succourance Seekers* and *Constricted*. These older consumers had some trouble adjusting to old age. This segment accounted for almost one in four older consumers. Both the Succourance Seekers and the Constricted, especially the latter, were particularly concerned about their health. The Succourance Seekers were also relatively dependent on others and perhaps, as a result, more socially active than the Constricted.

The third largest cluster accounted for about 17 per cent of older consumers. This cluster was regarded as being composed of three groups: *Apathetic*, *Angry* and *Self-Blaming*. Their lack of adjustment to retirement living meant that they

Table 3.1 Adjustment patterns for older consumers

Healthy adjustment

The Reorganisers have had success integrating themselves into retirement living. They attempt to stay active by reorganising their lives, substituting new activities for those that were abandoned after retirement. They enjoy life by seeking new experiences and social interaction.

The Focused group shows a mature approach to old age. Life has been and continues to be satisfying for them. The Focused people have chosen a rather small number of activities to which they devote time and energy.

The Disengaged are self-directed, calm and contented. They have accepted old age by reducing their activities to a relatively low level. Although interested in the goings-on of the world, they prefer to withdraw from most of their past personal associations and activities.

Fair adjustment

The Constricted people are preoccupied with their physical well-being. They have lived a satisfying life but view old age, new experiences, and social interaction as threatening that satisfaction. To avoid these threats, they structure a narrow set of activities for themselves which they pursue in a habitual pattern.

The Holding-On group contains achievement-oriented people who drive themselves hard. They are defensive about their age, fear the rocking chair image, and are reluctant to admit that they are indeed old. In keeping with this defensive posture they try to hold on to life by keeping busy.

The Succourance Seekers, although moderately active, prefer a passive life. They have strong dependency needs and lean on others for emotional support and responsiveness. Retirement for them is a refuge, a safe port after the turbulent working years.

Poor adjustment

The Angry group consists of aggressive, rigid and highly suspicious people who see themselves as victims of circumstance. They desire little pleasure from life and look back on the past as a series of disappointments. They view life as a failure but project the blame for that failure on to others rather than on to themselves.

The Apathetic group contains elderly people who have truly retreated to their rocking chairs. They feel that life is hard and there is not much they can do about it. Thus, they limit social interaction and make little effort to keep up with things outside their immediate surroundings.

The Self-Blamers look back on life as a series of unattained goals. These perceived failures have caused them to be highly critical and contemptuous of themselves. They sit in depression, showing little sign of ambition or initiative.

Source: French and Fox 1985

could be a difficult market segment to reach. The Angry, Apathetic and Self-Blaming were also socially inactive with a low level of self-esteem. They were seen to be somewhat dependent in that they would rather be served than serve themselves. However, they were not especially influenced by the opinions of others. These three groups, particularly the Angry, were especially cautious when spending money, a fact that is likely to indicate they have very limited spending power.

The *Holding-On* and *Disengaged* groups formed two self-contained clusters. Each of these segments represented about 10 per cent of older consumers. The Holding-On group were primarily concerned with maintaining appearance. They also enjoyed going out, indulging in the physical pleasures of life, and seeing their friends. The Holding-On group also claimed that they frequently thought about their health. They, like the Reorganisers and Focused, preferred to be self-sufficient. The Disengaged accepted the fact that they were getting old and adapted to this fate by withdrawing from many activities. Their average scores, across most of the opinions and perceptions measured, tended to be low. But the Disengaged exhibited a particularly low level of concern about how they appeared and did not generally go out much. The one respect in which they did exhibit a similar viewpoint to another group, namely the Holding-On group, was in their low level of agreement that they would rather be served than serve themselves in a retail situation.

PSYCHOGRAPHIC SEGMENTATION

Psychological measures have been used to distinguish between consumers across markets in general as well as in relation to the markets for particular product classes. The psychological tools for classifying consumers have derived from two sources: (1) clinically developed personality tests and (2) custom-built psychological profiles, designed specifically for use in the consumer behaviour context and usually comprising measures of consumers' motives for buying or values, beliefs and opinions about consumerism or about particular categories of consumer behaviour (Gunter and Furnham 1992).

Drawing upon personality theories and personality tests, marketers have attempted to discover whether certain deep-seated personality dispositions can be used to predict general consumer behaviour tendencies (Kinnear, Taylor and Sadrudin 1972) and more specific product tastes and preferences (Koponen 1986). This 'off-the-shelf' approach to psychologically classifying consumers has not consistently proven to be effective.

Generalised psychological profiles of consumers have been developed in an attempt to classify the entire population. Such systems are based on general value systems, or attitudes and beliefs which distinguish people in general. They aim to provide a general guide to the way people can be expected to behave in the consumer market context, rather than pinpoint the extent to which consumers will prefer one product or brand over another. The best known of these typologies are the Values and Lifestyles (VALS) system (Mitchell 1983) derived from the theoretical base of Maslow's (1954) need hierarchy. The initial classification system produced equivocal results as an indicator of consumer behaviour patterns. A second version was reported by Riche (1989) which introduced a new model of consumer classification, with purportedly better predictive powers. A rival system, called the List of Values (LOV) was developed by another research group (Kahle 1983; Veroff, Douvan and Kulka 1981), derived from a combination of Feather's (1975), Maslow's (1954) and Rokeach's (1973) work on attitudes, needs and values. The system, it was argued, was more closely related to the values associated with life's major roles, such as marriage, work and leisure, as well as consumption. VALS and LOV had a number of similar features. Both systems distinguished consumers in terms of characteristics such as need for achievement and need for belongingness or affiliation. Both systems also differentiated between people in terms of selfish, inner-directed drives and societally-conscious, outwardly-directed values. The developers of LOV, however, reported that their measure of consumer values provided better predictions of consumer behaviour than the VALS system in relation to a number of products (Kahle, Beatty and Homer 1986). Further tests of this opinion suggested that the advantage of LOV over VALS could be explained in terms of a number of demographic items included in the LOV item battery. Without these demographic items present, LOV proved to be no more predictive of consumers' product preferences than VALS (Novak and MacEvoy 1990).

Psychographics and the grey market

The segment aged 50 and over has in many ways a different set of activities, interests and opinions from those of younger groups. Older consumers, however, do not all share the same attributes or daily habits. For example, older people may exhibit tendencies to seek warmer climates during winter months, go to bed earlier, engage in less physical activity, have more time for leisure pursuits, and may show a more positive identification with their age than the negative stereotypes which often abound about them among younger people.

Some marketing researchers have suggested that the nature of values and behavioural norms among older people is changing. Age has become as much a state of mind as a chronological and physical reality for many people (Schiffman and Sherman 1991). Those who perceive themselves as 'younger' tend to experience greater life satisfaction and appreciate those products and services that allow them to do this. The concept of 'cognitive age' as a segmentation variable is discussed in more detail later in this chapter.

Some marketing researchers have examined the relative significance of psychographic characters alongside other variables (e.g. demographics) as predictors of consumer behaviour in relation to specific types of products, while others have tried to develop universal typologies for all consumers regardless of the type of consumer behaviour. Among older consumers, researchers have produced typologies for specific areas of consumerism such as fashion (Huddleston,

Ford and Bickle 1993). Here fashion leadership was predicted by three lifestyle factors linked to how outgoing and positive thinking older consumers were in their attitude towards fashion shopping, how socially active they were, and how prone to building up credit. These factors (rather than demographic characteristics such as age, income level, educational levels or occupational status) were the key predictors. Much psychographic research has been more concerned with producing useful universal typologies.

Values and lifestyles approaches

A number of marketing researchers have explored the efficacy of values and lifestyles measures in distinguishing among different categories of older consumer. As with other research into broad-based psychological consumer typologies, these classifications were concerned with mapping general consumer orientations rather than predicting specific product purchase habits.

Day *et al.* (1987) conducted a study which addressed two specific questions: (1) Is there empirical support for a segmentation approach within the elderly cohort? (2) If there appear to be distinct segments within the cohort, can those segments be reached effectively and efficiently? If so, how (i.e. through which media and what kinds of message)?

Day *et al.* (1987) decided to experiment with lifestyle measures. The sample they selected consisted of 112 married females over 65 who were not working outside the home. They were given 137 attitude, interest and opinion items. Following factor analysis this set of items was reduced to 21. Cluster analysis performed on the 21 psychographic variables yielded a two-cluster solution. Then, a second cluster analysis was performed on activity items only and this resulted in the two primary groups being divided into two subgroups each, yielding four groups in all.

The two major groups were designated the *Self-Sufficient* and the *Persuadable*. The first group exhibited a degree of self-sufficiency that reflected internal locus of control. This manifested itself in higher risk taking. The second group was more marked by an apparent susceptibility to persuasion – more akin to external locus of control.

Within the *Self-Sufficient* group one of the two subgroups comprised the *Active Integrated* – self-perceived opinion leaders who give rather than request information when interacting with others. They were affluent to the point of feeling capable of handling most situations, with their own decision-making ability not being overwhelmed by current social pressures. As well as being opinionated they were also politically conservative.

Members of this segment were characterised as perceiving themselves as competent to make decisions and handle life. They generally were better educated than other segments and believed that success came primarily from hard work. If they worked outside the home, they tended to demonstrate more nurturant and achievement-oriented rather than aggressive traits. In retirement they enjoyed life in a physical sense and were the most likely of the four groups to try new products.

Members of the second subgroup, the *Disengaged Integrated*, expressed opinions similar to the *Active Integrated* group, but these people lived within a more limited income. While less active than the first segment, their self-confidence carried them through most situations which they faced, the one notable exception being handling financial pressures. They entertained friends in their home and enjoyed a social drink. Generally the *Disengaged* were quite content with their lives. They were not social isolates. Self-directed, they were interested in more than their daily routine and kept abreast of what was happening in the world.

The two segments of the *Persuadable* group were differentiated along several characteristics. One segment, the *Passive Dependent* showed a resignation to life that approached apathy. Not only were they subdued but also had no desire to 'stand out'. New social contacts were minimal and they were content to make their homes the centre of their entire life. Their concern about their physical appearance was an after-thought, at best. They were generally unassertive and generally unconcerned about matters outside the home. They neither cared for nor adjusted well to major changes, relying for the most part on long-established behavioural patterns and habits. Members of this group usually had not worked outside the home and were at best only moderately satisfied with life.

Unfulfilled desires reflected the character of people in the second subgroup of the *Persuadable*. The *Defended Constricted* were highly sociable, sought acceptance and had the financial means to satisfy desires, especially those desires for something new and different. What they lacked was the self-confidence to complete the actions to fulfil those desires. They were somewhat averse to risk and sought assurance from others that they were indeed doing the wise thing. Their social orientation was a function of the fear that being housebound would cause them to miss the interesting facets of life. They tended to be preoccupied with health and/or trying to continue with the activities they enjoyed during middle life. Moreover, they tried to sustain a high level of activity and to like activity outside the home in order to ward off the image of incapacity due to ageing. Day *et al.* (1987) suggested that this information about older consumers' characteristics could guide advertisers in deciding upon campaign strategies to employ in respect of particular commodities.

With respect to creative strategy, advertising messages directed at members of the *Self-Sufficient* group, for example, should reflect their internal locus of control. That is, they should be portrayed as self-confident, independent and outgoing. In order to design advertisements to which these people can easily relate, scenarios might show these people as leading active lifestyles, for example entertaining friends, attending events outside the home, and looking the part of sociable, up-to-date individuals. In contrast, people in the *Persuadable* group are more likely to relate to scenarios centred on activities in and around the home.

For advertisers who want to target their messages more narrowly, the profiles of the four subgroups suggest ways of doing so. For instance, those people in the *Active Integrated* segment were more self-confident and therefore more self-reliant in their decision-making. They were more satisfied with their financial status and somewhat more adventurous. Hence, not only should the advertising reflect this self-confidence, but it should also provide factual information to enable this segment to make their own decisions. In contrast, the *Disengaged Integrated* women tended to seek advice from others when making decisions, so advertising depicting people seeking advice and information from significant others is more likely to be effective in communicating the selling message to this segment.

The two sub-sets of the *Persuadable* group also offered contrasts that could be useful in designing advertising messages. For example, those people in the *Passive Dependent* segment tended to fit traditional old-age stereotypes. In other words, they were more conservative, more emotionally dependent and more risk-averse than those people in the *Defended Constricted* segment. Moreover, the *Passive Dependent* were 'home bodies' and rarely ventured out, whereas the *Defended Constricted* were much more sociable and active. While the advertiser would not want to portray the *Passive Dependent* as dullards, sensitivity to their insecurities and lack of social contact could increase the effectiveness of advertising messages.

Gollub and Javitz (1989) reported a national US study of how older adults prefer to live in retirement. The study – Lifestyles and Values of Older Adults (LAVOA) – was sponsored by the National Association for Senior Living Industries (NASLI) and conducted by SRI International. The study was commissioned to provide a better understanding of how older adults think and how they differ from one another. It revealed six older-adult market segments defined by psychological, demographic and health factors. Each segment of older adults differed in how it wanted to live in retirement. Some wanted to live in single-family homes, while others wanted independent apartments, congregate-care facilities or life-care communities. Congregate-care facilities are retirement housing complexes that offer residents a variety of on-site services, including meals, for a monthly fee. Life-care communities offer unlimited care until death, including on-site nursing homes, for an entry fee. Some older adults wanted community and recreational amenities, and convenience and health services, while others were not interested in services, preferring to remain independent.

In a survey of 3,600 nationally representative people aged 55 and older, SRI identified four psychological factors that influenced these preferences. First, autonomy–dependence – the degree to which people are driven by the need to be on their own. Second, introversion–extroversion – the degree to which people are other-directed and seek social involvement. Third, self-indulgence–self-denial – how much people seek gratification. Fourth, resistance–openness to change – how adaptable people are. The SRI analysis also examined the health status of older Americans to determine how much people's functional ability affects their lifestyle preferences, apart from psychological or socio-economic factors.

Six distinct psychographic segments of older adults emerged from the study: (1) Explorers; (2) Adapters; (3) Pragmatists; (4) Attainers; (5) Martyrs; and (6) Preservers. Each segment has a distinct psychology and distinct preferences for how it wants to live in retirement. Gollub and Javitz (1989) provided a descriptive biographical synopsis for each type.

Explorers want to do things their way. They are self-reliant and less willing than any other segment to believe children have an obligation to assist their parents. They are also the most introverted segment, reflecting their individualism. This segment is in moderately better health, is slightly younger and is somewhat better educated than older adults as a whole. Explorers' rugged individualism reflects life experiences that taught them self-reliance; they have less faith in the ability of others to meet their needs. Their autonomy and tendency towards self-denial may reflect a distrust of institutions and poor self-image.

Adapters are the most extroverted segment and they are also open to change. But no other segment except Preservers is more dependent. Adapters are the socialites among their peers; personal relationships and material possessions play an important role in their sense of well-being. Along with Attainers, Adapters have the highest level of education and they are second only to the same segment in self-indulgence, health and wealth. Adapters are less willing to believe that children have an obligation to assist their parents than are older adults as a whole. Adapters are more likely than average older Americans to live with a spouse and children, and to like where they live, but they have also thought about moving. They are more inclined than the average to consider moving to an apartment. They rank second among the six segments (following Attainers) in their interest in moving to a better climate and changing to a new lifestyle.

Pragmatists are the second most extroverted segment (following Adapters), the second most willing to agree that children have an obligation to assist their parents (following Martyrs), the second oldest (following Preservers) and the third most self-indulgent (following Adapters and Attainers). Pragmatists are also slightly less well educated and wealthy, but healthier than the older adult population as a whole. They are average in their dependence and openness to change. Pragmatists are conservative and conformist in their values. While they are self-indulgent, their sense of well-being depends more than other segments on how they are perceived. They are also more family centred than the other segments.

Pragmatists are the second most likely group to live alone, the least likely to have thoughts about moving and the second most likely to think about moving to a nursing home, an older-adult housing complex, or to get help in caring for themselves. They are not interested in moving to an adult community, though they rank second in their concern about having social supports, and rank first in wanting to live with people of the same religion.

Among all the segments, Attainers are the youngest, most autonomous, self-indulgent, healthy and wealthy. Along with Adapters, they have the best education, and they are second only to Adapters in their openness to change. Next to Explorers, Attainers are the least willing to believe that children have an obligation to help their parents. This segment is average in its introversion/extroversion. Attainers are more impulse oriented than the other segments, and more capable of realising their objectives. Their values are oriented toward getting what they want.

Attainers are the most likely to own their own homes, the most likely to live with their spouse and the most likely to have children living at home. They are the least likely to want to move to an adult community with a service package. They are most likely to have thought of moving – particularly to another state – to a smaller home, to get cash from their current home or to live in a better climate with a new lifestyle and fewer chores. They are more likely to want children to be included in any community where they live, and they care about having movie theatres, cultural events, parks and colleges on site nearby.

Martyrs are resistant to change. This is the segment that most agrees that children should help their parents. Though Martyrs are the second youngest segment next to Attainers, they are second only to Preservers in being the least well-educated, the most self-denying, the least wealthy and the least healthy. They are second only to Explorers in being introverted. Martyrs stand out because they are less able to express and implement their values than the other segments (though they are not the poorest, or the least healthy group). They rationalise their helplessness through denial and introversion.

Martyrs are more likely than the other segments to live with their children or relatives, or to find their current home too hard to maintain. They are the segment most likely to want to leave the community, to want to move to a larger home, to want to move closer to shops and to consider moving to an adult community.

Preservers are by far the least healthy segment – almost all the survey respondents with serious health problems fell into this category. Preservers are second only to Martyrs in their resistance to change. They are highly need-driven compared with the other segments – their concern is with preserving what they have, and they have little. They look to helpers, whether family or professionals, to maintain their quality of life.

Preservers are the segment most likely to rent an apartment or live in older-adult housing in a high-rise building. They are most likely to live alone, or with children or relatives. They are the most likely to consider moving to older-adult housing, and they are most likely to feel that security, central dining, meal delivery, maid, maintenance and housekeeping services are essential in retirement housing.

Lifestyle characteristics were found elsewhere to be predictors of fashion opinion leadership for older consumers, aged 50–85 years, while demographic variables such as real age, income, educational level, house size and occupation, did not exhibit any significant links to fashion-related opinions (Huddleston, Ford and Bickle 1993).

Further American research found six lifestyle clusters among an older consumer sample which were called: Self-reliants, Quiet Introverts, Family-orienteds, Active Retirees, Young and Secures, and Solitaires (Sorce, Tyler and Loomis 1989). Strategic marketing suggestions were offered for each of these groups. Satisfaction would be increased if a product were designed and tailored to meet the needs of a particular lifestyle type. Moschis (1991) was critical of the segmentation strategies suggested by Sorce *et al.* (1989). First, he noted that 'age is usually not a major factor in determining older consumers' responses to marketing activities' (p. 34). Second, the inclusion of other variables may still not accurately define different groups of older consumers. Contradictions arise in fitting consumers into artificial categories. For example, in general, older people have more disposable income than younger people and are perceived as relatively well-off. However, they have higher medical care and insurance costs. They are considered to be thrifty and yet are in need of discounts. Moschis called for more data and less speculation on some of these older consumer psychographic typologies.

Research in the United Kingdom has been carried out by the market research agency, BMRB, using its Target Group Index (TGI) – a large scale consumer survey which obtains vast amounts of data from a substantial nationwide sample of respondents on a wide range of consumer-related matters. After conducting a cluster analysis on data collected in the 1993 TGI survey, five significant groups of consumer were identified in terms of their attitudes and behaviour. The context of this research was shopping. The resultant groups represented examples of the kinds of divisions which can be identified among grey market consumers.

The first group identified by TGI were 'astute cosmopolitans', who constituted just over 19 per cent of the 50 to 75 age-group and, as their name suggested, were discerning shoppers with a strong sense of style. By contrast, the 'temperate xenophobes', who made up 20.4 per cent of the 50 to 75-year-olds, tended to be unwilling to go abroad, eat foreign foods, or be even a little adventurous in their lifestyles.

The 'thrifty traditionalists' were the next group identified by TGI, and also made up 20.4 per cent of the 50 to 75 age-group. A further 19 per cent of the third-agers fell into the 'outgoing funlovers' group, and the largest group, making up 21.4 per cent of the 50 to 75 age-group, were dubbed the 'apathetic spenders'. These people used credit cards to buy things they could not afford, and did not like parting with cash.

One of the fundamental ways in which people can vary is in their general approach to life. One illustration of this is that certain individuals will be more prepared than others to take risks. Among older consumers, those who are less averse to risk taking may be targeted to try a new product. One group, identified as the New Age elderly, perceive themselves to be younger and more youthful than they really are, and are also less fearful of trying new products. They have been found to have greater confidence in their purchasing behaviour, buy new products selectively, and are particularly interested in inner growth and new experiences as opposed to physical possessions (Schiffman and Sherman 1991).

Elsewhere, this segment has been referred to as the New Seniors, who are creative, wise, active and concerned about the world. They are interested in an experiential lifestyle and intellectual growth. As a group, however, they tend to be poorly understood by marketers (Wolfe 1990).

Self-perceived age

Chronological age may not necessarily reflect how old a person feels. The belief that two people of the same age can be expected to exhibit consumer behaviour patterns which have greater similarity than patterns one would expect to find with two people of different ages, rests on an assumption that a person's actual age is the crucial defining variable. However, some people remain more 'youthful' than others, in a psychological sense, despite their actual age and this often has a bearing on how they perceive themselves and the world around them, in turn shaping the way they behave. Age can be a state of mind as much as being a physical state (Schiffman and Sherman 1991). Research on self-perceived age has indicated that how old people think of themselves may provide better insights into consumer behaviour than chronological age.

Opinions about 'getting old' tend to shift with the age of the individual. For many people aged over 60, old age may not be recognised to begin until 75. Many people aged 60 or more say they feel ten years younger (Brown 1986). This subjective age, or how old we feel, is related to health and financial conditions. It has also been shown that the way older people adjust to old age provides a useful classification system for differentiating market segments among them (French and Fox 1985). As a result of such factors as these, a variety of segmentation approaches for the older market has been offered. One review of 33 segmentation studies in the mature market found that five key variables were used: (1) discretionary income; (2) health; (3) activity level; (4) discretionary time; and (5) response to others (Bone 1991). Wide variations in the character of the older consumer can be found in respect of each of these variables. Consequently, older consumers represent a divergent group. It is important to realise, however, that chronological age may not be the best way to understand consumer need (*Marketing News* 1988). Older adults can occupy a number of different roles (Schewe and Balazs 1990) and exist in a variety of conditions, hence marketers must relate effectively to selected target groups by thoroughly understanding them (Miller 1991; Goodhead 1991).

Consumers' self-perceptions of their age have been referred to as 'cognitive age' (Barak and Schiffman 1981). While it has been observed that older people think and behave differently from younger people (Schewe 1990), older consumers cannot be regarded as a homogeneous age-group, even in terms of 'age' itself. Certainly, chronological age is closely linked to purchase levels for particular age-related products, especially medical products. In addition, though, there are wider differences in expenditure, both in terms of how much is spent and the types of commodities that are purchased (Lazer and Shaw 1987; Abrams 1990). Older people also manifest certain differences in their information-processing abilities, displaying qualitatively different patterns of product information usage (John and Cole 1986; Cole and Houston 1987; Cole and Gaeth 1990). Older consumers are more responsive to advertising which provides an informational appeal on behalf of the product, for example by pointing out the product's benefits and usefulness. Stylistic production techniques, special effects and lively music or other features designed to have an impact at an emotional rather than a cognitive level may be found distracting by older consumers (see Chapter 6 for a more detailed discussion of these issues).

It has been regarded as increasingly important, however, to understand how older consumers view themselves with respect to ageing. Failure to acknowledge this perspective can have unwanted consequences in the consumer context. For one thing, older consumers do not wish to be patronised or portrayed as a vulnerable group unable to cope effectively by themselves in taking informed consumer decisions.

Use of the cognitive age measure involves asking respondents to select the age decade (twenties, thirties, forties, etc.) to which they feel they belong for each personal age measure. There are four key dimensions: the age a person feels; the age a person thinks he/she looks; the age a person perceives him/ herself to act; and the age a person perceives to be reflective of his/her interests. Cognitive age is computed as the numerical average of the decade mid-points of the four sub-components.

Research using this measure has found that older consumers frequently align themselves in terms of age-related feelings and actions with a younger age group than their own (Barak and Schiffman 1981; Underhill and Cadwell 1983). This tendency to perceive oneself as being younger than one's real age occurs equally among men and women (Barak and Rahtz 1989). People who feel younger than their real age are generally more satisfied with life (Sherman, Schiffman and Dillon 1988). Cognitive age has also been linked to aspects of consumer behaviour. Cognitively 'younger' older women manifest higher self-confidence and greater fashion interest. They tend to be more work-oriented and exhibit greater participation in entertainment and culturally-related activities. Cognitively 'younger' older women were apparently still concerned about their personal image and this influenced their dress sense and clothing purchases (Wilkes 1992).

INFORMATION SEARCH SEGMENTATION

Several studies have performed market segmentation exercises on the basis of information sources used for making purchase decisions. The significance of identifying these features of the older consumer market rests on research findings which have indicated differences between older and younger adult consumers in the way they search for product-related information. Factors such as experience with the product category, familiarity with various brands and the information processing abilities of these different consumer segments have emerged as explanations for this difference.

A survey of car buyers found that older consumers searched less while shopping for a new vehicle and were likely to express greater satisfaction with their previous choices when compared to younger consumers (Furse, Punj and

Stewart 1984). It was suggested that age differences may have emerged in this case because older consumers had more experience to rely on than did younger consumers when they selected a car.

In another study, when selecting unfamiliar brands from four different product categories, older housewives considered fewer attributes and alternatives than did younger housewives (Schaninger and Sciplimpaglia 1981). In this study, it was reasoned that older consumers with diminished working memory capacity have difficulty holding in their heads details about numerous alternatives in a product range. As a result, they may engage in a much more limited search of product-related information than do younger consumers. It has even been suggested that the inability of older consumers to evaluate and process new information about different brands could lead to them making inferior choices (Janis and Mann 1977).

A further demonstration of this restricted search of product-related information has been found in the context of food shopping by older consumers. They are less likely than younger consumers to use nutritional information about food products. However, this difference between consumers from different generations could be reduced if consumers were required to write down the nutrition information provided with products. This could alleviate the effect of information processing limitations on the part of older consumers when having to make nutritional evaluations about food products (Cole and Bulasubrahmanian 1993). Individually delivered reminders to use nutritional information promoted more extensive searching and increased use of the nutritional information provided on product packaging among all consumers. Even then, younger consumers searched these guidelines more intensively than did older consumers and made more informed product selections.

Westbrook and Fornell (1979) identified four segments of major household appliance buyers based on use of information sources for making these purchases. Kiel and Layton (1981) identified three segments among Australian car buyers based on information sources used: 'low searchers', 'high searchers', and 'selective searchers'. These studies were concerned with purchases in which personal selling plays a dominant role, however, so the results might be somewhat removed from advertising decision-making. Lumpkin and Festervand (1987) identified three older consumer segments based on respondents' use of eight different product information sources.

A number of studies have been completed on use of information sources by older consumers. Some older consumers rely heavily upon interpersonal communication to find out about products, brands and where to shop. Others use a combination of information from other people, media advertising, and point of purchase impressions (see Klippel and Sweeney 1974; Schiffman 1971).

Lumpkin and Caballero (1985) found that those older consumers with an internal locus of control (perception that they are in control of their own lives) were more likely to rely on personal experience as an information source or on objective sources such as magazine articles. Older consumers with an external locus of control (a perception that they have little control over their own lives) tended to rely more heavily on catalogues, money guarantees, endorsements, and advice of family members. Davis and French (1989) also explored ways of segmenting the older consumers market. The objectives of their study were:

1   To identify potential audience segments among the older consumer based primarily on attitudes toward advertising.
2   To develop psychographic profiles for each of these potential audiences in order to provide insight on the make-up of these individuals and to facilitate comparison of results to those found in previous studies.
3   To examine media consumption among these audiences to determine whether the diversity identified with respect to information usage is reflected in media habits.

The study used a sample of 217 married female respondents aged 60 and over. Respondents were asked to rate agreement with over 200 psychographic statements, which dealt with a variety of attitudes, opinions and interests. They were also questioned about their sources of information about brands and products and their beliefs about advertising. Four statements of opinion were used to measure this last variable: 'I often seek out the advice of friends regarding brands and products'; 'Information from advertising helps me make better buying decisions'; 'I don't believe a company's ad when it claims test results show its product to be better than competitive products'; and 'Advertising insults my intelligence'. Three distinct segments of female older consumer were identified based on advertising attitudes and beliefs: Engaged, Autonomous and Receptive.

The Engaged agreed that advertising insulted her intelligence and did not believe a company's advertisement when it claimed that test results showed its product to be better than competing products. She often sought the advice of friends regarding brands and products and agreed that information from advertising helped her to make better buying decisions. In sharp contrast to the other two groups, these women relied upon the opinions of others in evaluating products. The level of social activity of these women makes it clear that they have not disengaged from society as some older consumers tend to do.

Autonomous women did not seek out the advice of friends regarding brands and products and were neutral about the value of information from advertising in making purchase decisions. These women also felt that advertising insulted their intelligence and were highly suspicious of competitive advertisements. These individuals did not seem to rely heavily on any external sources for information. They apparently relied more upon personal experience as an internal information source.

Receptive women did not believe that advertising insulted their intelligence, thereby differing from women in the first two segments. While this type was suspicious of competitive advertising, they believed that advertising helped them make better buying decisions. While these individuals seemed to utilise and rely on information from advertising, they did not tend to consult with friends about brands and products. The attitudes these women held towards advertising made this group a more receptive audience for advertisers.

Four psychographic profiles emerged following analysis of responses to the 200+ psychographic statements. These were: (1) a cosmopolitan dimension (e.g. 'I am interested in the cultures of other countries'; 'I enjoy looking through fashion magazines'); (2) importance of cooking and baking (e.g. 'I like to bake'; 'I like to cook'); (3) combination of innovativeness and concerns for personal and social issues (e.g. 'I try to select foods that are fortified with vitamins and minerals'; 'I am usually among the first to try new products'); and (4) negative outlook on business in general (e.g. 'Generally, manufacturers' warranties are not worth the paper they are printed on'; 'Most big companies are just out for themselves').

Engaged segment members would seem to be of special interest to companies introducing new products for older consumers. This group was more innovative than either of the other segments. The task of reaching this segment is aided by their media habits. This group used mass media to a considerable extent, especially news media. In addition, they were socially involved and often consulted with friends regarding products. This might aid in disseminating new product knowledge through word-of-mouth communication.

Autonomous segment members were the least innovative of the three groups and would not be as attractive as targets for new products. They did not use mass media as heavily as those in the Engaged segment and seemed to be more socially isolated. The Receptive segment members were a particularly attractive target for those businesses which rely on advertising to communicate with prospective customers. These women displayed fairly favourable attitudes towards advertising and business. Of special note was their use of television comedy programmes. Comedic appeals might be appropriate in reaching this group. Advertising done in connection with television comedy programmes would probably be more effective in reaching this group than either of the other two segments.

Consumers can be segmented not only according to their demographic characteristics but also in terms of their psychological profiles. Associated with the psychological divisions among consumers are the core values and lifestyles to which they adhere, and which can play an important part in shaping their product and service tastes and preferences. Psychological profiling can be as revealing among older consumers as it can among younger consumers. How older consumers perceive themselves can also represent a powerful factor through which to differentiate subgroups of the mature market which have relevance to understanding the consumer behaviour of people in this market segment.

In Chapter 2, actual age divisions among members of the mature market were found to be associated with significant differences in consumer activity. In this chapter, the concept of 'cognitive age' has been shown to have equally significant implications for understanding consumer behaviour among older consumers. The identification of psychologically distinguishing characteristics of older consumers can lead to a deeper level of understanding of their consumer behaviour, as compared with an examination of demographically distinguishing features, which are descriptive rather than explanatory in nature. A study of older consumer values, lifestyles and psychological make-up can uncover drives and motives underpinning consumer behaviour, and the objectives or goals which older consumers wish to achieve through their purchases.

4   Leisure and media use

One characteristic feature associated with entering the 'third age' is the slowing down of individuals in terms of their activities; these become reduced in range and variety and are pursued less vigorously than when they were younger. A closer examination of the changing nature of the older generation today reveals that this stereotype of the older person may be misleading and, for increasing numbers of them, essentially untrue. People over the age of 50 or even 60 or 70 are not necessarily past their sell-by date. Many retain youthful vitality and ambitions. What is more, growing numbers of people in this age bracket continue to enjoy good health, and when coupled with greater disposable income than younger people and more time in which to spend that money on leisure pursuits, this places them in the market for many different commodities.

From a marketing point of view, the grey market can be regarded as an increasingly attractive target group for many advertisers. The key question then becomes how best can this group be reached? Knowing the answer to this question requires some understanding of how older consumers use their time and, in particular, how different mass media fit into the picture. In this chapter therefore, we will turn our attention to the older consumer and leisure time usage. It will become clear that while older consumers at the younger end of their age spectrum remain physically active in many ways, as a group, they are major consumers of the mass media. The communications literature is replete with studies relating to reaching older consumers, although these studies have typically dealt with older persons as one more or less homogeneous group. As earlier chapters have demonstrated, however, older consumers can be differentiated into distinct subgroups on the basis of a variety of demographic, behavioural and psychological measures. Patterns of leisure time and mass media usage therefore need to be considered in relation to these factors whenever appropriate.

Older consumers exhibit a healthy appetite for many different media, including different types of print and broadcast media. Leisure-related and media-related behaviours do change as people enter their retirement years, with such changes reflecting the greater availability of time to pursue personal interests or hobbies, or simply to relax. Thus, the reallocation of time represents the most significant shift in general behaviour among older consumers. A retired person has more discretionary time than ever before and can thus allocate more time to certain activities than was possible while still employed.

Of course, not everyone aged over 50 is retired. Despite increased opportunities to take early retirement, there are still many people aged between 50 and 65 years who remain gainfully employed. The time constraints on their leisure and media-related behaviours may be every bit as tight as those which prevail with younger people. What it may be more important to examine among these people is any differences in taste for leisure pursuits and for media content which set them apart from individuals younger than themselves. In this chapter we will examine statistical evidence relating to older leisure and media consumers and explore the taste and interests of these people, and what motivates their leisure and media-related behaviours.

LEISURE AND THE OLDER CONSUMER

Earlier chapters have shown that older consumers cannot be conceived as being a single group with common interests, motives and personalities. They can be differentiated demographically and psychographically according to age, gender, socio-economic status, financial status, life stage, lifestyle and personality. These different factors may also influence the dispositions they exhibit towards consumer behaviour. The older consumer may reach a point where he or she has a greater amount of discretionary time. Being older in a purely chronological sense, however, does not necessarily mean becoming less active. Older people participate in a variety of pastimes and leisure pursuits. Many of these pastimes are mass media-related, which clearly has important implications for marketers. The older consumers' leisure time is not exclusively monopolised by the media though.

The importance of leisure

Just because an individual has stopped working does not mean that they should withdraw from life completely and do nothing constructive with their time (Woods 1994; Young and Schuller 1991). A retired person today can look forward to 10, 20 or even 30 years of retirement. By the turn of the century, it has been estimated that, given a life expectancy of 85 years, people will spend their first 20 years in education, the next 30 years in work, and the last 35 years in retirement (Kaplan 1979; Laczko and Philipson 1991). Retirement now heralds the possibility that it may in fact become the longest and most stable period in our lives.

For decades we have been used to opposing work and leisure. Work has been seen as the antithesis of relaxation, fun, amusement and idleness, with recreation being literally re-creation: that is, re-creation for yet more work. Thus, it is hardly surprising that for many older people leisure has come to be associated with notions of deservingness, of it being somehow earned through hard work. Retirement within such an ideological framework is consequently problematic, especially for certain groups of older people who may never have been in paid employment in a traditional sense: older women who, for example, may have devoted themselves to raising a family and looking after the home.

In addition, although the importance of work may have declined in temporal terms, its psychological impact is still considerable. The functional work ethic has tended to dominate many older people's lives. This attitude can make adjustment to retirement difficult for some people because they regard not working as being idle (Coleman 1993). A generation which values itself through the work that it does, may lose identity and self-respect once they have withdrawn from working life.

The difficulties of looking at retirement as leisure has meant that various approaches have been adopted in order to try to articulate what the experience of leisure is like in old age. Two perspectives have been alluded to in this context: the first relates to leisure time and the activities of which it is constituted and the second examines leisure as it relates to notions of adjustment, successful ageing and life satisfaction (Kelly 1990). With the first of these perspectives, research concerns have largely been taken up by issues such as delineating how much time individuals might have to spend on leisure, how levels of participation vary across different activities, and what roles might be ascribed to leisure in the absence of paid work.

Research that has concentrated on participation levels and activities tends to give a very restricted view of the potential of this phase of life. In fact, the impression given by this mode of analysis is one of declining participation, certainly as far as most activities outside the home are concerned (Kelly 1990).

In Britain, the Carnegie Enquiry into the Third Age presented a depressing illustration of retirement as constituting an abundance of leisure in terms of time, but in which very small minorities of older people took part in any kinds of leisure activities, particularly those of an active nature beyond the home (Midwinter 1991). The bulk of the leisure time spent by older men and women is on predominantly sedentary activities such as television watching and listening to the radio, accounting for three-fifths of the leisure time of the average older woman, and over half that of the older man.

Taking part in leisure activities is as important for older people as for younger people. It is a crucial dimension of well-being in later life (Bernard 1985; Havighurst 1963) and, despite the lack of any universally agreed definitions of adjustment or successful ageing, measures of the extent of engagement in various physical and social activities have often been used as an important element in studies of these kinds (Day 1991; Day and Day 1993).

European studies have highlighted the crucial part skills in leisure activities play in maintaining the individual's ability to function competently into old age. The Berlin Aging Study demonstrated how social and leisure activity contribute to a person's competence and hence to the quality of life in old age (Baltes *et al.* 1993). Regular participation in social and other activities outside the home has consistently correlated with higher levels of life satisfaction among older people (Kelly 1990)

There is an important gender-related perspective on the study of older people's leisure lives. One view is that men and women might move closer together in the time they respectively spend in pursuit of leisure during their retirement years (Bernard and Meade 1993a). Research has consistently shown that women have much less time for leisure than men and that this difference persists into old age. In Britain, of the 105 waking hours available to people each week, a retired man generally has around 92 hours of free time per week, and a retired woman about 75 hours (Central Statistical Office 1990). This appears largely to be due to the continuing preoccupation of women with domestic and family responsibilities (Mason 1987). While retired men between the ages of 50 and 65 spend as much time on shopping as women, they still tend to do less work around the house than women. Their additional free time is largely spent watching television, reading, talking and listening to the radio (Young and Schuller 1991).

Despite these observations, there is nevertheless increased participation in leisure pursuits in older life, among both women and men. In Britain, around 30 per cent of older women join social clubs, with about 13 per cent attending clubs that cater solely to older people, and 11 per cent play bingo. Indeed, in North America, women exhibit higher rates of attendance than do men at leisure centres or social clubs designed specifically for their own age-group (Freysinger 1993). In Britain, older women may be more involved than older men in church-related activities and other organized pursuits (Berry, Lee and Griffiths 1981). Both sexes show increased participation in voluntary work (Davis-Smith, 1992).

Some older people turn to activities which will improve their minds. Across Europe participation in education in all its forms is known to play a continuing and important role in the lives of older people (Norton 1992; Tokarski 1993). Men as well as women engage in activities of this sort (Schuller and Bostyn 1992). In contrast, physical activities, sports and other forms of outdoor recreation show relatively low levels of participation. In Britain, just 5 per cent of women aged 60 and over take part in keep-fit activities such as yoga and aerobics, with even smaller percentages engaging in pursuits like swimming or cycling. American studies have borne this out further, reporting higher levels of involvement for men in exercise, sports and outdoor recreation (Kelly, Steinkamp and Kelly 1986).

Social pursuits such as visiting friends and relatives and being visited play an important part in the leisure lives of older people. Maintaining these networks of relationships is especially important for older women (Jerrome 1993a, 1993b). A variety of surveys have indicated that older people enjoy extensive social networks. According to one investigation in Britain, at least half of all older people are in contact with friends every week. Women are more likely to see friends than are men. Contact with friends does not decrease substantially with age, although the pattern of visiting does vary. The 'younger' older person is more likely to go and visit others, while the 'older' elderly person is most likely to receive visits. Older people are generally very satisfied with the amount of contact they have with friends. Almost nine in ten express satisfaction with the contact they have. Those who would like to see more of their friends usually report that distance or health problems (either their own or their friends') are the reasons that prohibit more social contact. Neighbours also form part of the social network; the vast majority of older people report that they talk to their neighbours regularly, although this behaviour does decrease with age (Askham *et al.* 1992).

Another source of social contact and interaction is membership and participation in the events of various social groups and organisations. Included within this category are activities as diverse as church attendance or visiting the local public house. According to one study in Britain, two-thirds of over-70s had participated in some form of social activity in the week before interview. Even at the age of 85 years and over, four in ten (40 per cent) of people were still active in some form of social organisation. There was a marked difference between the sexes in the types of social clubs visited. Women were more likely than men to report church attendance, while men were more likely to report going to the pub (Victor 1994).

Table 4.1 indicates the extent to which men and women in different age-groups in Britain participate in various home-based leisure activities. Table 4.2 provides

Table 4.1 Participation in home-based leisure activities in Great Britain: 1993–94

	16–19	20–24	25–29	30–44	45–59	60–69	70+	All
Males (%)								
Watching TV	99	100	99	99	99	99	97	99
Visiting/entertaining friends/relatives	96	97	97	97	94	94	91	95
Listening to radio	93	95	95	94	91	86	83	91
Listening to records/ tapes	96	96	93	86	76	66	50	79
Reading books	55	58	56	60	61	59	58	59
Gardening	24	22	37	52	62	65	55	51
DIY	34	44	61	68	65	58	35	57
Dressmaking/ needlework/ knitting	2	3	3	3	3	3	4	3
Females (%)								
Watching TV	99	99	99	99	99	99	98	99
Visiting/entertaining friends/relatives	98	98	99	98	96	95	94	96
Listening to radio	97	95	92	91	88	84	77	88
Listening to records/ tapes	97	96	92	88	75	62	42	75
Reading books	75	70	70	71	71	74	67	71
Gardening	11	23	34	51	57	54	39	45
DIY	16	35	39	40	34	23	10	30
Dressmaking/ needlework/ knitting	19	30	30	37	44	48	38	38

Note: Percentages show proportion in each age-group participating in each activity in the four weeks before interview
Source: General Household Survey, Office for National Statistics

figures for participation by age-groups in a number of sports and more physically active pursuits. Among men and women, across all age-groups, watching television emerged as the most pervasive activity. There were virtually no differences among age-groups in the extent to which people claimed to watch television. It was a near-universal activity. Following closely behind the television was a non-media activity – visiting or entertaining friends or relatives. While this activity showed some sign of dropping off among older people, this trend was not very pronounced.

Listening to the radio was the third most popular pastime, with around nine out of ten tuning in at some time or another. The radio was clearly a more popular medium with younger people than with older people, with listening dropping away among those people in their 60s and 70s. An even more marked reduction with age occurred with regard to listening to records and tapes. Reading books remained quite popular throughout life, with very little variation in extent of reading across different age-groups. Reading, as a pastime, was generally more popular among women than men of all ages.

The biggest age-related changes in extent of participation occurred with non-media, home-based activities such as gardening, do-it-yourself and dress-making/needlework/knitting. Gardening was most common of all among people in their 50s and 60s. Do-it-yourself activities become established among people in their 20s, presumably as they begin to acquire their own homes, and remain a prevalent activity until people reach their 70s and become less physically able to carry out such jobs themselves. Among women, dressmaking, needlework and knitting become most firmly established in their 40s, 50s and 60s.

Table 4.2 Participation in most popular sports, games and physical activities in Great Britain: 1993–94

	16–19	20–24	25–29	30–44	45–59	60–69	70+	All
Males (%)								
Walking	45	46	48	48	47	45	33	45
Snooker/pool/billiards	56	47	34	23	14	8	3	21
Swimming	23	19	19	21	12	8	3	15
Cycling	37	19	21	16	11	6	5	14
Soccer	44	27	19	9	2	0	0	9
Golf	15	13	12	11	9	7	3	9
Females (%)								
Walking	40	41	41	41	42	36	20	37
Keep fit/yoga	29	28	26	22	14	8	6	17
Swimming	26	25	22	24	14	8	3	16
Cycling	14	12	8	9	7	4	2	7
Snooker/billiards/pool	26	17	6	4	2	1	0	5
Tenpin bowls/skittles	9	9	5	4	2	1	0	3

Note: Percentages show proportion in each age-group participating in each activity in the four weeks before interview
Source: General Household Survey, Office for National Statistics

Among the most popular physical pursuits outside the home are walking, swimming and cycling. Among men, soccer and golf, and snooker, pool and billiards feature prominently, while among women, keep fit or yoga are relatively popular. In the case of all these activities, except walking, however, there is gradual falling away of involvement with age, with significant reductions having occurred by the time people have reached their 50s and 60s.

THE IMPORTANCE OF MEDIA

The mass media feature prominently in the lives of older consumers. Television viewing is nearly universal, while listening to the radio is widespread. Reading newspapers is also important to older consumers. The media convey many consumer-related messages via advertising and sponsorship, as well as in programming and editorial content. The media also present representations of older people which may reflect or conflict with older consumers' self-perceptions. It is important in a marketing context therefore to understand how older consumers use the major media.

In the United States, for example, Steiner (1963) found that when older consumers were asked what media types were most important to them, they indicated newspapers, television and radio, in that order. In addition, these respondents perceived television to be an entertainment medium and newspapers an information medium. More recently, Stephens (1982) studied media habits among the older consumer and compared her results with those of Steiner. She found that older consumers seemed to place far more emphasis on television than on newspapers, but the remainder of Steiner's findings were confirmed.

Regardless of the particular mass medium being considered, research has shown that older people are relatively greater consumers of news and information than younger adults (Doolittle 1979). Many findings indicate that older people prefer media that provide information over entertainment (Phillips and Sternthal 1977). In terms of specific media, older people have been found to rank newspapers as the most important medium in contrast to younger people who rank television as most important (Schiffman 1971). However, there is no straightforward positive correlation between age and preference for newspapers over television. Among the mature audience, age-related differences of opinion about these media can be found. In one survey, newspapers emerged as the preferred news source for the 'young-old', aged 50 to 60, while television was favoured by the 'older old'. Newspapers and magazines with a generous news content are especially preferred by the affluent older consumer (Burnett 1991).

USE OF PRINT MEDIA

Reading is one of the most popular pastimes for the older consumer. Spring (1991) reported that Americans may spend only about two-and-a-half hours a week reading, but this still represented the third most popular leisure activity after socialising and watching television. In fact, the average adult spent only about 30 minutes more a week socialising than reading books, magazines and newspapers. The 55 to 64s spent more money on reading material per year than any other age-group. While reading expenditures overall in the United States dropped by approximately 6 per cent between 1986 and 1991, they increased during that period for the mature market, aged 55 and over.

Newspaper readership is significantly and positively related to age, education and income and negatively related to television viewership (Robinson and Skill 1995). In addition, newspaper readership begins to fall off for readers over the age of 65 or when their eyesight declines (Salisbury 1981). In the United States, just over 63 per cent of the older population read a daily newspaper and represent the largest group of subscribers to newspapers (Simmons Market Research Bureau 1991). Among the 55 to 64 age-group, just under 72 per cent read a daily paper as compared with around 55 per cent of the 18 to 34 age-group.

Newspapers appear to serve as an important source of news information and of consumer decisions by older consumers (Dodge 1958; Phillips and Sternthal 1977). An American study in Atlanta found that over half of the older consumers surveyed read a daily newspaper and almost 70 per cent read a Sunday newspaper (Bernhardt and Kinnear 1976). Similarly, Schreiber and Boyd (1980) found that 65 per cent of older consumers they surveyed named newspapers as the most influential medium in affecting buying decisions. This finding the authors attributed to the importance of food shopping among older consumers and the featuring of supermarket coupons in local newspapers. Newspaper reading, however, was seen to decline with age.

Research reported by Sturges (1990) based on a survey of people in Britain aged between 50 and 80 found that the majority read at least one newspaper every day, although as many as one in five did not read a newspaper at all. For those who did, reading a particular newspaper was a habit and they would be unlikely to change either the paper they read or the frequency with which they read it.

Tabloids and local newspapers were the most popular dailies with a small proportion reading the quality press. None of those interviewed read Sunday newspapers regularly, mostly because of their prices. Reasons for choice of newspaper included familiarity with the format; editorial style and content; habit; coverage of local news and the sports page.

Burnett (1991) found newspaper readership in the United States to vary among income levels of older adults. Specifically, he found that affluent older men read the news section, business section, travel section and magazine section of the newspaper more often than their less affluent counterparts. In addition, the affluent older male was more likely to read *USA Today* and the *Wall Street Journal* than older males with a more moderate income. Older females tended not to read the sports or business sections as much as men, but the affluent ones among them were more likely to read the news, food, lifestyle and travel sections of newspapers than their less affluent counterparts.

Unlike newspaper readership, which tends to increase with age, magazine readership tends to decline (Harris and Associates 1975; Phillips and Sternthal 1971; Schreiber and Boyd 1980) and drops off dramatically at the age of 70 (Chaffee and Wilson 1975). Thus, magazine readership is less widespread among the over-50s. The *Marketing Week* survey (Sturges 1990) reported that most older people in Britain did not read any magazines regularly, again, mostly, because they were too expensive. One in four of those questioned said they read magazines occasionally, usually when they were given to them by a friend or at the hairdresser's or doctor's. Some interest was expressed in a magazine which offered practical, money-saving ideas, but most were not interested in the concept of a new magazine targeted at old people.

Danowski (1975) reported that older people in the United States tended to spend about 30 minutes a day reading magazines, but other estimates have been lower. Later research reported that 16 minutes a day was probably closer to the average amount of magazine reading time indulged in by older people (*TV Dimensions '86* 1986). Such general estimates for the mature market as a whole conceal differences among older consumers in their magazine reading habits. Better-off older people read magazines more often than the less well-off and read many more different magazines (Burnett 1991). The affluent older consumer, who also tended to be better educated, showed preferences for reading news-heavy magazines such as *Business Week, Newsweek, New Yorker, Time, US News and World Report, Forbes, Fortune, Money* and *National Geographic*. There is clear evidence also that mature consumers have different magazine reading tastes from younger people (Mundorf and Brownell 1990). The only magazine which appeared to be read by everyone, regardless of age, was *TV Guide*.

READING BOOKS

Newspapers do not represent the only print medium of significance to older consumers. We saw earlier that older people read books for pleasure. The General Household Survey in Britain showed that by the beginning of the 1990s more than six in ten people aged 45 to 59 years (62 per cent) and 60 to 69 years (66 per cent) read books on a regular basis (Eckstein 1992). *Cultural Trends 1992* presented further statistics compiled originally by Book Marketing Ltd about reported book ownership and reading habits, and about book buying habits. Comparisons made between consumers aged 15 to 24 and aged 65+ revealed some interesting age-group differences in book consumption patterns (see Tables 4.3 and 4.4).

The over-65s were significantly more likely to have read a book for interest or pleasure in the past four weeks and to be currently reading a book for pleasure than were the under-24s. The older age-group also indicated spending more hours per week reading books than did the younger age-group. Indeed, well over half the older age-group read for pleasure. In contrast, younger readers were more likely to read purely for information or reference. This probably reflects the fact that among younger respondents, reading was closely linked to formal study

Table 4.3 Book ownership and reading habits

	Age-group percentages[a]	
	15–24 (%)	*65+ (%)*
Read book for interest or pleasure in past 4 weeks	53	63
Used books for information or reference in past 4 weeks	53	39
Currently reading a book for pleasure	40	56
Reading books is one of my favourite activities	16	40
Finished reading last book for pleasure a year ago or less	74	75
100 or fewer books in home	55	61
More than 100 books in home	45	39
Books at home:		
Bible	57	63
Dictionary	58	69
Use or read books to help:		
with job[b]	22	2
with study	45	2
Spend over 10 hours per week reading for pleasure[c]	18	36

Source: Books and the Consumer, Book Marketing Ltd 1991
[a] All percentages are based on all respondents in the given categories except in (c) below
[b] 29 per cent in 25–34 and 35–54 age-groups
[c] Basis: those who read a book for pleasure in previous 12 months

rather than leisure. Despite this, three out of four respondents – young and old – claimed to have read a book for pleasure within the past year. Younger respondents were more likely than older respondents to have more than 100 books at home. Most young and older respondents had a bible and a dictionary at home.

Around one in four respondents in this survey aged 15 to 24 and 65+ claimed to have bought 10 or more books in the last 12 months. Of those who had bought any books for themselves in the past year, more than four in ten (43 per cent) of those aged 65+ and over half of those aged 15 to 24 (55 per cent) said they had bought themselves a new paperback within the previous 3 months. Among the same respondent base, one in five of those aged 65+ (21 per cent) and one in four of the younger age-group (26 per cent) also claimed to have bought a handbook for themselves within the previous 3 months.

Books were most likely to be bought from a bookshop or stationery store. The next most likely purchase location was newsagents. Over one in ten were bought from a chain store and a similar proportion from a supermarket. A slightly more popular book buying location than the latter two was a railway station or airport bookstore. Around one in seven readers over 65 had purchased a book by post, and three in ten had purchased a second hand book in the past 12 months. More

Table 4.4 Book buying habits

	Age-group percentages	
	15–24 (%)	*65+ (%)*
Bought 10 or more books in last 12 months[a]	24	29
Bought new paperback for self within past 3 months[b]	55	43
Bought new handbook for self within past 3 months[b]	26	21
Type of shop bought book from in past 12 months:[c]		
Bookshop	51	49
Book/stationery shop	76	64
Chain store[d]	12	12
Museum/tourist gift shop	8	6
Newsagent	30	22
Station/airport	12	15
Supermarket	10	12
Bought book by post in past 12 months[e]	14	14
Bought books second-hand in past 12 months	23	30
Have a library ticket	68	56

Source: Books and the Consumer, Book Marketing Ltd 1991
[a] All those buying books in previous 12 months
[b] All those buying books for self in previous 12 months
[c] All buying for self who ever visit bookshop or book section of shop
[d] 21 per cent in 35–54 age-group
[e] All respondents

than half the over-65s had a library ticket, compared with two out of three individuals aged 15 to 24 years.

RADIO LISTENING

The over-50s are regular users of broadcast media. As we will see in later sections of this chapter, older people are the heaviest viewers of television and attach a great deal of importance to this medium as a source of information, entertainment and companionship. Rather less attention has been paid by media researchers to the use of radio made by older listeners. Research carried out in the United States has shown that radio usage generally increases with age (Simmons Market Research Bureau 1991). The typical older adult listens to between one and two and a half hours a day (Beyer and Woods 1963; Danowski 1975; Parker and Paisley 1966). Even so, national radio listenership data for the USA collected by the Simmons Market Research Bureau suggest that older consumers are significantly less likely to use the radio on a typical day than their younger counterparts. Younger people may spend more time listening to the radio in the car, however.

When older consumers listen to radio, they prefer country music, talk radio, adult contemporary music, news and nostalgia programming (Simmons Market Research Bureau 1991). A closer examination of radio usage suggests that the over-65s are no more likely to listen to talk or news programming than the 55 to 64 age-group, but both are more likely to listen to talk or news than the 18 to 34 age-group. The latter are usually more inclined to listen to music. Generally, older consumers listen to daytime AM radio and very little FM (Phillips and Sternthal 1977; Schiffman 1971; Schreiber and Boyd 1980). Radio listenership among older consumers may vary with their level of income. Older men and women with better incomes have been found to prefer easy listening, whereas less well-off men and women exhibit more allegiance to country and western music, religious or gospel music and sports.

In the United Kingdom, the over-55s represent more than 30 per cent of the radio audience. Indeed, their representation as a segment of the audience for this medium is greater than their proportional presence in the population in general (see Table 4.5) (Day and Cowie 1990). Older radio consumers exhibit varied listening tastes, however, as is evident by the extent to which they tune into different radio stations.

Table 4.5 Radio audiences: demographic profile

	All Radio (%)	Population (%)
4–15	4	16
16–24	15	16
25–34	20	14
35–44	17	14
45–54	14	12
55–64	15	12
65+	15	16

Source: Day and Cowie (1990), BBC Broadcasting Research Department

It is clear that different radio stations have varying degrees of appeal to particular age-groups. Some radio stations, most notably BBC Radio 1 appeal mostly to the under-44s, while others, such as BBC Radio 2, Radio 4 and BBC Local Radio have greater appeal to the over-44s, and greatest appeal of all to the over-55s (see Table 4.6). Across the late 1980s and early 1990s, the over-55s radio audience exhibited a movement away from BBC radio stations and towards independent (commercial) local radio stations.

THE USE OF TELEVISION

Social scientists have investigated the place of television in the lives of older viewers over many years. Media research has shown that television viewing

Table 4.6 Audience shares of radio listening by age

	4–15	16–24	25–34	35–44	45–54	55–64	65+
Radio 1							
1985	53	64	47	26	12	4	3
1990	37	52	45	26	12	3	2
1991	32	48	44	26	13	4	2
Radio 2							
1985	4	3	8	19	29	33	27
1990	2	1	2	8	20	34	35
1991	1	1	2	6	16	30	31
Radio 3							
1985	—	—	1	2	3	3	3
1990	—	1	1	2	3	3	3
1991	—	—	1	2	2	4	4
Radio 4							
1985	1	1	8	14	14	17	24
1990	2	1	6	13	14	16	21
1991	2	1	6	14	15	16	20
Radio 5							
1990	1	—	1	1	1	1	1
1991	1	—	1	1	1	1	1
Any BBC							
1985	64	71	69	71	74	79	83
1990	46	57	59	59	64	78	85
1991	40	53	57	56	62	75	82
ILR							
1985	26	20	26	26	25	20	17
1990	44	35	36	38	32	20	14
1991	45	38	37	40	35	23	17

Source: BBC Broadcasting Research Department, Daily Survey
Notes:
(a) UK population aged 4 and over. Service share of listening is defined as the percentage of total listening time accounted for by each service, i.e. hours of listening to a service per week per head of population as a percentage of total hours listened to all services
(b) Radio 5 began broadcasting on 27 August 1990
(c) ILR: Independent Local Radio includes 'new wave' or 'incremented' services from 1st quarter 1991

increases from middle age to about 70 years, after which there may be a slight decline (Bogart 1972; Bower 1978; Chaffee and Wilson 1975; Kubey 1980). There is widespread agreement among them regarding the importance of television and its functions. Glick and Levy (1962) first characterised older viewers as 'embracers'. This term describes a population with a particularly close identification with the television experience. Further, they tend to be less discriminating than the general population. Their attitude is one of acceptance, even strong appreciation. Finally, embracers tend to make great use of the medium.

Television watching has been and continues to be the most frequently reported daily activity for older people in countries such as the United States (De Grazia 1961; Schramm 1969; Spring 1991) and viewing levels are highest of all among the widowed and retired older person (Davis and Kubey 1982; Kubey 1980). The reason for this higher than average level of viewing appears to be associated with the greater than average amount of spare time available to older adults for viewing (Danowski 1975).

Research over many years has shown that the elderly population watches television in greater amounts than any other age-group (Comstock *et al.* 1978; Graney and Graney 1974; Real, Anderson and Harrington 1980; Ross 1982; Samli 1967; Stephens 1982). Schramm (1969) and De Grazia (1961) found that older people listed watching television as the most frequent 'leisure time' activity. A Harris poll in 1974, in the United States, found that more people over 65 spend time watching television than spend time reading newspapers, listening to the radio, or reading books or magazines.

Past research has shown that the importance of television viewing for old people is relatively independent of their living arrangements. Schalinske (1968) investigated television in the lives of a small sample of institutionalised elderly. He conducted an intensive in-depth study of a select group of institutionalised old people and their use of television. He concluded that personality patterns and viewing activity in this population were similar to those of the general elderly public.

The significance of television for institutionalised elderly has been corroborated by other research. Peterson (1973) looked at a highly active, well-motivated group of older people; people moving into a southern California retirement community. All but one of the respondents indicated that they watched television daily, and this particular activity had the highest reported incidence of any.

Historically, studies of viewing behaviour among older populations can be traced back at least forty years. One of the earliest studies of time spent viewing was by Ripley and Buell (1954). Two samples of male viewers were compared and it was found that men aged over 61 years reported viewing 3.15 hours per day on average. This was compared with men aged 19 to 31 years whose average was 2.35 hours. Similar higher rates were reported for female viewers who, as a rule, tended to watch more hours per day than did males.

De Grazia (1961) questioned people regarding their recent daily activities and found that 'watching television' appeared more often than any other activity for both 'yesterday' and again in the things they did 'in the last four weeks'. In a similar survey of 5,000 social security beneficiaries in four areas of the USA, Schramm (1969) found that the most frequently named daily activity was watching television.

Cowgill and Baulch (1962) interviewed 224 older consumers resident in Wichita, Kansas, whose daily viewing time averaged more than 5 hours. Schalinske (1968) found that residents of a retirement community watched for around 3.5 hours per day, while Schramm (1969) found that 70 per cent of 5,000 social security recipients watched television every day for an average of around 3 hours. Bower (1978) looked at data collected from a national sample of 1,900 adults and found that those aged 60 and over viewed an average of 4 hours on weekday evenings and on weekends. Danowski (1975) interviewed residents of a retirement community in Michigan, finding the 162 respondents viewed as much as 6 hours a day. Korzenny and Neuendorf (1980) found that the elderly watched 4.5 hours a day, with 5 per cent of their respondents reportedly watching more than 60 hours a week (8.5 hours a day).

Some researchers have employed techniques other than questionnaires and self-report interviews to measure viewing time among the older consumer. Davis and Edwards (1975) installed automatic recording devices on the television sets of older viewers who were residents in care houses and convalescent centres. They found that the amounts of viewing in these groups were 3.2 and 4.1 hours a day respectively.

Robinson (1981) had older consumers record how they spent each hour of the day in a diary and found that they averaged 2.2 hours a day of viewing. Fouts and Abraham (1986) presented 60 to 80-year-olds with a diary in which they merely checked programmes as they watched them. They found that their respondents watched 5.3 hours per weekday.

In the United Kingdom, official television industry audience statistics produced by the Broadcasters' Audience Research Board (BARB) have revealed the oldest viewers in the population to be the heaviest consumers of television (see Table 4.7). Between the ages of 55 and 64, viewers were registered as watching between 28 and 36 hours per week across the 1985–1993 period (figures for last quarter of each year). This equates to around 4.5 to 5 hours per day. During the same period, the over-65s watched 35 to 40 hours per week (well over 5 hours a day).

Table 4.8 confirms the significance of older consumers' television viewing. When represented on an index basis, where 100 represents the overall average level of viewing across age-groups, it is clear that older age-groups are heavier users of television than younger age-groups. This difference has remained largely unchanged over many years.

Thus, estimates of time spent viewing television among the older consumer, though varying between 3 and 6 hours per day, have revealed a population segment that is very attached to the medium. Individual viewing patterns have been found to vary in turn according to certain other viewer characteristics such as level of education, state of health and living circumstances (e.g. living independently or living in a nursing home) (Fouts and Abraham 1986).

The significance of television for the older consumer is underlined by the importance attached to it compared with other activities. For example, it has been noted that older viewers spend an average of 22 per cent of their waking hours watching television (Moss and Lawton 1982). Indeed, older people spend more time watching television than doing any other activity except sleeping (Atchley 1974; Davis 1971; Marshall 1987; Rubin 1982). Thus, television

Table 4.7 Total amount of weekly television viewing by age

	1985	1986	1987	1988	1989	1990	1991	1992	1993[a]
4–15	21.1	23.2	21.8	21.4	21.2	18.9	21.8	18.3	18.9
16–24	17.2	17.3	16.7	18.8	18.7	18.0	21.3	19.9	19.6
25–34	26.5	27.2	26.6	26.0	25.5	24.1	28.0	24.3	25.2
35–44	23.2	25.2	24.4	24.4	23.2	23.0	27.0	23.1	24.5
45–54	27.4	29.4	28.4	29.3	26.6	26.6	29.2	24.6	25.2
55–64	33.4	35.0	35.8	35.1	33.8	31.3	34.7	28.3	} 33.6
65+	37.1	38.2	39.7	39.6	37.3	35.3	39.2	35.4	

Source: Up to 1992, Broadcasters Audience Research Board/Audits of Great Britain/Research Services Millward Brown; 1993, Trends in Television, AGB Television Information Systems
[a] Calculated by multiplying *daily* amount of viewing by 7.0

Table 4.8 Indices of total amount of weekly television viewing by age

	1985	1986	1987	1988	1989	1990	1991	1992	1993[a]
4–15	78	85	80	78	81	75	76	74	73
16–24	63	64	61	68	71	72	74	80	76
25–34	98	100	97	95	97	96	98	98	98
35–44	86	93	89	89	88	92	94	93	95
45–54	101	108	104	107	101	106	102	99	98
55–64	123	129	131	128	129	125	121	114	} 130
65+	137	140	145	144	142	141	137	143	

Source: Up to 1992, Broadcasters Audience Research Board/Audits of Great Britain/Research Services Millward Brown; 1993, Trends in Television, AGB Television Information Systems

viewing exceeds all other important activities including visiting with friends and reading (Hendricks and Hendricks 1981).

Time of viewing

In countries such as the United States, fairly consistent patterns of viewing have generally been found during different times of the day. Viewing patterns do not vary a great deal between age-groups. Older viewers do tend to tune in somewhat earlier than younger viewers, usually to catch the late afternoon and early evening news. Older viewers continue watching in large numbers throughout peak-time programming, but phase out of the viewing situation between 9.30 and 10.00 pm.

Prime-time viewing in the USA (7.00 pm to 10.00 pm) has been found to account for approximately 55 per cent of total viewing among the older consumer, with decreasing amounts of time spent viewing between 4.00 pm and 7.00 pm and 1.00 pm and 4.00 pm respectively (Rubin and Rubin 1982b). Korzenny and Neuendorf (1980) reported a similar trend, with 58 per cent, 27 per cent and 15 per cent of viewing time taking place after dinner, in the afternoon and in the morning, respectively.

A trimodal distribution of peak viewing times was found by Rubin and Rubin (1981). The greatest peak occurred between 8.00 pm and 9.00 pm with smaller peaks in the early afternoon and between 10.00 am and 11.00 am.

Channel viewing profiles

In Britain, older consumers exhibit distinct channel viewing preferences. While some mainstream channels, such as BBC1 and ITV, emerge as channels viewed by all viewers, regardless of age, others tend to attract proportionately more viewers in particular age-groups. Both BBC1 and ITV show age profiles with a bias towards older viewers, but this simply reflects the fact that older people watch more television in general. BBC2, however, attracts a markedly higher proportion of older viewers than does BBC1. On the commercial side, Channel Four has a more distinctly youthful viewing profile, while attracting relatively few older viewers (Eckstein 1994).

The newer satellite channels have an age profile which differs significantly from the mainstream terrestrial channels. More than one in five viewers of satellite channels are aged under 15, while over half are aged under 34 years. This compared with around 35 per cent of BBC1's viewers being under 34. The bias of the satellite channels towards younger viewers becomes significantly evident when compared with the age distribution of the general population. These channels had a much smaller share of viewers aged over 55 than are found in the population as a whole.

In the United States, despite their heavier overall television viewing, older viewers were found to be much less likely to subscribe to cable television. The over-65s, for example, were the least likely of any age-group to subscribe to cable channels (Universal Almanac 1991).

Programme preferences

Although it is clear that television viewing is an important activity for older people, there is less consensus regarding their preferred programmes. The ambiguity may simply reflect the fact that older people are very diverse in their attitudes, values and preferences. Nevertheless, many research findings do suggest some support for Meyersohn's (1961) contention that older people prefer factual non-fiction programmes rather than fictional material. Hopf and Bedwell (1969) reported an increase with age in such preferences, but a decrease in scripted drama of all types. Tennant (1965) recorded an increased interest in variety shows, 'old-time' music, and quiz programmes in addition to news and current affairs, with a decrease in taste for detective dramas, comedies and love stories.

Gunter, Sancho-Aldridge and Winstone (1994) asked UK viewers for their opinions about general programme types to provide a broad indication of their likes and dislikes. Survey respondents were asked to indicate their personal degree of interest in watching each of 35 broad programme types. In each case, they were invited to say if they were 'very', 'quite', 'not that' or 'not at all' interested in watching that type of programme.

The programme types which respondents in general most often said they would be *very* interested to watch were national news, nature and wildlife programmes, and recently released films. Other popular types of material were international news, and local and regional news. All except one of these programme types were widely endorsed by older respondents, aged 55 to 64 years or 65+ years. The exception was recent film releases which were of significantly less interest to older respondents than to younger respondents.

Indeed, substantial age differences were observed in preferences for at least 15 programme types. All kinds of factual programmes were preferred more widely with increasing age. Older respondents exhibited greater interest in all kinds of news and in current affairs. The over-65s were especially interested in plays and drama serials, older or classic cinema films, holiday and travel programmes, quiz and panel game shows, variety shows, and religious programmes (especially church services).

Programmes the older consumer prefer watching have typically been assessed by surveys and interviews. Older viewers are frequent consumers of news and factual programmes. They generally have a preference for serious programmes, although they also watch certain less serious dramas and game shows avidly (Davis 1971; Wenner 1976; Korzenny and Neuendorf 1980). Rubin and Rubin (1981) found that they watched news the most, followed by game shows, and then a tie among dramas, music-variety and soap operas. A year later, Rubin and Rubin (1982a) again reported that news programmes were viewed the most, but were followed in descending order by music-variety programmes, documentaries, dramas, game shows, talk interview shows, sports and situation comedies.

Davis (1971) found that the top three kinds of programmes in descending order were news, music and drama. Davis and Edwards (1975), using an automatic recording device attached to the television set, found that news and public affairs programmes were the most watched, followed by game shows, situation comedies and drama. Davis *et al.* (1976) found lower viewing levels among an older persons sample than Nielsen (publishers of official network television audience ratings in the United States) had shown for the USA, based on self-report measures. They concluded, however, that self-reporting of television viewing habits by older viewers is unreliable when the dependent variable is one of physical viewing patterns rather than content or preference statements.

Fouts and Abraham (1986), using a television diary, found that news/human affairs programmes were the most preferred, followed by (in descending order) dramas, soap operas, situation comedies, game shows and movies. Only one study (Durand *et al.* 1980), an advertising study, reported that news was not the most watched type of programme. Using a diary method, they found the order of preference (in descending order) to be mystery-drama, situation comedies, and news. Although researchers occasionally categorise some programmes differently and use a variety of assessment techniques, the appetite for news and information is the most documented finding in the literature involving television and the older consumer. Preferences for other kinds of programmes are far from clear, and this variation is, in fact, due to a wide range of variables, such as sampling of older consumers, and time of year. Nevertheless, it is known that older viewers watch game shows, dramas, soap operas and situation comedies in large numbers. This is a reflection of the availability of such programmes as well as the combination of motives which a majority of older viewers have for any important activity, namely, involvement, stimulation and enjoyment.

The news preferences of older consumers tend to be even more pronounced among those who are more affluent. Better-off older people are more attuned to news media generally (Burnett 1991; Doolittle 1979), but show a special interest in televised news (Rahtz, Sirgy and Meadow 1989).

More recent studies from the United States have confirmed that older viewers exhibit a clear preference for news programmes, being more likely than younger age-groups to watch national and local news programmes (see Robinson and Skill 1995). Using self-report measures, Goodman (1990) found that older males and females rated news and public affairs programming as their favourite. Males in this sample also reported a strong liking for sports programmes, while females expressed a liking for educational programming. In contrast, preferences for soap operas tend to be much more prevalent among young viewers than older viewers (Mundorf and Brownell 1990).

Orientation towards television

Orientation towards television refers to the analysis of the motivating forces which underpin older people's use of television. Changing circumstances in the older person's lifestyle can result in shifts in the way they use television. This is partly a function of reallocation of time to different media, with the increased availability of discretionary time, but also results in part from changing attitudes towards television. Older people are generally less likely to feel uncomfortable about the amount of time they spend watching television. Their reasons for watching, however, can vary with their individual personalities and social circumstances.

In a nationwide survey of public opinion about television in the United Kingdom, respondents of all ages were asked what they felt about the amount of time they spent watching television. More specifically they were asked if they felt they spent too much time viewing or whether they watched what they felt was the right amount. In general, six out of ten respondents said they watched the right amount of television and did not over-indulge. Just under one in five felt they spent too much time watching, while a similar proportion claimed they did not have a chance to see enough (Gunter, Sancho-Aldridge and Winstone 1994). Older respondents were even more likely to say they watched the right amount of television and were less likely than people in general to say they watched too much.

Another British poll found more people aged 65+ (44 per cent) or 45 to 64 years (41 per cent) admitting that they watched more television than they had done 10 years earlier, as compared with the national average (38 per cent). The over-65s (42 per cent) were much more likely than average (29 per cent) to regard television as a necessity rather than a luxury. Despite this last finding, however, older consumers (13 per cent) were less likely to look forward to a dramatic increase in television channels than were people generally (21 per cent) (Key Note 1995).

Before looking at specific reasons given by older people for watching television, a number of more general hypotheses have been put forward to account for the orientation of older consumers towards television. Smith, Moschis and Moore (1985) hypothesised that reliance on the media should increase with age. Disengagement theory (Cumming and Henry 1961) posits that society and the elderly enter a process of mutual withdrawal from one another as a consequence of ageing, leading to a reduction of social interaction and an increase in personal isolation. Once the social withdrawal is complete, a new social equilibrium, which society and the older person find mutually satisfying, is established. The reliance on mass media is one way to combat total social disengagement and to help the older person establish a new social equilibrium of disengagement and mutual satisfaction (Schramm 1969).

Activity theory (Lemon, Bengston and Peterson 1972) suggests that older people are forced to disengage from society through social imposition. When faced with this contraction of life space, the older person attempts to locate alternative activities to fill the gap created by the forced loss of previous social roles. The older person who successfully finds alternative activities adjusts more readily to the disengagement experience. Alternative activities may include television viewing.

Socialisation theory (Dowd, Sisson and Kern 1981; Smith and Moschis 1984; Smith, Moschis and Moore 1982, 1984, 1985) posits that older people can be socialised into their new life stage. Socialisation is envisaged as a continuous learning process spanning a person's entire lifetime. It allows a person to adapt to ever-changing life conditions and life experiences through acquisition of requisite social skills, and the creation of ever-changing personal cognitions, attitudes and behaviour. Regardless of whether social disengagement is voluntary or involuntary, with ageing, older consumers face increasingly contracted life spaces. Thus one would expect that in order to adapt to the loss of interpersonal, social-influencing contacts, many older people turn to the impersonal learning gained from mass media sources as attention paid to mass media provides the major source for learning substitution (Graney and Graney 1974).

Rahtz, Sirgy and Meadow (1989) studied two samples of people aged 60 and over in the United States to explore social psychological and demographic correlates of television orientation. Orientation to television was measured using a seven-item scale ('Television shows life as it really is'; 'Magazines are more interesting than television'; 'I frequently watch daytime television'; 'Television shows older people the way they really are'; 'Television gives useful information about health'; and 'I pay very close attention to television advertisements about health').

A psychographic instrument was developed which measured Low Morale ('I feel old'; 'I often find myself feeling lonely'; 'I am not in good physical condition'; 'Getting around town is difficult for me'); Limited Activity ('I stay home mostly'; 'I would rather stay at home than go with friends'); Financial Concern ('I am very cautious when spending my money'; 'I often worry about financial security'): Personal Concern ('I frequently think about my health'; 'I often think about my personal safety'); and Lack of Respect ('My opinion on things doesn't count'; 'Not many people respect senior citizens').

Results indicated a negative relationship between television orientation and morale, outside home activity, perceived respect for the elderly, income and education; and a positive relationship between television orientation and concern for one's personal and financial well-being. According to activity theory, physical pain or limitations may be a strong influence on the level of morale. Further, lack of physical mobility and activity may lead to feelings of dissatisfaction. Due to physical handicaps, dissatisfied elderly may turn to television viewing as the only viable means of remaining 'active' and alive.

Television orientation seemed to have a negative effect relative to older persons' perceptions of their own opinions and respect for senior citizens. This perspective may be the result of extended interaction with a medium which often shows the older person in unenviable roles or situations (O'Toole 1981). A strong orientation towards television was linked with a state of concern about personal well-being. Studies in the United States and elsewhere indicated that heavy television viewers held increased expectations of being crime victims (Doob and MacDonald 1979; Gerbner *et al.* 1980a, 1980b). This elderly crime victim scenario could often be viewed on television dramas. A multiple regression analysis was used to established the key demographic and social-psychological predictors of television orientation. Education, activity and morale emerged as the most significant predictors.

Motives for viewing

What motivates older people to watch television? Researchers have investigated numerous motives. One general observation is that television is relatively inexpensive and convenient. It is readily accessible and can be enjoyed while performing other activities at the same time. It can be a diversion but also the source of various specific types of gratification.

Particular constellations of motives lead viewers to be highly selective in choosing programmes which satisfy underlying needs. For example, those who engage in higher levels of social interaction watch television for a variety of reasons (e.g. for topics of conversation, stimulation); with their viewing preferences matching their perceived motives (e.g. talk shows). Older viewers who have low levels of life satisfaction and health and mobility problems watch television to pass time and for companionship, resulting in a preference for game shows and soap operas (Rubin and Rubin 1982b).

As we will see, there is no doubt that information seeking and utility motives for watching television are important among older viewers. Davis and Edwards (1975) suggested that television provides the older person with connection to the surrounding world, a means to structure the day, a feeling of keeping occupied and a sense of companionship. Elsewhere, it has been proposed that television (and other media) use can serve to combat loneliness, isolation or 'disengagement' by providing a sense of contact with others and participation in society (Schramm 1969; Hess 1974), and to substitute or compensate for lessened or lost personal interaction or information channels (Peterson 1973; Graney and Graney 1974; Davis *et al.* 1976; Stephens 1982). Indeed, many researchers believe that television viewing by the older person is generally motivated by a number of particular motives. The most prominent of these to emerge will be examined below.

Information source

Television is a convenient and valued source of information. The need for information was indicated by several early communication researchers (Davis 1971; Schramm and White 1949; Steiner 1963). One observer wrote that the older person may have a special interest in obtaining information about the world because as they reach Erikson's (1950) final stages of psychosocial development (ego integrity), they are 'merging with the world' (Kubey 1980).

Out of a list of 14 different motives for watching television, Rubin and Rubin (1982b) found that information-seeking was clearly the motive most often checked. Fouts and Abraham (1988) found that 66 per cent of their older persons' sample checked this motive from a list of 32 motivational statements. Wenner (1976) conducted a study with a small sample of people aged 65+ using a Q-sort technique and found that older people are highly motivated to keep up with current events, especially those which concern their local community. The precise nature of these motives depended upon the personal and social circumstances of the older person. More socially mobile people might use television deliberately to isolate themselves socially when it suited them. Socially isolated older people, in contrast, viewed television as a source of companionship and to compensate for a lack of face-to-face social interaction with other people. Thus, television, for these people, served a kind of quasi-informational function. A further category of older person, who were also socially isolated, used television as a conversational topic to initiate and build social contacts.

This information-seeking is expressed in a variety of ways. Older people watch considerable amounts of news and current affairs programming on television. Some viewers become hooked on information programmes and talk shows, watching them throughout the day. In the US, they have been found to be heavy subscribers to all-news cable stations. Other older viewers, while still very interested in factual material, may exhibit more selective tastes for programmes such as local news or nature and science documentaries (Fouts 1989). For older viewers, television can be a 'window to the world' (Davis 1971). News programmes can enable all individuals to know the same facts, scandals and disasters as everyone else.

Entertainment

Viewing for entertainment is another major motivational factor. This has consistently emerged as a key reason for watching television among people aged over 55 years (Korzenny and Neuendorf 1980; Rubin and Rubin 1982a; Fouts and Abraham 1988). In a study of hospitalised older patients, Rubin and Rubin (1981) confirmed the importance of entertainment value of television to this age bracket. Tan (1979) used a technique of removing television sets from people's homes and asked them what they missed the most. It was found that older people missed the entertainment more than informational aspects of programmes.

Viewing patterns arising from a strictly entertainment motive are difficult to elucidate, although Rubin and Rubin (1982a) did find that such viewers tended to watch game shows, action and adventure programmes, and situation comedies. The difficulty in establishing patterns of entertainment-motivated viewing is that what is entertaining or enjoyable involves viewers' perceptions rather than an objective aspect of content. Programmes can gratify entertainment-seeking *and* information-seeking motives. Both motives may operate together to drive viewing behaviour.

Other motives

Media researchers have identified a variety of other motives which underpin the viewing behaviour of older people. Television can serve as a source of topics for conversation (Meyersohn 1961; Doolittle 1979; Rubin and Rubin 1982b). One study revealed that older people report using television more than any other source to find topics of conversation of mutual interest with friends (Ostman and Jeffers 1983) although the amount of information that they actually retain from such conversation is in some doubt (Cavanaugh 1983).

Older consumers also appear to use television to help schedule their daily activities, sometimes referred to as 'daypart bracketing' (Davis 1971). For instance, they may decide not to go shopping until after watching a particular programme.

Watching television for substitute companionship has been suggested by several researchers (Graney and Graney 1974; Schramm 1969; Rubin and Rubin 1982b). This 'parasocial' dimension of television viewing may be important to the popularity of news programmes, talk shows and serialised drama with regular presenters and characters becoming established as 'friends' whom viewers invite into their homes by switching on their television sets. This motive may be particularly salient among older viewers who report being lonely. Such individuals are known to be heavier viewers than people who do not report being lonely (Perlman, Gerson and Spinner 1978). Schramm (1969) argued that television may help to combat loneliness and alienation by compensating for lost interpersonal channels of communication.

Television also offers older viewers a way of relaxing and passing time. It offers the opportunity to fill time that may otherwise remain unoccupied. Fouts and Abraham (1988) found that more than seven in ten of an older persons' sample they studied occasionally used television to relax. This feature of television viewing has been observed by other media researchers (Kubey, 1978). Other motives have also been reported such as arousal (Rubin and Rubin 1982b), prevention of boredom (Rubin and Rubin 1982b), and escape (Fouts and Abraham 1988; Korzenny and Neuendorf 1980; Kubey 1980).

The specific motives for viewing mentioned above include personal (e.g. relaxation) and social motivations (e.g. topics for conversation). Another social motivation, noted by Fouts (1989) is sharing the viewing experience. Fouts observed that many older viewers reported enjoying watching with their adult children, grandchildren and great-grandchildren whenever the opportunity arose. Usually, the programmes were selected by the person in whose residence the viewing took place; often, the selection was based on mutual interests or the interests of the younger viewers. The underlying theme conveyed was that the older person just liked being with their family, and shared viewing was one of a number of shared activities which afforded this sort of opportunity.

Fouts and Abraham (1988) examined the relationship between variety in motives and amount of viewing. Their respondents checked as many of the 32 motivational statements with which they were presented as applied to themselves and kept a television diary for 3 consecutive days. On average, 11 motivational statements were checked by each viewer, with 'positive' motives (e.g. information-seeking, sharing the viewing experience) and 'negative' motives (e.g. escape from depression, passing time) accounting for 67 per cent and 26 per cent of the statements, respectively (there were equal numbers of each type of motive which could be checked). Apparently, they watched television for the same positive motives as for any other quality activity such as reading and collecting stamps, namely because it was enjoyable, relaxing and informative.

The greater the number of motives they had for watching television, the significantly more time they spent watching it, indicating that the more functions it served for them, the more they used the medium. An implication of this finding is that as older consumers acquire more reasons for viewing due to life circumstances (e.g. loss of a loved one, immobility), an increase in viewing can be expected.

Television may play a part in bolstering the self-concept of older viewers. Concerns have been expressed by some observers, however, that television may impart negative images of the older person. The next chapter will explore the depiction of old age on television and the impact it might have on public perceptions of older people. The interplay between television and the viewer's self-concept may represent a motivational factor which shapes viewing behaviour.

Korzenny and Neuendorf (1980) reasoned that when older viewers' self-concepts are positive, they will be motivated to watch informational programmes in order to maintain and reinforce their involvement with the world; whereas viewers with negative self-concepts would watch more fantasy and escapist programmes (e.g. situation comedies, game shows). Older viewers with positive self-concepts were found to watch fewer escapist programmes, with those having negative self-concepts avoiding news programmes.

Fouts and Abraham (1986) tested the same hypothesis, using a self-concept scale containing the six dimensions of self-concept suggested by other researchers, namely self-esteem, mobility, physical health, independence, life satisfaction and social involvement (Markides and Bolt 1984; Wober and Gunter 1982) and a television diary to assess programme preferences. Self-concept was found to be significantly and positively related to watching soap operas and game shows. These findings are consistent with the notion that informational programmes satisfy the motive of active and satisfying involvement with the world, with escapist programmes being viewed in order to distract attention from everyday concerns.

Gunter *et al.* (1994) reported a nationwide UK survey in which respondents were provided with a list of 16 statements dealing with various reasons or motives for television viewing and were asked to say how often each reason applied to

Table 4.9 Reasons for watching television

Base	All (%) 1421	55–64 (%) 202	65+ (%) 164
I watch to see a specific programme that I enjoy very much	76	73	84
I watch to see a special programme that I have heard a lot about	40	43	35
I watch just because it is a pleasant way to spend an evening	28	27	40
I watch just because I feel like watching television	23	22	33
I watch because I think I can learn something	20	19	35
I watch because there is nothing better to do at the time	16	13	20
I turn on the set just for company	14	14	21
I start watching one programme and then find myself watching for the rest of the evening	13	10	17
I watch in case I'm missing something good	12	11	18
I watch as an escape from everyday concerns	11	7	13
I watch to be sociable when others are watching	10	9	13
I start watching because someone else in watching and seems to be interested	10	9	9
I watch just for 'background' while I'm doing something else	8	6	8
I keep watching to put off doing something else I should do	8	4	3
I watch a programme because everyone I know is watching	6	7	6
I watch to ignore or get away from others	5	4	5

Note: Percentages are of those respondents saying each reason 'often' influences their viewing
Source: Gunter, Sancho-Aldridge and Winstone 1994

their own viewing behaviour. Results are summarised in Table 4.9 where the items are ranked in terms of percentages of respondents saying that a reason 'often' applied to their own viewing. The opinions of people aged 55 to 64 years and over 65 years are separately displayed.

One reason stood out above the rest. Three out of four respondents said they often watched television to see a specific programme that they enjoyed very much. The second most often endorsed reason was to watch a special programme that they had heard a lot about. Watching for relaxation or learning were reasons endorsed as often influencing by at least one in five respondents. Older people exhibited similar reasons for viewing. Indeed, respondents aged 55 to 64 did not differ much at all from respondents in general. The over-65s, however, were more likely to say they often watched television to see a specific programme they enjoyed very much, because it is a pleasant way to spend an evening, because they felt like watching, or to learn something. The over-65s were also more likely to watch for something to do or for company.

Sensory decline

Kubey (1980) and Heatherton and Fouts (1985) have suggested that deterioration of sensory abilities associated with ageing influences a person's use of mass media. For example, a diminution in auditory ability may result in a shift from listening to the radio for news to viewing television news, since the association of visual cues with auditory cues may allow a person to fill in many of the perceptual gaps. Sensory decline is physiologically based, directs specific behaviours, and influences the persistence of viewing; thus, it can be viewed as a generalised motive.

There are several aspects of the *visual system* which deteriorate with age, three of which have particular relevance to television viewing. Acuity appears to decline slowly from 50 years on and then rapidly deteriorates after age 70 (Marmor 1977). Although acuity problems can often be corrected by wearing glasses and surgical procedures, some declines cannot be totally corrected and many older people either do not seek correction (e.g. because of cost, immobility), accept the decline is part of ageing, or are unaware of the decline. Consequently, reading often decreases and is visually replaced by another medium, such as television.

Programme preferences may also be related to changes in acuity. It has been shown that the older person has more difficulty in recognising faces and this difficulty is partially the result of an acuity decline (Owsler, Sekular and Boldt 1981). Heatherton and Fouts (1985) argued that the news and soap operas on television use close-up views of anchor-persons and major characters, thus preferences for these programmes may increase through facial recognition.

A reduction in contrast sensitivity often makes it difficult for the older person to detect low-contrast images (Owsler, Sekular and Boldt 1981), thus requiring three times more contrast than younger people to detect and discriminate faces. Davis and Edwards (1975) found that increases in contrast in a television picture were preferred by older viewers more than younger viewers. Similarly, there is a reduction of light reaching the retina; that is, only one-third of the light that reaches a 10-year-old's eyes will reach the retina of a 60-year-old (Ordy, Brizzee and Johnson 1982). These reductions of light with age have several implications for television viewing. For example, programmes such as mysteries which use diminished light or low contrast for artistic and dramatic effect may be less enjoyable. Too much light in the viewing situation, particularly when it is reflected on the television screen, may be more bothersome for older viewers than for younger viewers.

There are two aspects of the auditory system which have been shown to deteriorate with age and which may influence television viewing. Hearing or pitch loss is referred to as presbyacusis and becomes apparent after 50 years of age for pitches of about 100 Hz (Botwinick 1970; Oyer, Kapur and Deal 1976). Only 21 per cent of older people who have hearing difficulties attempt to correct them by using hearing aids (Kasten 1978); many do not know they have losses, or do not want to correct the losses for personal or economic reasons. With pitch loss, speech discrimination decreases, resulting in greater difficulty in following and understanding conversation in interpersonal situations, thus predisposing them to seek other auditory experiences in which the volume is readily controllable, for example radio and television (Kubey 1980). Heatherton and Fouts (1985) agreed that older people often prefer watching the news because the anchor-persons have typically received training in diction, thus facilitating comprehension. This person is also presented in close-up which provides visual cues (mouth movements), cues which contribute to comprehension.

The second change is the decreasing ability to ignore irrelevant and distracting auditory stimuli (Layton 1975). The introduction of such stimuli produces frustration and declines in learning (Phillips and Sternthal 1977) and thus may influence the television experience. Fouts (1989) reported that a survey of older people he carried out revealed that they preferred watching television alone so that they could follow the programme more effectively. A few also complained about programmes and commercials that had loud background music which distracted them from fully understanding the plot or information being presented.

ROLE OF TELEVISION IN EVERYDAY LIFE

The role of television in the lives of older consumers varies according to the personal circumstances and characteristics of individual viewers. Many early studies examined older people's patterns of television use within contexts of relative degrees of confinement. While some researchers suggested that television viewing is of great importance to older people regardless of social setting (Davis 1971), for a long time it was not obvious from the research literature if there were changes in television use when individuals found themselves outside of their usual daily environment. Davis and Edwards (1975) found that older viewers living in a convalescent centre watched television 28 per cent more than comparable viewers without health problems. Doolittle (1979) reported that older people with higher educational levels watched more news programmes; those with lower levels watched out of habit and because television was inexpensive (Rubin and Rubin 1982a).

Rubin and Rubin (1981) found that entertainment and information were two important home viewing motivations. Viewing to pass time or to relieve boredom seemed to have important meaning for both older people and confined individuals. Viewing to pass time, a principal use of television by older people in their home environments, also became the primary motivation for watching television of all patients in a hospitalised and more isolated context. The hospitalised sample of Rubin and Rubin preferred comedies and news programmes and, to a large extent, shunned musical and variety programmes. According to these researchers: 'The confined, isolated situation seemed to produce needs to fill idle time and to keep in touch with the outside environment. Comedy viewing would seem to provide a means of time consumption and escape for forgetting one's own problems for a period of time' (1981: 10–11).

On reaching the later stages of their life, more and more older people regard this as a time for relaxation and enjoyment. The image of retirement is changing. No longer seen as the final, running-down stage of life in which one prepares for death, retirement is now regarded by increasing numbers of older people as a period in which they can begin a new life, seek new goals and realise fresh ambitions. Improved health and financial circumstances for many means that they remain active during these autumn years. Those who are sufficiently self-reliant and motivated enjoy a variety of outdoor and indoor hobbies and pursuits. They may also have more time, of course, to simply sit back, relax and read, listen to the radio or watch television.

Older consumers value the mass media as sources of entertainment, distraction, relaxation, escape and, most of all, information. The media are regarded as important information sources, with television being seen by many as one of life's necessities. Although attaching great value to television, however, older people do not invariably welcome the changes that the medium is currently undergoing. Even so, many of their number find their lives enriched through engagement with a variety of media, old and new. Although this burgeoning market segment shares many interests in common with younger media consumers, its membership also displays distinctive tastes and needs which they wish the media to cater for.

The combination of ageing processes and changes in life circumstances are likely to interact and influence the communications needs of the older consumer. As knowledgeable consumers of television, older consumers not only are selective in their use of television, they also have definite suggestions for improving its content. For example, Real, Anderson and Harrington (1980) found that 91 per cent of older viewers wanted more information and discussion of issues related to their age-group; Adams and Groen (1975) reported that approximately 50 per cent of older viewers desired more programming dealing with pensions, health and government services. Older viewers have also been found to use such information when it is available.

It is important for marketers to take note of these needs and interests. The impact of the mass media upon the older consumer requires careful consideration not just of their specific subject matter preferences, but also of the way in which this age-group is represented in and treated by the media. The next chapter examines this issue in more detail.

5 Representation and image

IMAGES OF AGEING

The images associated with particular groups within society embrace sets of impressions and expectations which other people hold about them. Images as such may take on a verbal or non-verbal form and express symbolically actual or assumed attributes which are used to characterise and define that group. In general once a set of images becomes attached to a particular group, it tends to stick. The group thus becomes stereotyped. Where ageing is concerned, stereotypes often tend to refer negatively to aspects of physical appearance, mental functioning and social competence. Stereotypes play a central role in social life. Most people are dependent, to some degree, on them as a means of communication (Lippman 1922). Stereotypes can shape an individual's perceptions of others and represent an almost inevitable consequence of living in a complex social environment in which information overload would be regularly experienced unless some system emerges for ordering and categorising the bewildering variety of people, groups, institutions and events with which an individual will come into contact. It is easier if individuals can be pigeon-holed in a pre-existing category than if discrete new categories have to be created for each new individual who comes along. This 'averaging' of characteristics across individuals who appear to belong together in the same category, may lead to misleading and inaccurate impressions emerging which, though convenient to deploy, nevertheless fail properly to represent the true character of the individuals thus grouped together.

Such stereotyping of specific social and demographic groups can affect the way they are perceived within society and has important implications for marketing of products and services. In the case of the older consumer, prevalent unflattering stereotypes may influence the way older consumers see themselves and the impressions which others, including marketers and advertisers, hold about them. These impressions may in turn influence the approaches adopted by marketing strategies in trying to reach older consumers. Advertisers may be similarly affected and create promotional campaigns and messages that utilise unsuitable images which older consumers will reject and fail or refuse to identify with.

Before examining images of older consumers within advertising, this chapter will examine images of ageing in a wider perspective. In so doing, it will reinforce the importance of understanding the nature and genesis of prevailing social images of ageing and old age, how they have evolved over time, and their current status within today's society. The general mass media have played a part in promoting stereotypes of old age. This representation of the grey market can be found not only in advertising, but also in other print and broadcast media content, especially in television programmes. In getting across effective marketing messages to older consumers, it is crucial to know where certain images of ageing will be disavantageous and why. Research into media depictions of ageing and old age has provided useful insights into where there have been tendencies to project images of older people which do not always go down well, and which, frankly, fail to reflect reality.

Origins of stereotypes

The stereotyping of the elderly begins with the attribution of certain psychological traits to that age-group which then influence sets of generalised ideas which people hold about the members of that age-group (Hamilton and Trolier 1986). In general, older people are thought about in positive and negative ways, but the negative characteristics tend to outnumber the positives (Mueller and Ross 1984; Mueller, Wonderlich and Dugan 1986).

The term 'ageism' has been coined to describe the pejorative images of older people. Ageism may be defined as systematic stereotyping and discrimination against people because they are old. Ageism is similar to sexism and racism in that it is discrimination against all members of a particular group. Implicit within the term is the notion that the old are in some way different from everyone else and are not subject to the same wants, needs and desires as the rest of society.

Old people are associated, for example, with a shrivelled appearance. This is not too surprising since wrinkles are perhaps the most significant visible sign of ageing (Liggett 1974). The body, although easier to conceal, also gradually reveals signs of ageing. Movement becomes more restricted as the older person takes on a more stooped gait, weight may be gained around the midriff and some shrinkage in height may occur. There is a further belief that mental faculties lose their edge with increased age, and that older people become more forgetful, more muddled in their thinking, less able to concentrate and focus on what is happening around them. Socially, there is a view that older people become more dependent upon others and are less able to cope for themselves in respect of dealing with the basic necessities of life. Victor (1994) listed the following stereotypes of old age:

(1) All elderly people are alike.
(2) Elderly people are socially isolated.
(3) Most older people are in poor physical and mental health.
(4) Retirement is more problematic for men than women.
(5) Elderly people are isolated from their family and neglected by them.
(6) Elderly people are not interested in, or capable of, an active sex life.

(7) The old cannot learn.

(8) Intelligence decreases with age.

(1994: 78)

Many of these stereotypes have no basis whatsoever in truth. Although the realities of ageing do not fit the commonly held stereotypes, the myths about ageing continue to find common currency and expression in everyday life.

Sometimes beliefs about older adults reflect a general view that certain characteristics or abilities naturally change across the life span. Memory, for instance, is expected to peak in a person's mid-20s, but decline significantly in later life (Ryan 1992). Other intellectual abilities may not become fully developed until middle age before declining in old age (Hendricks *et al.* 1988). Across a range of personality traits, there is a tendency to identify more losses than gains in desirable abilities and characteristics with advancing age (Heckhausen, Dixon and Baltes 1989).

Young people may hold a range of contrasting opinions about older people, in some instances perceiving them to be characteristically miserable, inflexible and dependent on others, while in other instances regarding them as open-minded, cooperative, friendly, cheerful and able to take care of themselves (Rothbaum 1983; Schmidt and Boland 1986; Hummert *et al.* 1994). Researchers have also found distinct groupings of traits about older people indicating multiple stereotypes of this age-group (Brewer, Dull and Lui 1981; Hummert 1990). Conceptions about older people can vary markedly among different age-groups. Older people tend to hold more complex and varied sets of impressions about their own age-group than do younger people (Hummert *et al.* 1994).

An American study looked at what adults under 65 perceived as the main problems of ageing. These expectations were then compared with the experience of a sample of over-65s (National Council on Ageing 1975). At the most general level, virtually none of the non-elderly adults could envisage the years after their 60th birthday as being the best years of their life. At least a third saw them as having advantages as well as disadvantages. The biggest disadvantages were perceived as being illness, decreased mobility, poverty and loneliness.

Public expectations about later life saw old age as a time of fear of crime, poverty, poor housing, inadequate medical care, poor health and lack of social interaction. Elderly people consistently rated these features as much lesser problems than the non-elderly population. The discrepancies between the two groups were enormous. Six out of ten non-elderly respondents (60 per cent), for example, thought that loneliness was a serious problem of old age compared with just over one in ten (12 per cent) of elderly respondents. More than half (54 per cent) of the younger respondents also believed that not feeling needed was a serious problem for older people compared with just 7 per cent of older respondents themselves.

The concern about such stereotyping of older people among the rest of society is that they may influence the way older people are treated by others. Many prevailing stereotypes about older people carry the message that they are a non-productive group within society with little influence or significance. They can therefore be ignored (Victor 1985). As well as influencing the behaviour of others towards older people, stereotyping can also affect the way older people view themselves and shape the behaviours they deem to be appropriate for them. This has been observed to occur especially when older people are in the company of younger people, further reinforcing the stereotyped expectations which younger people already hold about them. Young people often construct negative images about people whom they regard as old, and often hold relatively few counter-balancing positive impressions of them. At the same time, older people themselves may adopt a style of conversation and topics, and choice of vocabulary which reinforces the age difference between themselves and younger people. Ageing therefore becomes not simply a function of biological change and decline, but a psychological disposition and attitude to life (Coupland, Coupland and Giles 1991; Giles and Coupland 1991).

Many modern stereotypes about ageing conform with the view of dis-engagement theory, introduced in Chapter 1, and suggest that older people should withdraw gradually and gracefully from professional and social life, and accept a more passive and dependent existence. By regarding older people as a distinct group, separate from the rest of the population, with their own idiosyncratic and often not particularly attractive or appealing attributes, ageist attitudes develop which may disadvantage this group. Such stereotypes may cause older people to define themselves in a certain way. One impact of this may be that wealthier and healthier older people may regard themselves as exceptions to the norm, rather than rejecting as inaccurate the 'norm' which has been set by ageist stereotypes (Victor 1994).

Historical perspective on ageism

Concepts of older people and ageing have changed over time. Historically, the diminished resources of physical strength, money and social influence that accompanied getting old left many older people totally dependent on the goodwill and charity of family or neighbours. In the period spanning 1300 to 1840, evidence suggests the existence of ideals of charitable Christian duty towards elderly people. Old people who had made little provision for an independent old age could otherwise find themselves neglected and treated as outcasts (MacFarlane 1986). Older people could expect a comfortable later life if they had accumulated and retained sufficient material resources (Thomas 1976). Despite the more general image of respect afforded to older people in pre-industrial Britain, they could still find themselves stigmatised if they had no material means of retaining a position of authority and influence in the community.

The traditional view of old people was that they were a group who, regardless of their actual age, had become helpless and dependent upon the support of others. A labourer permanently incapacitated by injury or ill-health could therefore be regarded as 'old' at the age of 40 (Shorter 1983). The belief that industrial society destroyed the support older people could expect to receive from their community when most people lived in close-knit rural environments has received little empirical support (Haber 1983). There is some doubt that old people ever gained a position of respect simply because of their age even in pre-industrial times (Fischer 1978; Stone 1977; Haber 1983).

As society moved into an industrial age, however, conceptions of ageing began to change in certain subtle respects. An increased preoccupation with health and retaining youthfulness for as long as possible, resulted in some sections of society, usually the better-off, becoming more concerned about a youthful vision of life rather than its prolongation (Kastenbaum 1974). The traditional images of older people, while retaining their broadly negative stereotyping, began to recognise distinctions among members of that age-group. One study showed how these distinctions were reflected in the different visions of the elderly present in children's stories, songs and games in the nineteenth century. Three different types of elderly person were identified: the *good-old*, comprising wise, moral old people who were generally friendly and supportive of younger people; the *bad-old*, comprising people who do not act their age, who go to lengths to disguise how old they are, and refuse to conform to the stereotypes prescribed for them; and finally, the *past-it*, comprising generally senile individuals, who are physically impaired and the butt of jokes (Tamke 1978).

Distinctions between different old-age types prevail even today. In a small study of men and women in Aberdeen, Williams (1986) located positive and negative attitudes towards ageing. Such attitudes were found to have a long history. A distinction was drawn between a 'green old age' and 'the last stage of withering'. A further distinction was made between 'the honoured and despised old, the honoured retaining their faculties through wealth and moral effort, and the despised losing theirs through poverty and moral weakness' (Williams 1986: 4).

Perceptions of ageing and old age have changed in the light of industrial and technological developments which have rendered many of the skills and the knowledge of the older generation redundant. As a consequence, old people have become devalued and irrelevant to the modern day economic and production process (Dowd 1980). This climate of industrial and technological change has gradually produced a shift in the image of ageing which has become established in the wider society. In modern western industrialised societies such as Britain and the United States there has been a social reconstruction of traditional ideas about ageing. Key manifestations of this shifting view occurred during the years between the First and Second World Wars in the twentieth century. This period, for instance, witnessed the emergence of the consumer culture. Changes in the political economy of the western world placed a greater premium on the value of being younger and having a youthful workforce with a modern outlook (Achenbaum 1978; Victor 1994).

The introduction of new production methods and the effects of economic depression forced many workers to become unemployed and in this context of unsettling social ferment, the idea of retirement as an appropriate stage of life for ageing workers took hold of the public imagination (Graebner 1980; Phillipson 1982). The concept of the old age pension had already been accepted and both on humanitarian grounds and grounds of expediency; retirement came to be seen as a natural resting place, even a reward, for men in their 60s. During the inter-war years too, women (many of whom were dependent on a male wage earner) began to be treated as a distinct category who were increasingly seen as requiring special treatment (Roebuck and Slaughter 1979).

Against this background, the images of retirement as a 'normal' consequence of reaching the age of 65 for men and 60 for women gradually emerged and added an extra layer to the traditional belief that as people got older they became more useless and should therefore gradually 'disengage' from active life. The difference between traditional and modern images of old age as uselessness is that in pre-industrial Britain such 'retirement' was the consequence of a physical inability to work whereas in modern Britain, as elsewhere in advanced societies, it is determined by a bureaucratic decision based on fashionable stereotypes of ageing which have little to do with the actual capacity of many individuals to carry out productive activity (Cain 1974).

Since the Second World War there have been a number of developments linked with cultural and socio-economic change which have affected images of ageing. First, advances in medical science have made people more conscious of the internal state of their bodies and of their external appearance. Second, the increase in life expectancy means that more people are living beyond their 70s and dying of diseases associated with old age. Third, the impact of consumerism as a method of promoting mass-produced goods in terms of their capacity to enhance one's lifestyle. This development has important implications for the social construction of ageing because these promotion techniques rely heavily on an image of the consumer as a person with the youthful energy to continue renewing his or her purchases. Fourth, the expansion of the mass media which reproduce stereotypes and circulate images at a faster pace and to a wider audience than ever before. Fifth, society has become increasingly multicultural and incorporates a diverse range of ethnic identities, each of which has its own set of images of ageing.

The emergence of middle age

As the stage of retirement took on official status, thus defining in fairly precise terms when the onset of old age would begin, a stage of life known as 'middle age' also came more clearly into focus. One significant feature of middle age was to draw a clear distinction between this stage and 'old age'. One way in which attempts were made to achieve a distinctive and positive image was to re-define middle age as 'mid-life' which was portrayed from the 1920s onwards as an extendable phase of vigorous and self-fulfilling life (Hepworth and Featherstone 1982).

A new, modern image of middle age therefore emerged which shifted emphasis from the traditional characteristics of this stage of life, such as putting on weight, hair loss, impaired vision, on to the fact that it could represent a vibrant, challenging period of life in which individuals could still enjoy youthful energy coupled with the additional benefits of experience and continue to achieve various personal and professional goals. There were already signs during the nineteenth century among the better-off social classes that men and women were taking steps to delay the onset of signs of ageing, by watching their diet, taking exercise and so on. The emergence of consumerism in the 1920s placed further emphasis upon the need to challenge an assumption that middle-age weight gain was inevitable. During the 1920s and 1930s the idea that graceful ageing, health, and physical and moral attractiveness were interrelated began to exert a heightened influence on the social reconstruction of middle age.

The signs of ageing on face and physique were increasingly portrayed as visible evidence of an unwise and socially unacceptable way of life, particularly when they became noticeable during middle age. The new values expressed a view that the ageing process should be deferred as long as possible. The accelerating impact of consumerism during the inter-war years sharpened awareness of the central role of the body in social life and the influence of imagery on the evaluation of individuals in a world of appearances (Featherstone 1982). Throughout this period, too, middle age was steadily presented as a time of opportunity for taking stock and self-development. According to Knopf 'At a certain age people have to realise that tomorrow will never come' (1932: 226). The emergent philosophy of life was that people should not live in the past, they must live for the day and waste no time in striving to achieve personal growth and fulfilment.

Changes in the imagery of middle age reappeared to even greater public acclaim in Britain in the 1970s where concern over the problems of mid-life showed no signs of waning. In a study of portrayals of ageing women in American popular films, Stoddard (1983) observed that the 1970s represented a crisis period for men and women in terms especially of self-fulfilment. Coupled with concerns about whether one has achieved enough was the deepening anxiety about the proximity of old age.

Images of retirement

Each year in Britain, about half a million people retire and, for many of these, the problems of adjustment can be enormous. One of the most significant difficulties for any retiring person in western societies is adapting to the fundamental role change associated with giving up the highly valued work role. According to some observers, acceptance of retirement is probably not helped by negative stereotypes which many people hold of older adults and which gerontologists believe contribute to many of the dysfunctions associated with old age. Some researchers have pointed to unfavourable characteristics of the older person on television which may serve to reinforce and even engender 'ageist' stereotypes.

Negative stereotyping of older people by sections of the general population is consistent with gerontological studies of attitudes towards age and ageing (Harris 1975; McTavish 1971; Tuchman and Lorge 1953a). Other research has shown that children internalise and accept dominant stereotypes of the older person at very early ages (Hickey *et al.* 1968; Jantz *et al.* 1976; Page *et al.* 1981).

Not all images of ageing and retirement have been negative. A few concerted attempts have been made to redress the balance and to present a more modern, varied and positive outlook on retirement. From its first appearance in Britain in 1972, the retirement and leisure magazine *Choice* (originally entitled *Retirement Choice*), the first in what is now an expanding range of popular retirement magazines, set out to dismantle the traditional image of retirement. In the second issue of this magazine Lord Raglan, the president of the pre-retirement association, argued that having contrived the age of retirement and its condition, society should play a full part in providing pre-retirement education to help people adjust to a new way of life (Raglan 1972).

The new magazine set itself the task of confronting and dismantling the traditional image of retirement which associated the end of full-time employment with passive old age. Retirement should become a positive stage in life. Fashion pages, for example, told women to adopt a modern outlook in the clothes they wear.

During the 1970s, the magazine continued to fight against the public stereotype of retirement. Men and women of retirement age were still a dynamic part of society; people stay younger and healthier for longer. By 1974, *Retirement Choice* became *Pre-retirement Choice*, adopted a glossier image, and featured interviews with and profiles of celebrity figures from politics, showbusiness and the media – all of whom were ageing gracefully and some of whom expressed no intention of retiring. The accent was now on preparation for retirement planning for a new generation of men and women in mid-life, who could not be expected to be attracted by images of retirement and old age, but who might reasonably be expected to have a long-term interest in leisure planning. By 1975, the word 'pre-retirement' was dropped, leaving the title of the magazine as *Choice*. The magazine continues to present retirement as an extended leisure lifestyle.

A more positive view of retirement emerged during the 1970s. Instead of being regarded as the beginning of the end of life, it came to be seen instead as a new stage of life offering its own distinct challenges. This change was embodied in the emergence of more active lifestyles for older people in a period that was increasingly being referred to as the third age (Bernard and Meade 1993a; Young and Schuller 1991). Income was recognised as having a crucial part to play in the status of retired people. Traditionally, reduced income following retirement generally meant a reduction in roles because of a shortage of funds. However, those individuals who benefited from occupational pensions or who had amassed substantial savings were found to enjoy retirement. For these individuals it opened up the possibility of having time to enjoy many new activities.

Awareness of the changing nature of retirement, combined with the focus on gender issues, has helped redefine or reconstruct images of retirement. From the late 1980s, the focus shifted toward the varied types of experiences affecting people either in the transition to, or within, the period of retirement.

Some research has investigated the difficulties of coping with early retirement. Here it is important to distinguish between a minority of people who choose to retire early (because they have sufficient income), and who often report satisfaction with the decision (McGoldrick and Cooper 1989), and the much larger number of workers who retire early because of health problems (Bone *et al.* 1992). This latter group appear more likely to report uncertainty about the future and to experience problems of adjustment (Cribier 1981; Parker 1980).

Early retirement may lead to some tensions, even where resources are relatively secure and there are no health problems. Byteway (1986) in a study of Welsh steelworkers who had experienced redundancy some 4 years prior to interview, found dissatisfaction being expressed, with men feeling that their skills were being wasted. Walker's (1989) research on the impact of redundancy among steelworkers in Sheffield found those who had taken the early retirement option to be evenly divided between those relieved to be leaving work and those expressing regret.

Guillemard (1986) related the problem of the early retired to ambiguities in their social position. She saw such people as neither really unemployed nor actually retired. Very few accept the label senior citizen, yet society has no category or role in between that of worker or pensioner. Guillemard (1986) highlighted the way in which, during a period of economic recession, old age is being redefined to incorporate people from middle age onward. This perspective emphasises the fluid nature of the social boundaries surrounding chronological age, with economic and ideological changes often having a decisive impact on the meanings attributed to particular periods within the life course (Hockey and James 1993).

Another area of differentiation concerns the question of women in retirement. Women's experience of retirement is affected by both their position in the labour market and ideologies regarding their role as carers (Bernard and Meade 1993b). Early research argued that entering retirement was less stressful for women, partly because work had been a less important element in their lives, and partly because of the maintenance of the role of housewife (Donahue, Orbach and Pollak 1960). However, Dex (1985) suggested that the later research literature indicates strong similarities in the attitudes of men and women toward work. Women have been found to be more economistic or instrumental than was thought to be the case (and men less so), and both experience variations through the life course in their orientations to work. Martin and Roberts' (1984) analysis of the Woman and Employment Survey found that the majority of working women had a high financial dependence on working and enjoyed working.

Loss of work may, therefore, have profound implications for women. At the same time, the type of work carried out by women workers also raises difficulties for their retirement. Many women are in low-paid jobs with non-existent or very low pensions (Abdela 1991; Davies and Ward 1991). This may be one reason why women have been found to be less positively disposed towards retirement than are men (Jacobson 1974).

AGEING AND THE MASS MEDIA

Agencies, such as the mass media, have been implicated in a number of studies as sources of misleading or unhelpful stereotypes of older people. Negative images of older people have been noted in studies of jokes (Davies 1977; Palmore 1977; Richman 1977), novels (Loughan 1977), magazine cartoons (Smith 1979), birthday greeting cards (Demos and Jacke 1980), television commercials (Francher 1973), television drama (Harris and Feinberg 1977), and television programming in general (Ansello 1978).

Newspapers, especially the popular tabloids, have been accused by some critics of being interested in older people only if they are victims of crime or family neglect, as manifestations of the perceived decline in moral standards or as examples of the burden of old age. A survey by Victor (1994) indicated that newspapers were not interested in normal ageing but only in more shocking and exceptional aspects of growing old in modern Britain. Women's magazines tend to be aimed at the young or middle-aged and only pay attention to the necessity of preventing the onset of old age rather than to the more positive and rewarding aspects of later life. The 'empty-nest' stage of life is often portrayed as a time of crisis for women rather than as a time of opportunity. The apparently straight-forward reporting of events may also be highly ageist. For example, the ages of 'elderly' judges are reported when they err in their judgement but when younger judges err their age is more often excluded from the report.

Negative conceptions and attitudes about older people may affect the way in which they are treated, and stereotypic notions regarding the needs and responses of older adults may affect actual behavioural response to them (Bennett and Eckman 1973; Butler 1961). Recognising that older people are vulnerable to these myths, and that television is one potent source which may perpetuate them, it is important to examine the nature of television output to ascertain the extent to which it is projecting misleading messages about them. Once the pattern of depiction of older people has been established, the next question is to what extent are viewers influenced by these images? The second part of this chapter will examine research evidence on the influences of media portrayals of older people on the way they are perceived by others as well as by themselves.

As this chapter will reveal, however, positive as well as negative images of older people have been recorded in the mass media. Buchholz and Bynum (1982) conducted a content analysis of newspaper articles about older people in 1970 and 1978 in *The New York Times* and *The Oklahoman*. They found that the two newspapers pictured older people 'more favourably than the media critics might lead one to believe' (1982: 87). Furthermore, most stories 'presented neutral image stories of the elderly, and of the remainder, positive image stories outnumbered the negative image stories 2:1 . . . Significantly more stories depicted the elderly in active roles than in passive or neutral ones, and the number of active role stories increased significantly between 1970 and 1978' (1982: 87). Seltzer and Atchley (1976) conducted a content analysis of children's books from 1870 to 1960. Contrary to what they hypothesised, the findings did not support a generalised negative picture about older people. There were generally fewer negative images than had been expected. There is also some evidence that ageing is becoming a more viable subject for the mass media and that greater interest is being paid to the positive aspects of ageing. The major British television channels have started to produce special programmes for older viewers, probably in response to the increasing size of the 'ageing' market. These represent exceptions, however.

The portrayal of older people on television, especially as it may relate to any effects on public perceptions of older people in reality, is an important issue for two main reasons. First of all, television plays a singularly important role in the lives of older people, for whom it provides a source of information, escape and companionship. Viewing figures show that people aged over 65 watch more television on average than any other age-band. Secondly, older viewers represent an already substantial, but more importantly, a growing segment of the television audience.

OLD PEOPLE ON TELEVISION

Before counts are taken there has to be a set of criteria established for designating on-camera characters as old. Casatta *et al.* (1980) studied the content of 13 daytime television serials for a two-week period during the summer of 1978. Characters were determined to be older when content defined them as being aged 55 or older, they were seen as being the eldest of at least three generations, they were depicted as a grandparent, a resident of an institution for the aged, a retired person, or any character who appeared elderly. If the actual age of the actor or actress playing the character was known, that, too, was taken as an indicator that the character was old.

Elliott (1984) monitored appearances made by older people in two daytime soap operas over a four-week period. For this study, an older adult was distinguished by being 'about' 65 years old or older, a judgement made on the basis of appearance. In addition, old people were in roles of great-grandparent, parent of a child aged 30 or more, or designated as retired. If the character had lines that described him or her as being an older person, or if such a description was applied to that character by others, then they were defined as being old. Again, if the actual age of the actor or actress was known, this qualified for inclusion in the old category.

Old people in programmes

According to Davis and Kubey (1982) television presents stereotyped characterisations of older people which perpetuate myths about old age; for example, that being old involves loss of libido and of mental faculties. Such stereotyped portrayals, which are commonplace on prime-time and daytime television, do not reflect the way older people necessarily are and may thus cultivate distorted public impressions of older members of society. For this reason American researchers have compiled detailed inventories of role models which will shape viewers' impressions of themselves and their position in society.

Many content analyses of television output have indicated that television does not give older people as much coverage as it gives younger people. Mertz (1970) analysed over 500 television programmes on the American networks to assess the role played by older persons. He found that not only were older people under-represented but also that over 80 per cent of elderly role portrayals fell into what he categorised as stereotypical characterisations.

In an examination of prime-time American television from 1969 to 1971, Aronoff (1974) reported that older people are typically omitted from major character roles on peak-hour television shows. Out of over 2,700 characters who were monitored, a mere 5 per cent were classified as 'elderly'. This was about half their share in the US population at the time. Furthermore, Aronoff observed, even when they did appear, elderly characters were usually cast as evil, unhappy and generally dependent on more youthful characters.

Peterson (1973) sampled 30 US commercial network half-hours between 8 pm and 11 pm in 1972. She counted as old those people whose real-life age was at least 65 and those playing roles judged by an observer to be at least 65. In all, out of 277 characters observed, she located 32 old people, three of whom were women. Old people comprised 13 per cent of that television population, substantially discrepant from the Aronoff (1974) study, but based on a smaller sample. Observers rated these older characters along 21 bipolar adjectival scales. Eighteen per cent were rated negatively and 59 per cent positively, but no comparative data for other age-groups were provided, so we do not know whether older people were perceived as significantly better or worse than any other character type.

A subsequent study of one week's prime-time drama programming on the major US television networks in 1974 indicated again that older people were under-represented and negatively portrayed relative to other age-bands (Northcott 1975). In this analysis, 'older adults' were those in their late 50s to mid-60s and 'aged' were in their late 60s or over. Just seven (1.5 per cent of the 464 characters recorded) were judged as aged over 64 years, compared to their actual census incidence of 10.1 per cent in 1973. Television was found greatly to over-represent the vigorous and competent adult male and attractive, youthful adult female. The elderly, on the other hand, were more often presented as incompetent, in bad health and involved in crime, usually as helpless victims.

Ansello (1978) analysed 238 half-hour segments of programmes and advertisements in 1977 and 1978. He found that the elderly accounted for 6 per cent of all characters portrayed, with females and non-whites substantially under-represented. Comparing older females with older males, the findings showed that the females were more likely to give information and be nurturant and less likely to ask questions and solve problems.

While Northcott's study (1975) could find little evidence of specific stereotypes traditionally associated with old age (such as poor physical health, senility, poverty, institutionalisation) it must be remembered that during the period of the study only seven significant portrayals of elderly characters were recorded at all; hence the study failed to accumulate sufficient data to suggest in which specific ways television may routinely stereotype the elderly.

Harris and Feinberg (1977) collected data on the frequency and nature of elderly role portrayals on the three US television networks for programmes broadcast throughout the day among seven days of the week over a six-week period. Older characters, it was found, were most often seen on comedy shows and news and talk programmes. Kubey (1980) observed that when the elderly did make more frequent appearances it was often in a comic context. They might be shown, for example, involved in behaviour normally associated with people a lot younger, such as riding motorbikes or performing modern dance. However, because such portrayals, which were in sharp contrast with traditional stereotypes, were presented in a comical way, they might actually reinforce those stereotypes.

The portrayal of the aged on prime-time television during the mid-1970s was analysed extensively by Greenberg, Korzenny and Atkin (1979). They assessed the frequency of portrayal, personal attributes and social behaviour of the elderly for composite sample weeks of national network TV fictional series at the beginning of the 1975, 1976, and 1977 seasons. One episode of each regular series broadcast between 8 and 11 pm and on Saturday morning between 8 am and 1 pm was videotaped. Special sports events, variety shows, and network movies were excluded. Altogether about 60 hours of programming were recorded per sample week. Each speaking character in each series was included in the analytic framework, giving 1,212, 1,120 and 1,217 characters respectively for the three years.

The crucial measure of age was assessed by coding decisions on age to the nearest full year. Other manifest attributes coded included sex, race and programme type, and also whether the character was a law-breaker. In addition, social behaviours performed by these characters were coded and analysed, which included various displays of pro-social, affectionate and aggressive behaviours.

Variations in the distribution and number of the aged occurred as a function of the time and type of programme. Larger percentages of older characters appeared on Saturday morning shows during the second season and larger percentages were also observed in late-night shows. Considerably fewer older characters were found from 8 pm to 9 pm.

Characters assessed as aged 60 and over were found more often in situation comedies than in any other programme type. All age-groups dropped in representation in crime shows during the third season because there were fewer of these items broadcast, but the two oldest age-groups declined in occurrence by twice as much as did characters aged 20 to 49 years. In summary, the oldest characters on TV were found in equal proportions in situation comedies and crime shows; all other adults were found primarily on crime shows.

There were differences between age-groups in some social behaviours but not in others. There was an absence of any strong or systematic differences between older and younger characters in the display or reception of either affection or altruism. There were differences, however, in the commission of acts of physical aggression. The two oldest age-groups were much less likely than others to perform physical aggression; older characters, though, were more likely to be verbally aggressive.

This content analysis revealed that the aged represented a small and decreasing proportion of all television characters, with a decline in their presence occurring from 4 per cent to 2 per cent of the television population over the three seasons monitored. Greenberg *et al.* (1979) compared the age distribution of television characters with census data from the same age-groups. Relative to the real world, the television world was overpopulated by those in the 20–34 and 35–49 age brackets. The over-65s were under-represented, but characters in the 50 to 64 age-band were represented on a par with their occurrence in the population (around 15 per cent).

The most extensive analysis of prime-time television in the United States, spanning the period 1968–80, revealed a distribution of age-groups on television differing substantially from that manifest in the real world (Gerbner *et al.* 1980b). The television age curve bulged in the middle years and grossly under-represented both young and old people. More than half of television's dramatic population was between 28 and 55 years, while those over 65, representing in actuality about 16 per cent of the US population, made up only 2.3 per cent of the fictional population. Children's programming had even fewer older people than prime-time – only 1.4 per cent of all weekend daytime characters were over 65.

Ratings of older programme characters by codings along several personality attribute scales indicated that more older characters were treated with disrespect on screen than were any other age-groups. Older men were found to play fewer serious roles and had greater relative presence in comedy contexts. About 70 per cent of older men and 80 per cent of older women were judged to be held in low esteem and treated discourteously. Also, older characters were frequently portrayed as foolish, incompetent, eccentric, held in low esteem and lacking in common sense. This research went further and claimed that heavy viewing of television was not only related to, but probably also resulted in the development of, a negative image of the elderly. Heavier viewers were ready to call a person 'elderly' at an earlier age on average than were light viewers.

In another study, Signorielli (1982) analysed the content of over 400 programmes on American television, recorded over a four-year period between 1975 and 1979. Nearly 1,300 major adult characters were identified. Older characters were relatively rare. Where they did occur such characters were often depicted as separated, widowed or divorced. Ten years later, findings emerged which exhibited a departure from the more usual pattern of portrayal of old age. Bell (1992) examined the title sequences of five prime-time programmes on American network television that were popular with older audiences. Four of these programmes were dramas and the other was a situation comedy. In these programmes older characters were portrayed as central characters and in most of these cases they appeared as relatively powerful, independent and affluent.

Further, they were depicted as asexual, though as still physically, mentally and socially active, and they were generally looked up to by other characters.

These pieces of American evidence suggest, therefore, that the amount of television viewing may affect the ways in which people perceive the demographic structure of the television population, and their ideas about characteristics of various segments of the real world population. In contrast, however, the only available content analysis of the elderly on British television, carried out by an elderly group (the University of the Third Age) themselves reported that age as such was not devalued. They did emphasise, however, that older women were less fairly represented than were older men (Lambert, Laslett and Clary 1984). In this exercise, all programmes transmitted in a two-week period in the winter of 1983 were reviewed by a team of 14 monitors aged 33 to 73 years. For the purpose of this exercise elderly people were defined as those aged 60 or over. In the programmes monitored, people within the target age-group appeared in 62 per cent of programmes transmitted by BBC1, 51 per cent of programmes on BBC2, 57 per cent of programmes on ITV, and 63 per cent of programmes on Channel Four. This relatively high profile of older people was significantly accounted for by the inclusion of world leaders, almost all of whom were older males, in news and current affairs programmes.

When news and current affairs programmes were excluded, older people were far less visible. They were relatively inconspicuous in plays, serials, action dramas, comedies and children's programmes. When older people did appear in fictional programmes, they were rarely the central character. Rather, they tended to be background characters moving into and out of the action as the story necessitated.

The overall balance of evidence from this study was that British television in the early 1980s depicted older people as reasonably fit and healthy. Within this broadly favourable conclusion there was still considerable selection bias in the way that older people were depicted. There was a significant trend to play down the sexual aspects of later life, and to minimise the financial hardships of age by exaggerating levels of income. There was also a difference in the characteristics of 'young' and 'old' elderly. The young elderly were seen as being much more active and less passive than older elderly. Additionally, despite their numerical dominance in the population, older women were less likely to appear than older men. Furthermore, the images depicted of older women were not very appealing. They had to overcome the double stereotype of ageism and sexism.

Dail (1988) revealed a slightly more favourable picture. In 12 programmes examined, 193 elderly characters made 3,468 'verbalisations and behaviours'. This represented a more prominent positioning of this age-group than had typically been found in other studies. Even so, male characters were numerically dominant.

Robinson and Skill (1995) analysed programmes appearing on four US television networks – ABC, CBS, Fox and NBC – over a four-week period in 1990. The sample included 260 fictional series. All speaking characters were catalogued in each programme and coded for gender, race, age, marital status, social class and religious allegiance. An elderly character was one who appeared or was known to be aged 65 or more. Older characters were those aged 60 to 64.

Out of 1,446 characters coded, 19 per cent played a main role and 55 per cent were cast as supporting players. Nearly 67 per cent of the 34 characters aged 65 or more were cast as supporting players and only 9 per cent were main characters. Of 196 characters aged 50 to 64 years, just over 19 per cent were leading and 58 per cent were supporting characters. Of the three characters aged 65 or over in main or central roles, two were females and one was male. There were 38 characters aged 50 to 64 in main roles, of whom 21, or 55 per cent, were male.

Females aged 50 to 64 were far more likely to be divorced or widowed than their male counterparts. Over 60 per cent of characters aged 65 or more with unknown marital status were females, and males and females aged 65 or over were equally likely to be widowed. Just over 88 per cent of characters aged 65+ were white, and more than half of the characters in this age-group (55 per cent) were classified as upper middle class.

Older people were found to remain a relatively invisible generation on television, comprising just 2.4 per cent of all characters. In a related investigation, Robinson and Skill (1993) had noted that significant increases in the number of characters aged 65+ had not occurred over the previous 15 years, nor had characters of that age cohort improved in terms of the prominence of their roles on television. The number of male characters aged 50 to 64 had not changed either, while the number of female characters aged 50 to 64 had increased.

Images of age in serialised drama

A small number of studies of the portrayal of older adults has focused specifically on their appearances in soap operas. American research on serialised dramas has indicated that although not widely shown, older people have tended to be afforded more respect and status in this genre (Downing 1974). Older adults in day-time dramas were shown as valued sources of advice among their children and grandchildren.

Monitoring 13 daytime US television serial dramas over a four-week period, Elliott (1984) found that older actors comprised 8 per cent of the characters. Older characters in this study were those who were judged to be about 65 years of age or older. This level of representation compared favourably with figures produced by Gerbner *et al.* (1980a) who coded them as representing only 2.3 per cent of the fictional television population. Gender differences of significance emerged. Older males had more diversified roles than did older females. The women had strong family roots, while the men occupied positions of importance in a more professional sense.

Casatta, Anderson and Skill (1980) examined 10 episodes of 13 daytime serials in the United States in 1978. A total of 365 characters were identified from these programmes, of whom nearly 16 per cent were 55 years of age or older and about 9 per cent were 65 years or older.

Dail (1988) content analysed 44 half-hour or hour-long episodes from 12 different family-oriented television series to assess the portrayal of older adults, judged to be aged 55 years or more. These characters were then classified in terms of mental stability and alertness, physical condition and health status, emotional stability and level of social interaction.

In all, 193 characters aged 55+ were identified. Older people when compared with younger people were found to be shown in a more positive light in terms of mental condition, physical behaviour and social behaviour. Thus, if any message was being transmitted at all about older people, it was that life can be good with increased years.

Images of age in children's programmes

A small number of studies have examined the representation of older characters in programmes made especially for children. The importance of this work lies in the assumption that children may be particularly susceptible to the influences of stereotyped portrayals of old people.

Under-representation of the older population was observed to occur in weekend children's programmes on American television in the early 1970s. Levinson (1973) reported a study of all continuing cartoon series appearing on one local and three network channels in Atlanta over three consecutive Saturday mornings in May 1973. Of 644 human characters observed, just 4 per cent were described as 'elderly', among whom 77 per cent were male. This study, like several others, however, did not indicate how 'elderly' was defined.

In studying a sample of shows on the American networks viewed by children, Jantz *et al.* (1976) found that not only were older women, children and minority groups under-represented, but out of 85 half-hour segments there were only four child–older person interactions.

The old have been found to be under-represented in cartoon programmes. This is a genre specifically targeted at younger children. It is often concerned with the struggles that children have between one another and with authority. Authority is usually held by the parent generation, not the grandparent generation. So not only are older adults not likely to be seen in cartoon land, but when they are, they are benign. Negative roles are assigned to younger adults, or to non-humans who are not old. These findings of content analysis done by Bishop and Krause (1984) demonstrated that ageing and old age were not dominant themes or even subordinate themes in American Saturday morning television programmes.

Bishop and Krause (1984) examined 106 cartoons, broadcast on American television over six weeks, with the conclusion that older people were not often prominent and, when they were, they were framed in a rather stereotyped, negative fashion. Neither the overall themes of the programmes nor the portrayal of primary characters reflected an emphasis on ageing or old age. Out of 378 primary characters, 7 per cent were judged to be 'old'.

Despite its absence as a major theme or character attribute, age did emerge as an incidental topic within cartoons. One in five cartoon programmes contained some reference to ageing or old age. These references were typically made in a largely non-positive manner. Indeed, out of 21 remarks recorded, 19 were classed as 'negative'.

TELEVISION VIEWING AND CONCEPTIONS OF OLD AGE

Content analysis studies have revealed that older people have often been depicted in a stereotyped way by the mass media. Television programmes, in particular, have been acknowledged as providing a source of potential misconceptions about older people. Establishing that individuals are portrayed in a particular fashion by the media is not sufficient to demonstrate that public conceptions or public attitudes are being affected. In this section we turn to evidence concerning the possible effects of mass media depictions of older people on the way they are perceived, with the initial focus being on the role of television programmes in this context. In the next section, we examine the depiction and impact of older people in advertising.

Despite the weight of findings from content analysis research supporting the view that the media are unfair to older people, this 'conception' is not necessarily transmitted to and absorbed by media consumers. In the UK, for instance, there is evidence that most people hold a positive opinion about the way older people are treated by the media. Indeed, there is a prevailing view that the media often make older people appear better than they are thought to be in real life (Midwinter 1991). Interestingly, older people were slightly more inclined to adopt that view than were younger people who were surveyed (see Tables 5.1a and 5.1b).

Table 5.1a View of media portrayals of older people as compared with what they are really like

	Total (%)	19–54 (%)	55–69 (%)	70+ (%)
Much better	30	24	33	32
About the same	41	43	39	41
Much worse	26	28	25	23
Don't know	4	5	2	4

Table 5.1b Real level of older people's problems compared with media coverage

	Total (%)	19–54 (%)	55–69 (%)	70+ (%)
More widespread than media	48	53	48	41
Media reflects existing level	30	31	27	32
Media exaggerates problems	19	14	22	23
Don't know	3	1	3	4

Source: Midwinter 1991

Evidence from the United States has confirmed that older people may turn to media portrayals of their own age-group with a view to gaining certain emotional gratifications from them. The nature of the gratifications sought and obtained, however, may depend upon the standpoint of the individual. Despite the case that has been made against the alleged disproportionate negative portrayals of old age in the media, research findings have indicated that such portrayals may sooth some older viewers rather than upset them. A key factor appears to be whether older viewers themselves are lonely or not in their own lives. Some individuals may make social comparisons between themselves and their own current situation and the depictions of same-age people shown on television. Unhappy, lonely viewers may actually be cheered by witnessing portrayals of older people in similar or even worse circumstances than their own. In contrast, older people who are happy with their own lives may suffer the opposite reactions to portrayals of sad, lonely dependent people of their own age-group (Mares and Cantor 1992).

Seminal work about public conceptions of old age and older adults emerged during the early 1950s (Tuchman and Lorge 1953a, 1953b, 1958), since when there has been continued interest in understanding attitudes towards old age and the ageing process (see Bader 1980; Lutsky 1980). One major challenge facing researchers has been to develop an understanding of those factors that are responsible for particular attitudes (Kogan 1979; Lutsky 1980; Palmore 1982).

Implicated as a possible influential agent in this context has been television (Kubey 1980). One theory of the impact of television viewing on perceptions about older people was advanced by Gerbner *et al.* (1980b) who argued that television presents a distorted and negative view of older people and that the more time viewers spend watching television, the more likely they are to adopt such impressions.

In support of their contention that television's portrayals do more than simply reflect or positively contribute towards ideas about older people, Gerbner *et al.* (1980b) reported survey findings which indicated an association between television characterisations and audience conceptions of older people, the strength of which varied with amount of viewing. Heavy viewing was related to a negative image of older people and the quality of their lives but was never associated with any positive images of older people. Heavy viewers, for example, tended to believe more often than did light viewers that older people are unhealthy, sexually inactive, narrow-minded and largely helpless. Conceptions of the young about when people become old were also distorted. When groups of adolescents were asked: 'At what age does a man (or woman) become elderly or old?', light viewers tended on average to say 57, while heavy viewers felt it was 51.

An individual's perceptions of the self and society are based largely on interactions and comparisons of oneself with others. Retirement, for many people, usually results in meeting fewer people and under these circumstances, television may become an important social reference from which an older person derives information about his or her current role and status in society. Content analysis studies of American prime-time television drama have indicated infrequent and highly stereotyped portrayals of the aged on television which may in turn cultivate a severely distorted public image of the older person in real life. It is possible, furthermore, for this material to carry its influence to the British viewing public, as it is largely American prime-time drama that makes up the 14 per cent of imported material used on British television, again mostly in prime-time. However, the interpretations and conclusions drawn by Gerbner and his colleagues depend on the fundamental assumption that the overall amount of viewing is the crucial variable in the relationship between television portrayals and audience response. Yet the effects of television portrayals on public attitudes are mediated by, and may depend more importantly upon, the ways in which viewers use and perceive television content than simply on how much of it they actually watch.

Korzenny and Neuendorf (1980) examined the links between television viewing habits and the self-perceptions of groups of older people and indicated the necessity to qualify such relationships with, (1) the functions served for the viewer by television; and (2) the viewers' perceptions of television portrayals of older characters. Neither of these factors was considered by Gerbner and the cultural indicators team and this restricts quite seriously the value of their findings. For most of the people sampled by Korzenny and Neuendorf, television performed two main functions – escape ('it takes my mind off things') and information ('to gain new knowledge', 'it provides useful information'). Older characters on television were seen as being portrayed in four different ways by older viewers: as assets to society; burdens on society; respectfully treated; or humorous. The following relationships between these factors were observed.

Older people who watched television mainly for escapist reasons from everyday problems tended to view more fantasy content, perceived older characters on television as burdens on society, and also tended to have somewhat negative self-images. The aged who watched mainly for information, however, saw more real (i.e. news) content and perceived older characters on television and themselves in a less negative light.

In a small study by Ward (1980), 59 respondents were given an opportunity to express their opinions about certain television programmes. Forty-five per cent thought television provided a poor reflection of older age, while 35 per cent disagreed. Four in ten (40 per cent) thought that older people were seen less often on television than in normal life.

Gerbner *et al.* proposed that television is 'the wholesale distributor of images of our popular culture' (1980b: 37), but that the images it presents do not correspond with the world of everyday experience. Heavy television viewers are hypothesised to use television to define and interpret everyday reality more often or to a stronger degree than light viewers because of a heavier reliance on this medium for their information about the world.

To test their notion of cultivation, Gerbner *et al.* conducted content analyses of television programming to infer the nature of the television 'world'. They then conducted partial correlational analyses to determine whether a relationship exists between television viewing and attitudes, with a possible third variable cause of such a relationship (e.g. age, race, income and education) held constant. Following their early research which focused on the impact of television depictions of crime and violence upon viewers' levels of fear and anxiety, critics challenged the way Gerbner and his colleagues had interpreted their data. They were accused of using inadequate statistical controls for relevant extraneous variables and of being selective in the variables selected for analysis from largely secondary survey source (Hirsch 1980; Hughes 1980).

In responding to these criticisms, Gerbner and his co-workers refined their theory. They introduced a new 'mainstreaming' hypothesis, according to which heavy television viewing should channel beliefs into the television worldview only among social groups that do not already subscribe to that view. Thus, middle-class and working-class viewers may hold disparate views about levels of crime in society. However, heavy viewers among both social classes would hold more similar opinions than light viewers, as television shapes their perceptions of the world. Thus, television is hypothesised to produce a convergence of social perceptions even among people who, on the basis of their demography, would normally be expected to hold differing world views.

Gerbner *et al.*'s (1980b) statements about the role of television in shaping public conceptions of older people were further examined and the original data were revisited by Passuth and Cook (1985). Computing fresh statistical analyses on the same data set, Passuth and Cook reached different conclusions from the Gerbner group, and found that the effect of television viewing on knowledge and attitudes about older people was small, restricted to younger people, and not consistent across a range of measures of viewing and attitudes.

This research examined the effects of television viewing, age, education, income, race, gender, life satisfaction and psychological well-being upon knowledge about adults aged 65 and over, and attitudes about this same age-group. Television viewing was measured with two questions: (1) 'About how many hours did you spend yesterday watching television?' and (2) 'How much time do you personally spend watching television – a lot of time, some but not a lot, or hardly any time at all?'

Using the same data set as Gerbner *et al.* (1980b) Passuth and Cook (1985) replicated the finding that an inverse relationship existed between reported hours of television viewing and knowledge levels and attitudes about older people, but when they controlled simultaneously for a variety of other demographic and psychographic variables, the relationship held for only one age-group (young adults under 30) and then for knowledge about older adults but not for attitudes. These results were interpreted as offering only limited support for the cultivation hypothesis. Little evidence emerged, either, to support the idea of mainstreaming.

The absence of any evidence for cultivation effects or mainstreaming effects was explained in part as a function of the under-representation of older people on television which meant that even heavy viewers would receive little exposure even to negative stereotypes. A second reason was the observation that television portrayals of older people were not overwhelmingly negative anyway. While Gerbner's (1980b) own content analysis revealed older people to be depicted as stubborn, eccentric and foolish, and more likely to be treated with disrespect, they were not shown as less useful members of society or as any more lonely than younger characters. A third factor was that other social forces may be more powerful than television in shaping viewers' perceptions of older people, which include newspapers, books and personal experience. Both newspapers (Bucholz and Bynum 1982) and books (Seltzer and Atchley 1976) have been found to depict positive images of older people as much as negative ones. Research on the role of personal experience has produced less definitive conclusions (Bader 1980). Young people with living grandparents are less likely to stereotype old age and older people negatively than those without living grandparents (Bekker and Taylor 1966; Rosencrantz and McNevin 1969), and it seems that personal experience with grandparents makes this difference.

To sum up so far, much of the research in the United States has indicated that 'ageism' is a discernible and influential feature of prime-time network programming which falsely shows old people as less effective than they really are, and in so doing distorts (for the worse) both the public image and self-image of older people. However, some discrepant results have emerged to cast doubt on powerful cultivation effects (Passuth and Cook 1985). Furthermore, these findings may not be generalisable to non-US audiences, even in countries such as Britain which import substantial quantities of dramatic television programming from America.

Previous research has shown that relationships among American samples between television viewing and public attitudes concerning personal safety and trust are not always found to occur with British samples. Furthermore, American investigators have not comprehensively examined relationships between viewers' impressions of different kinds of television portrayal of older people and their perceptions of older people in reality. Thus, although Korzenny and Neuendorf (1980) showed that information on amount of viewing by itself is not sufficient to predict effects on attitudes towards older people, in reality their study suffers from two limitations. First, their sample consisted of old people only, who tended to give biased opinions of their own age-group anyway (Schreiber 1979); and secondly, they did not examine how perceptions of the way older people are depicted on television vary from one type of programme to another – which they might be expected to do if different categories of television content have different functions for viewers.

In British research, efforts were made to explore these distinctions and also to distinguish viewers' perceptions of older people in the real world. Further, perceptions of old age portrayals were distinguished for additional types of programme, and in relation to amount of viewing among different age-groups of these different kinds of programmes.

British research

Perceptions of ageing and the possible role played by television in their cultivation has been examined in a small series of studies in Britain. This research explored television-related influences in the context of the cultivation model proposed by Gerbner *et al.* (1980b). In an initial study, members of a London-based viewer panel were asked for their perceptions of the age of onset of old age. Specifically, they were asked: 'what is the first age at which you consider it is fair to describe a person as old?' The modal age that emerged was 70. While the answers to this question did vary with the age of the respondent, they did not vary significantly with amount of television viewing when viewers' own age was controlled (Wober 1980).

Most people had very positive responses to questions on the nature of old age. Indeed, heavier viewers had a more positive attitude to older people in that they perceived such people to be very cheerful despite their handicaps. This latter finding was true of heavier viewers regardless of their own age. With regard to portrayal in different types of television programme, viewers felt that old people are treated with respect in 'actuality' material (news, documentaries and game shows), but they did not consider, on balance, that old people were treated with respect in television comedies.

Exploring distinctions between parts of the television world further it was found that more viewing of television was linked with a better impression of how old people are portrayed in comedy programmes and with impressions that old people are treated with respect in news and action-adventure programmes. Overall, therefore, this early study indicated that television viewing was associated with generally positive perceptions of the depiction of old age (Wober and Gunter 1982).

In examining the role of television in shaping public perceptions of old age and older people, however, it is necessary to go beyond an analysis of the overall amount of television watching that takes place. The representation of older people on screen can vary across different programme genres. One view of old age can emanate from soap operas, another from factual programmes.

In Britain, public service broadcasting requirements have traditionally encouraged programming diversity designed to meet a wide variety of public viewing tastes and interests. This philosophy has resulted in programmes targeted at different age-groups. A survey of viewers in the mid-1980s asked whether programmes for different parts of the age spectrum were rarer or more commonplace than they had hitherto been (Wober 1984). There were widespread opinions that programmes aimed at adults but not suitable for children as well as programmes aimed specifically at children had both become more frequently occurring. This perception was not found to be widespread in respect of programmes for all groups. Thus, there was a tendency for most viewers to believe that television programmes were becoming more age-specific in their orientation.

The same survey also asked people to estimate the 'first age at which you consider it fair to describe a person as old', but this time they were also asked the 'first age at which you consider it fair to describe a person as adult', and similarly the age at which a person is 'no longer a child' and 'no longer a toddler'. Results were that, on average, the toddler was seen as ending at 5, and the child at just under 15; adulthood was seen as beginning at just under 19, on average, and old age at 62. These milestones define a perceived span of childhood and of the teenage phase with the first fairly closely tied to the formal years of compulsory schooling and the second rather shorter than the actual teen years.

A further finding was that for people who watched more television overall, and most of its separate categories (except news) there were small but significant negative correlations linking the amount of viewing with the perceived onset of old age. These correlations applied when any mutual relationships with age, sex and class were partialled out. A similar effect, though at a weaker level and located mainly with news and soap opera material, linked heavier viewing with earlier perceived age of the start of adulthood. Two explanations are available for these findings. One supposes that it may be an 'effect' of watching more television to believe that adulthood, and more noticeably old age, have an earlier onset. The other is that people with such beliefs tend for some reason to watch more television. In attempting to judge between these possibilities, or to suggest any other, it should be noted that there is no connection whatsoever between amounts of viewing and the perceived age of the end of childhood and no significant link overall (though tiny positive relationships involving soap opera and sport viewing) with the perceived age of the end of toddlerhood. This tends to dismiss any possibility that there may have been a 'polarisation' or extremist tendency expressed in the judgements of those who prove to be heavy viewers.

Detailed examination of the actual average scores of perceived onset of old age, amongst subgroups who are themselves of different ages or who watch television in differing amounts, shows that the 'effects' if any are very small; and they are not unidirectional. Thus, among those aged 20–29, heavy viewers give a younger onset of old age than do light viewers. However, if it is argued that this is an 'effect' of registering impressions from the content of television it might be expected that people a decade older, who have been watching television that much more, would show this pattern equally or more clearly. Instead, amongst viewers aged 30–39, heavy and light viewers have an equal point of perceived onset of old age (medium viewers place it higher). In fact, the highest average values of perceived onset of old age occur among light and medium viewers aged 50–59. It seems probable therefore that the overall result – which is a small one in any case – of a link between amount of viewing and the first age at which people are thought to be old is not a result of the amount of television watched. Instead, both this perception and the amount of television watched are an outcome of other, as yet unidentified, personal characteristics.

THE OLDER PERSON IN ADVERTISING

Until fairly recently, there was little research on the consumer behaviour of the older person. This has begun to change with more research now being done, especially on the older consumer's media habits. Research on mass media use of the older person has consistently demonstrated that television is the most important medium in their lives. As Rubin and Rubin have noted: 'Television is the preferred mass medium for the elderly, who have been found to watch up to six or more hours each day and to display a considerable affinity with the medium, particularly for news and information programming' (1982a: 242). In fact, this age-group spends more time with television than any other age-group, including young children (Schreiber and Boyd 1980).

Not surprisingly, older people use television as an important source of consumer information. For example, Schreiber and Boyd (1980) reported in their survey of 442 older adults that a majority of them felt that television commercials, particularly those for health and food products, were both useful and positive in their portrayals of older adults. Rubin and Rubin found that, in line with previous research, 'information learning is the most salient reason for using television . . . [among] . . . older respondents, who also indicate an obvious partiality to news and informational programming' (1982a: 142).

A study of older consumers' use of media for fashion information (Kaiser and Chandler 1985) revealed that although television was used less often than newspapers and magazines for fashion ideas and purchase information, 'it is unlikely that these media [newspapers and magazines] can provide as much information on the contextual appropriateness of clothing styles as television' (1985: 206). According to these researchers, demographic and contextual variables apparently do have an impact on the use of television for fashion information, as demonstrated by the findings that those older men with relatively high clothing expenditures were significantly more likely to use fashion information from television than were those older men with relatively low clothing outlays.

Studies on motivations for television use by the elderly generally show, according to Davis and Westbrook (1985), that older consumers '(a) are "embracers", accepting with little judgement what is placed before them, (b) overwhelmingly prefer news and public affairs programmes, and (c) perceive the viewing experience as a benefit because it provides companionship, a sense of involvement, and a meaningful structuring of time' (1985: 210–211).

Although older consumers have been found to mostly reject the notion that they are influenced by television advertising (Davis and Westbrook 1985), other evidence suggests that advertising in the media, and television especially, can play a part in shaping older consumers' product preferences (Smith, Moschis and Moore 1985). The mass media may have an important role in consumer socialisation which stretches far beyond children and teenagers, to influence the consumer behaviour patterns of older adults as well.

If advertising presents a distorted view of society, offering us a world in which everything is glossier, bigger, or more beautiful than in real life, perhaps its biggest distortion is that of age. The advertising industry's obsession with the cult of youth means that people over the age of 50 are rarely seen in advertisements, except in the role of grannies or pensioners: by appealing to the young, who are open to new ideas, advertisers hope to keep their image fresh and build loyalty that will last a lifetime. This attitude, however, may result in the exclusion of a sector of the population with increasing significance for marketers. Older people can no longer be considered as an underprivileged section of society simply waiting to die, but instead represent a group that now has great spending power and wants to use it.

Creating advertising for the older market has been an especially difficult challenge. Certain products may have appeal only to older people, and certain products can appeal to a broader range of consumers. In creating copy, sensitivity has to be exercised since it is assumed that most people do not want to be appealed to through their age status primarily. Although being old is not something that bothers all people, it can be assumed, being talked down to or patronised because of being old is something that does bother most people.

In a study on stereotypes of the aged (Hess 1974), it was stated that advertisers shy away from old people because 'they are "poor copy"; they remind us of role loss, deprivations and ultimate demise, none of which is a helpful product association'. Comfort (1988) blamed this attitude on the mercenary nature of advertising.

A cumulative body of research has indicated that older people are to a great extent less favourably treated than they could be in advertisements (Moschis 1987; Lexchin 1990; Wolfe 1990). Content analyses on the portrayal of older people in advertising in America have found that older people were under-represented in comparison with their numerical representation in the population (Kvasnicka *et al.* 1982; Ursic *et al.* 1986; Swayne and Greco 1987; Bramlett-Solomon and Wilson 1989) and that this was particularly true of older women (Gantz *et al.* 1980; England *et al.* 1981).

Not all the news about older adults in advertising has been bad, however. Even in the 1970s, some researchers noted upward trends in the extent to which older people were featured in television advertising. Furthermore, this trend was in contrast to shifts in the age distribution of the population. In the United States, for example, Schneider and Schneider (1979) analysed television commercials contained in 27 hours of prime-time (7–10 pm) network programming aired over three Minneapolis/St Paul, Minnesota network affiliates during October 1976. A total of 287 distinct commercials for different types of products were identified. Advertised commodities included food, snacks, soda; personal and beauty care; automobiles and accessories; restaurants and retail outlets; drugs and medicine; household appliances; furnishings; institutional/public services; alcoholic beverages; pet food and related products; household cleaning agents; clothing; finance and real estate; various others.

Comparisons were made with findings from an earlier study by Dominick and Rauch (1971). An overall shift was observed away from young adult characters in television commercials between 1971 and 1976. Both young male and young female characters appeared in 10 per cent fewer advertisements in 1976 compared with 1971. Most of this shift was taken up with an increased use of characters aged over 50. Older adults accounted for 6 per cent more female characters and 10 per cent more male characters in 1976 than in 1971.

The nature of older role portrayals

Concern about the representation of older people in advertising stems not simply from observations about the frequency with which they appear, but also refers to the way they are shown. Quality of representation is just as important as quantity, if not more so. The images that are cultivated about being over 50 or over 60 and so on, are shaped by the character of the roles older actors are given to play in commercials. A longitudinal study of the representation of older people in magazine advertisements found that this age-group was often featured. Not only did older people achieve prominence, but also they were often depicted in relatively prestigious work situations (Ursic, Ursic and Ursic 1986).

Zhou and Chen (1992) conducted a content analysis of the national advertisements in the December 1990 editions of ten largest circulating Canadian consumer magazines. The specific research questions asked were: (1) How frequently did advertisements present older characters? (2) How were older characters portrayed? (3) How did the portrayal of older and younger characters differ? The findings indicated that the problem with the portrayal of older people in Canadian magazine advertisements was one of both quantity and quality. Older people exhibited only a marginal representation. Only around 5 per cent of the characters in the advertisement sample were judged to be 50 years of age and older and no one aged 65 or older, despite the fact that this population segment was known to have a considerable share of consumer purchasing power.

The portrayal of older people, when it did occur, was generally stereotypic, although not blatantly so. Older female characters were very uncommon in magazine advertisements, in contrast to their presence in the population. Older characters were portrayed as uncharacteristically less capable in terms of their occupations; they were cast in less important roles to the advertisement's theme or lay-out, and they were portrayed as tending to stay at home and be less physically active when compared with younger characters. As a whole, the images of the older characters were largely in their negative stereotypes. From the perspective of older people, their insignificance and poor image in advertisements may lead them to think that they are not considered as valuable customers by marketers or as valuable members of society.

On a positive note, older characters were seen in social and 'transgenerational' scenes and not totally socially isolated. Although the patterns on the products and product types associated with older and younger characters differed, there was no strong tendency only to use older characters with 'old age' products. They were used to promote goods aimed at the average consumer.

Advertising on television has been observed to be orientated toward young people, while the older end of the age spectrum were disenfranchised (Francher 1973; Harris and Feinberg 1977). Furthermore, older men appeared more frequently and more often in a work environment (Ursic *et al.* 1986) and were used as the major role adviser much more frequently than older women (Harris and Feinberg 1977; Swayne and Greco 1987). Older women were also more often judged to be negatively stereotyped (Harris and Feinberg 1977). Moreover, older people were most often seen in advertisements selling corporate image rather than a particular consumable product (Gantz *et al.* 1980). Especially for characters past the age of 50, they were portrayed as having suffered a decline in their physical activity with health becoming a problem (Harris and Feinberg 1977) and tended to be seen at home or in non-working settings (Swayne and Greco 1987).

Francher (1973) assessed a sample of 100 television commercials for their ageing content and found only two commercials with any older characters. A majority of the commercial messages focused on youth, youthful appearance, or the energy to act youthful.

Harris and Feinberg (1977) found that people classified as over 60 years old represented nearly 11 per cent of total characters analysed in a sample of 80 television commercials from US network television. Older characters were less likely than younger characters to be advice givers or authority figures. This decline in authority with age was more pronounced among female characters than among male characters.

Age of character was found to be connected with particular product categories as reproduced below:

Clothing: Of eight people counted in clothing advertisements, all were women under 40.

Appliances: Of 24 people in appliance adverts, only one was over 60.

Health Aids: Of 37 people in health aids advertisements, eight (21.6 per cent) were over 60.

Personal care and Cosmetics: Approximately 83 per cent of all people in personal care and cosmetics adverts were under 30. Only one person, a male, was over 40.

Car Advertisements: of 17 people in car advertisements, 23.5 per cent were from the 50 to 60 age-groups. None was over 60.

Food: Of 50 people in food advertisements, only three (six per cent) were over 60.

Cleaning products: No people over 60 were counted in cleaning product advertisements. Sixty-six per cent were under 40.

(Harris and Feinberg 1977: 467)

Three streams of research seem to dominate the literature on the use of older people in advertising. The first stream consists of content analysis studies. The earlier studies (Harris and Feinberg 1977; Gantz, Gartenberg and Rainbow 1980; Langmeyer 1983) suggested that older persons have been both under-represented in advertisements and poorly stereotyped in unflattering, unhealthy and un-interesting ways.

Ostman and Scheibe (1984) reported that a month's US network television commercials (taped in March 1981) portrayed fewer aged than their proportion in the population. The television older population had, nevertheless, risen significantly above the coverage level noted in previous content analysis. They attributed this to a feedback process involving research and pressure-group activity; but another interpretation could well be that it represented a sampling fluctuation.

More recent content analyses (Ursic *et al*. 1986; Swayne and Greco 1987) have found that when older people are portrayed in advertising they do not play major roles in the majority of cases but instead appear with people in other age-groups and are not necessarily negatively stereotyped. Ursic *et al*. (1986), for example, found that in over one-half of 469 magazine advertisements containing older people (aged 60 and over), they were shown in working situations, mostly in prestigious occupations. Thus, there are some indications that the advertising industry is beginning to move toward more positive portrayals of older characters.

On a more positive note, however, the role of adviser in television advertising was frequently assigned to older men and women. When older people appeared in advertisements they were often placed in home settings where other, younger generations were also present. This style of older consumer presentation was most often associated with advertising for food products (Swayne and Greco 1987).

A second research stream has investigated the reaction of the older consumers' market to being identified as a separate market and has considered the desirability of having special age-related advertisements directed to this age-group through the use of older adult models (Gronhaug and Rostvig 1978; Bartos 1980; Rotfield, Reid and Wilcox 1982; Klock and Traylor 1983; French and Fox 1985; Barak and Stern 1985). These studies raise the question of whether people aged 60 or 65 or older actually see themselves as belonging to that age-group and consequently if they need to be reached from more than a purely age-based approach.

In this vein, it has been suggested that many older people see themselves as 10 or 15 years younger than their chronological age (French and Fox 1985; Barak and Stern 1985) and therefore may not identify in a positive way with spokespersons their own age. Gronhaug and Rostvig (1978) and Klock and Traylor (1983) found that attitudinal change and interest to purchase, respectively, were not positively affected by the use of older models in advertising directed to that age-group. Rotfield, Reid and Wilcox (1982) found that middle-aged housewives gave the highest evaluation to advertisements that had a match between model age and product orientation. This study found that an older model would not repel audience members' attitudes because of a lack of identification with audience self-images. Instead, it was more important that the model's age should fit the product orientation. These findings indicated that it may not be appropriate to feature older characters in advertisements for products even if older consumers are the intended market.

Other evidence has emerged that the age of a model or actor in an advertisement can affect the credibility of the message among older consumers. The model does not necessarily need to be the same age as the target market. In the case of advertising directed at the over-65 market, however, a same-age or middle-age (35 to 59 years) model is assigned much greater credibility than a young, under-35 model (Milliman and Erffmeyer 1990).

There are signs too that advertising executives have begun to realise the potency of using actors or models in advertising with whom older consumers can identify. In a survey of American advertising executives, an opinion clearly emerged that older spokespersons may be preferable for marketing messages aimed at older consumers (Greco 1988).

Advertising and adaptation to older age

The third stream of enquiry has investigated the effects of advertising on older consumers from a socialisation perspective (Smith, Moschis and Moore 1982, 1984; Smith and Moschis, 1984). The socialisation perspective maintains that older consumers who experience role losses through retirement, children leaving home, death of friends and/or spouse may look increasingly toward the mass media and advertising for cues to advise them on how to act and how to view themselves (Ahammer 1973; Smith, Moschis and Moore 1982, 1984).

Television advertising emphasising youth appeals was found to be related to negative self-images among older consumers (Kubey 1980). These findings were replicated in another study in which self-images among the older consumer were related to more elaborate measures of mass media advertising (television, newspaper, radio, and magazine advertisements) (Smith *et al.* 1982). Another finding was that older consumers' exposure to media advertising was negatively associated to their ability to filter puffery in advertisements.

This research stream suggests that mass media advertising, because of its impact on role-related perception, may be a socialising agent for the older consumer. These findings also suggest that the older consumer feels that advertisers do not portray older people in a positive or desirable manner, and are supported by other findings that heavy television viewers of all ages are more likely to have negative images of older people, even when heavy viewers are older people themselves (Gerbner *et al.* 1980b; Korzenny and Neuendorf 1980). These findings have led Smith, Moschis and Moore (1982, 1984) to recommend that advertisers should include more older spokespersons in positive portrayals in advertisements for products aimed at the older consumer in keeping with the 'ageing' of the general population.

Greco (1988) surveyed over 280 advertising executives for their opinions about the use of older people as spokespersons in advertising. Most (68 per cent) agreed that the use of older people as spokespersons helps gain awareness for new products. A smaller proportion (43 per cent) believed that older spokespersons help to get the audience's attention. Forty-three per cent of the respondents felt that older spokespersons were effective at gaining message comprehension, while a majority (74 per cent) also felt that older people could be effective in persuading audiences to switch brands. Forty-four per cent of the respondents felt that older spokespersons were effective for gaining purchase of a product, and just 32 per cent agreed that older spokespersons would be effective for gaining intention to purchase.

Giving more general views, a great majority of the advertising executives (83 per cent) acknowledged that stereotyping of older characters occurs in advertising, though more than one in two (51 per cent) felt that advertising portrayed older people in a positive manner. Over half (57 per cent) also felt that older spokespersons posed no greater risks of negative effects on general audiences than did younger spokespersons.

The problem of the older person on television seems to be one of quality rather than of quantity. While some content analysis studies have indicated that older people are represented in numbers reasonably close to their population distribution, it is the way they are portrayed which is problematic.

The use of older people in advertising aimed at that market segment may have the advantage that consumers will identify more with same-age spokespersons and perceive such commercial messages as more credible as a result (Milliman and Erffmeyer 1990). Another factor here is an acknowledgement that while older spokespersons may be effective in advertising aimed at the mature market, they may be less so for other target age-groups (Greco 1989).

COMMUNICATING WITH THE OLDER CONSUMER

In targeting products to the older consumer, marketers must not only take into consideration their needs and motivations, but also be careful not to embarrass them or make them feel uneasy about their age. In a classic marketing blunder, Heinz some years ago introduced a line of pureed 'senior foods' when it learned that many older people with chewing difficulties were buying baby foods. The new product failed because older consumers were ashamed to admit that they required strained foods. Instead, they preferred to buy baby foods which they could always pretend were for a grandchild.

Studies have indicated that older consumers often perceive that they are negatively portrayed in advertisements. Therefore, marketers should be careful that their advertising does not contain negative stereotypes of older people, but does in fact cater to their preferences.

Poor promotion, especially advertising, appears to have contributed to the alienation of older consumers (Festervand and Lumpkin 1985). Much advertising today stereotypes older people and often does so in a negative way. For example, *The Wall Street Journal* states that 'older people in TV ads are recognizable most often by their stereotypes; half-deaf codgers, meddling biddies, grandfatherly authority figures or nostalgic endorsers of products that claim to be just as high quality as they were in the good old days. Rarely are older people shown just as ordinary consumers' (Abrams 1984).

Although those over age 55 comprise approximately one in four (26 per cent) of American adults, several studies have shown that they account for only about one in ten (10 per cent) of television commercial characters – usually those in need of laxatives, denture adhesives, and sleeping pills. Older consumers do appear somewhat more significantly, however, in magazine advertising (Ursic *et al*. 1986).

It is understandable that marketing messages fail to hit the right notes with older consumers given that misleading and stereotyped beliefs about the communication competence of older people and about the most appropriate styles of communications to use with this market segment abound among other age-groups (Giles, Coupland and Wiemann 1992; Hummert *et al*. 1994; Ryan and Cole 1990). Indeed, not only the young believe that older people experience communication problems. Research with young and old people has indicated that both may perceive older people to have greater problems effectively receiving information as well as in expressing themselves, than do younger people (Ryan *et al*. 1992). In particular, older people are believed to have difficulty understanding what others are saying in noisy situations, lose track of conversations more readily, and are unable to remember who said what in a conversation.

Common negatively-edged stereotypes about older people may shape wider public beliefs about the general communication competence of this age-group. Such attitudes towards older people and perceptions of their cognitive abilities might affect the way people attempt to communicate with them. This outcome may occur not only in situations of face-to-face conversation with older people, but also in marketing contexts where mass mediated commercial messages are concerned. Awareness of these stereotypes and how they colour the perceptions and beliefs people hold about older people may help to offset the style of communications used when targeting messages at mature markets.

Older citizens are a prime market and thus promotions should be directed to them in a way commensurate with their value. Many business people, however, are reluctant to solicit trade from older people. A study by the National Council on Aging found that local store managers, even when convinced that older consumers represented a sizeable market, refused to direct any advertising or promotion efforts toward them for fear it would 'hurt their public image' and tend to keep away their most desirable age-group – the youth (Knauer 1988). On the other hand, care has to be taken not to single out older consumers as a marketing target. Many older consumers do not wish to be reminded that they are old (Greco 1989).

The following suggestions have been made for developing effective themes in promotional messages aimed at older consumers (Wisenblitt 1989):

1   Focus on the solution, not the problem
2   Don't portray age per se – appeal to the issue
3   Avoid stereotypes and ageism
4   Use appropriate semantics, actors, and spokespersons
5   Portray intergenerational decision-making and interaction
6   Portray experiences rather than 'things'
7   Use self-perception and cognitive age
8   Portray older consumers as dynamic and vigorous

9 Portray older consumers as part of the mainstream
10 Stress quality, reliability, and value
11 Stress comfort, security, and dependability
12 Stress independence and being in control.

Another facet of advertising to the older market is the way in which messages are presented. It is important to understand that older consumers process information differently from younger buyers because of changes in vision, hearing, and memory (Schewe 1989). Consequently, marketers should follow certain guidelines when selling or advertising to older consumers. First, advertisements and packages should not be cluttered with too much visual information. Second, action in commercials should be relevant and not distracting. Humour may also distract and clutter the message. Third, fast-speaking characters and those who do not enunciate clearly, should be avoided. Fourth, pictures should be clear, bright and sharp. Fifth, the language and message should be simple, focusing on one or two selling points. Finally, new information should relate to something with which they are already familiar (Abrams 1984). In Chapter 6, we take a closer look at how older consumers respond to advertising.

6 The importance and effectiveness of advertising

A case has been made in earlier chapters that older people, aged 50 and over, represent a potentially important market segment characterised by growing affluence and consumer activity. Concern has been raised about negative stereo-typing of older people in the mass media which gives an impression of people in this age-group which is at odds with reality. The real worry about such media imagery is that it may cultivate beliefs about older people which make them less attractive to marketers.

The neglect of the mature market by advertisers, however, is not justified on the basis of how older people respond to advertising. Indeed, research has revealed that many people in this market segment hold positive opinions about advertising. Reception and retention of advertising can also be as good as that found among younger people, although aspects of memory do begin to fail among older people once they have passed a certain age.

CONSUMER INFORMATION SEEKING

One of the key reasons for marketers to develop a better understanding of the psychology of older consumers is that they have been found to be active processors of consumer information when they are faced with making product-related decisions. Older consumers turn to a variety of information sources about products and services and place different degrees of trust in particular sources depending upon the nature of the purchase. In many instances, older consumers may turn to the same sources of product information as do younger consumers. Depending upon the type of product these information sources may include promotional leaflets, catalogues, packaging, point-of-purchase displays, and the advice of other people. The way older consumers use different types of information differs from their younger counterparts. Older consumers attach more weight to guarantees or warranties and to product or in-store information. They like to use salespeople for advice and are more concerned to have a personalised service than are younger consumers. The mass media also feature as significant information sources for older consumers (Lumpkin and Festervand 1987).

One particular mass media source to which older consumers may turn is advertising and they often report having been influenced in their eventual purchase decisions by advertising messages (French and Crask 1977). Many older consumers switch brands and experiment with new products on the strength of information they have obtained from advertisements (Hanson 1987). One particularly important finding for marketers is that older consumers who are attuned to advertising messages indicate that they have greater regard for those manufacturers who target their promotional efforts at their age-group, and may in return exhibit greater loyalty to products or to retail outlets associated with promotional efforts designed to appeal specifically to the mature market (Mason and Bearden 1978b).

Older consumers like to gather as much information as possible about a product or service before making a purchase (Campanelli 1991; Swartz and Stephens 1984). This observation is consistent with the finding that older people tend to be more cautious than younger people and seek a great deal of certainty in their decisions before they commit themselves to a purchase (Botwinick 1970). This might mean that older consumers may be among the last to adopt new products or services (Phillips and Sternthal 1977; Uhl, Andrus and Paulson 1970). This last point applies especially to older people's attitudes towards new technologies, which they tend to be suspicious about and slower to adopt than younger people (Pommer, Berkowitz and Walton 1980; Gilly and Zeithaml 1985).

This generally cautious approach to consumerism among members of the mature market has important implications for marketing to them. For one thing, it affects their opinions about different consumer information sources. As noted earlier, older consumers may utilise information from a variety of sources. Sometimes, they may rely heavily on their own past experiences or the recommendations of people they trust, while on other occasions, they may turn more to less personal sources such as advertising and packaging or point-of-purchase information (Schiffman 1971). Word of mouth or professional recommendations can hold significant sway with older consumers (Michman, Hocking and Harris 1979). Sales staff may be particularly important information sources for older consumers (Martin 1979). Not all members of the mature market behave the same way, however. On differentiating between older consumers in terms of their risk-taking tendencies, Klippel and Sweeney (1974) found that lower risk takers relied more heavily on the recommendations of family and friends, while higher risk takers placed more value on advertising messages.

According to some consumer behaviour researchers, older consumers display a progressive decrease in the range of information sources they consult to help with their shopping decisions as they get older. This is most notable among older consumers after retirement (Phillips and Sternthal 1977). Other writers, however, have challenged this observation and indicated no apparent effect of age on consumers' propensity to seek shopping-related information from a variety of sources (Davis, D. 1980).

While some investigations have indicated that older consumers attach great importance to various sources which may add credibility to a purchase, including advertisements, guarantees, store reputation, the way salespeople behave, and other independent sources of information (Lumpkin and Festervand 1987), the value attached to any particular source can depend upon the nature of the purchase. Looking across different product categories, different information sources have been found to come to the fore in guiding older consumers' purchase decisions. In a study of the information sources used when considering the purchase of a new salt substitute product, Schiffman (1971) found that older consumers relied on personal experience as a major source of information. Elsewhere, Reid, Teel and Vanden Burgh (1980) found personal experience to be the major factor informing small appliance purchase. Swartz and Stephens (1984) observed that older consumers relied primarily on the recommendations of other people and secondarily on the mass media in relation to a variety of services. In relation to clothes purchases, however, television and radio were found to have a negligible role to play in informing older consumers' purchase decisions (Lumpkin and Festervand 1987). In contrast, television and newspapers represented important sources of information for grocery items (Mason and Bearden 1978a; Mason and Smith 1977). Newspapers were also described as a major source (along with friends, spouses and salespeople) for clothing items (Lumpkin and Greenberg 1982; Lumpkin 1985).

One survey of the American mature market reported that two-thirds of the older consumers interviewed indicated significant use of retail advertisements as information to aid in retail shopping. More than eight in ten respondents in the same survey (84 per cent) also believed that they usually attempted to take rational decisions about their shopping choices and generally undertook product comparisons prior to making purchases (Mason and Bearden 1978b).

Strutton and Lumpkin (1992) examined the significance of a variety of information sources in relation to older consumers' acquisition of information about various new health care products. These sources included aspects of product marketing such as packaging, store displays and salespeople; interpersonal sources including spouse, family members, friends, neighbours and other people; medical expert sources such as doctors and pharmacists; independent expert sources (television programmes, government reports, magazine articles, newspapers articles); and mass media sources including advertising and celebrity endorsements. Distinctions were made between 'continuous innovations' and 'discontinuous innovations' in relation to new products. Continuous innovations comprised generic drugs, such as non-branded medications which could be bought in a pharmacy, and involved fairly minor alternations on a previously existing product. Discontinuous innovations comprised self-diagnosis products such as blood pressure or sugar level monitors and represented completely new products unlike anything previously available.

Findings showed that older consumers relied more upon medical sources for products which involved fairly simple modifications to previous products, but placed greater reliance on marketing dominated and mass media sources in respect of the completely new products. The authors recommended that for new products which represent continuity of an existing line, advertisers should limit their involvement to efforts conducted via the mass media designed to increase general product awareness. The role of advertising in this context would be to stimulate interest in the product and encourage potential consumers to consult other trusted information sources about it. For radically new products, however, the approach to marketing should be somewhat different. Here, a more significant role of the mass media was envisaged in not just raising awareness but also persuading older consumers to purchase the product. Here, the recommendations and endorsements of trusted and dependable spokespersons in advertising, whose credibility and authority in that context were in no doubt, could play a significant part in influencing older consumers' opinions about the product and their intentions to purchase it.

While older consumers do not generally appear to be different from younger consumers in their overall choice of information sources in certain product fields (e.g. clothing), they do attach particular weight to product guarantees, product or in-store information, and the standards of customer service supplied at the point of purchase (Lumpkin and Festervand 1987). Older consumers appreciate assistance from sales staff in a store in selecting appropriate merchandise, providing additional product-related information, and offering a personalised service.

ATTITUDES TO ADVERTISING

Attitudes to advertising are important regardless of the market segment. The credibility of any persuasive appeal is a significant factor in relation to eventual message impact. Credibility may stem critically from audience perceptions of the message source or spokesperson (Caballero, Lumpkin and Madden 1989; Petroshius and Crocker 1989). The attitudes that consumers form towards the advertising itself can play a significant role in enhancing positive attitudes towards the product or service being advertised (Homer 1990; Stayman and Aaker 1988).

Among older consumers, attitudes towards advertising can vary, particularly with regard to general liking (Rotfield *et al.* 1982) and message spokesperson credibility (Milliman and Erffmeyer 1990). Older consumers may attach greater importance to the information presented in an advertisement if they also rate the source of the message or the spokesperson in the advertisement as having a high level of expertise or credibility (Sternthal, Phillips and Dholakia 1978). Older members of the audience have been found to rate a television advertisement as more credible when it has a middle-aged or older-aged spokesperson than a younger-aged person appearing or speaking on behalf of the advertised product (Milliman and Erffmeyer 1990).

The general feeling about advertising in Britain has been found to differ little between 55 to 64-year-olds and people aged 16 to 54. People over 65 years, however, are less favourably disposed towards advertising. Those aged between 55 and 64 are much more likely to be favourably disposed than unfavourably disposed towards advertising (Bennett 1989). People who supported advertising on television outnumbered those who rejected it by four to one, the over-55s included.

Research has regularly found that older consumers generally recognise that advertising contains important information about products and services. The majority of older consumers endorse advertising as particularly important in relation to choosing retail outlets from which to shop and in guiding certain product purchase decisions (Bearden and Mason 1979).

The attitudes which older consumers hold about advertising may also depend upon how affluent they are. Burnett (1991) found that affluent older male consumers as compared with more moderately well-off same-age counterparts, agreed more that 'advertising insults my intelligence' and disagreed more that 'information from advertising helps me make better buying decisions'. Affluent older female consumers as compared with middle-income counterparts agreed more that 'TV advertising is condescending toward women' and that 'advertising insults my intelligence', while they disagreed more that 'information from advertising helps me make better buying decisions'. Thus, better-off older consumers hold generally more negative attitudes towards advertising and its usefulness to them in the consumer context.

Opinions about television advertising

A number of studies have focused specifically on older consumers' opinions about advertising on television. Evidence presented in Chapter 4 indicated the importance of television to the mature market. The significance of the medium applies not only in the case of gratification older people obtain from its programmes, but also from the advertising it carries.

One American survey investigating how older people perceive television advertisements reported that two-thirds of those interviewed believed advertising on television to be a useful source of information about products and services (Schreiber and Boyd 1980).

In a British study, Bennett (1989) reported findings from a national survey of viewers' opinions about advertising on television. Comparisons of different adult age-groups revealed that older adults were somewhat less likely to see television advertisements in a positive light on such measures as 'entertaining' or 'good way to find out about new products', but more likely to see them as informative about products. The over-65s were less likely than other age-groups to perceive advertisements on television as truthful.

Older adults were more likely than younger adults to say that television advertising causes annoyance, but were less likely to perceive advertisements on television as 'misleading'. The over-65s were somewhat more likely to say that television advertisements were confusing to understand, but older and younger adults did not differ in terms of believing that advertisements on television interfere with enjoyment or treat you as foolish (see Table 6.1).

There was widespread belief among the over-55s in Britain that advertising brings a wider choice of products to the notice of consumers and thereby extends

Table 6.1 Opinions about advertisements seen on television

	All Adults (%)	Age groups 16–54 (%)	55–64 (%)	65+ (%)
Positives				
Informative about products	35	33	38	38
Truthful	36	38	40	31
Good way to find out about new products	44	46	44	38
Entertaining	49	52	45	41
Negatives				
Interfere with enjoyment	35	35	34	37
Cause annoyance	25	23	28	34
Same ad on too often	58	58	60	55
Treat you as foolish	35	37	35	39
Misleading	28	30	23	25
Confusing to understand	8	8	9	12

Note: Percentage saying TV ads very/fairly often like this
Source: Bennett 1989

choice. The amount of advertising on television was not perceived to be excessive. Indeed, nearly two-thirds of 55 to 64-year-olds and nearly six in ten of those aged over 65 surveyed believed that the quantity of advertising on television was reasonable (Bennett 1989) At least half of the over-55s believed that advertising was good for the economy.

Television advertisements were more widely seen as having been checked for truthfulness than press adverts, especially by people aged 55 to 64, with 53 per cent believing this to be true for television as against 33 per cent for newspapers. The over-65s were less often convinced of this for both television and the press (38 per cent and 29 per cent respectively). Older people, however, largely rejected the view that there were more advertisements on television about things of interest to them (only 23 per cent agreeing with this sentiment), and were far from convinced that advertising helps keep prices down, with only 15 per cent believing this to be true .

In general, advertising on television is much more liked than advertising in the press and on radio. More than one in two British viewers (53 per cent) said they liked television advertisements, compared with 24 per cent for newspapers and 21 per cent for radio. The strength of this opinion was not so pronounced among adults aged over 55, however. While older and younger adults were equally likely to express some liking of advertisements in newspapers (24 per cent and 23 per cent) and on the radio (22 per cent in each case), older adults were less likely than younger people to like advertising in magazines (29 per cent versus 36 per cent) or on television (44 per cent versus 56 per cent) (Bennett 1989).

The role of advertising in providing useful consumer information has the support of over one in four (26 per cent) of over-55s in Britain, not greatly less than for all adults, among whom around one in three (32 per cent) endorse this function of advertising. It is worth asking whether the over-55s figure might be higher if more advertising was tailored and directed to their needs and tastes (Bennett 1989).

THE INFORMATIONAL EFFECTIVENESS OF ADVERTISING

Attitudinal surveys have revealed that older consumers have a well disposed frame of mind to advertising in general and to television advertising in particular. Thus, there would seem to be no great hurdle of animosity to overcome to promote advertising receptivity among members of the mature market. What impact do commercials have in terms of retentiveness? Even here, evidence has emerged from marketing research that indicates very positive signs. As we will see later in this chapter, memory abilities do change with age. Cognitive psychologists have found that certain aspects of memory change with age more significantly than others. This research carries important implications for marketers who are trying to reach older consumers with their advertising campaigns. Before examining this research, however, it is worth first taking a look at evidence from research in the field which has attempted to measure more general memory for advertisements.

Bennett (1989) reported research conducted by London Weekend Television which examined consumers' recognition of television commercials. Tests were run in which samples of respondents were exposed to showreels of current advertisements with brand names and insignia blanked out. Usually, there was a high level of brand recognition and brand name recall across most consumers, although the lowest rate of recognition or recall occurred among the over-55s. While the shortfall was quite substantial for older consumers, Bennett observed that this was against the background that many of the commercials in the showreels were not in product fields in which they had an inherent interest or in which they could readily identify with the characters portrayed.

Further evidence of consumer memory of television advertising which compared older and younger people was published by the Independent Television Association, and cited by Bennett (1989). This evidence derived from a survey among 419 video-recorder owning adults of whom one in five were aged over 55. Ostensibly the study was designed to gauge reactions to an early evening Australian soap opera (*Home and Away*) but commercials were also included in a design that rotated them both at normal speeds and fast-forwarding speeds. After viewing, a questionnaire elicited recall of the commercials, first spontaneously and then with prompting. The main purpose of the study was to discover whether commercials seen in fast-forwarded mode could be remembered as well as at normal speed. Correct identification for the over-55s was nearly eight commercials at normal speed and nearly six at fast-forwarded speed, only slightly down on the scores for all adults. No sign of failure to register the message because of decaying memories was found (see Table 6.2).

Table 6.2 Recall of 'outstanding' advertisements as a function of medium

	All Adults (%)		16–34 (%)		35–54 (%)		55+ (%)	
	1987	1988	1987	1988	1987	1988	1987	1988
Penetration								
Any media	59	59	67	65	53	60	54	52
Television	50	51	57	54	48	52	45	46
Posters	3	3	4	4	2	4	2	1
Magazines	1	1	1	2	1	1	0	1
Radio	1	1	2	2	1	2	1	1
Share								
Television	86	87	86	86	90	86	83	89
Posters	5	5	7	6	4	6	4	2
Newspapers	5	3	2	3	4	2	9	3
Magazines	1	2	2	3	1	2	0	2
Radio	2	3	3	3	1	3	1	1

Source: Bennett, 1989

Does the medium matter?

Advertising messages are conveyed to older consumers via a number of different mass media. It has already been noted that older consumers hold varying opinions about the advertising they see which are, in part, a function of the medium of transmission. According to some writers, television, for a variety of reasons, is the medium best equipped to get advertising across to the mature market.

One British survey, which compared the informational effectiveness of advertising in different media, found that television advertisements were perceived to be among the most outstanding more often than advertisements in other mass media. This was equally true of older and younger consumers. When national UK survey samples in the late 1980s were asked to mention 'outstanding advertisements' seen in the last four weeks, television consistently had by far the highest share of mentions compared with newspapers, magazines, posters and radio. Among the over-55s, television was just as frequently mentioned in this context by older consumers as it was by younger consumers (see Table 6.3).

One advantage of television advertising which has been identified by some writers is that it can allow for high frequency of presentation which may increase the probability of advertisement recall for all ages (Stephens and Warrens 1984). Older consumers, however, are better able to process information if they have control over the pace of the communication, which would not be the case for television advertising (unless it had been video-recorded).

In order to design advertising which will be maximally effective with older consumers, it is essential that marketers understand more about the psychology of that market segment, particularly in respect of the cognitive information processing abilities of older people. There are various factors which relate to the production of advertising messages and to the cognitive abilities of older

Table 6.3 Television advertisement recall from a soap opera

VCR owners' ability to recall TV commercials played in fast forward mode	Average number recalled	
	All	55+
Spontaneous recall of 10 commercials		
Total	2.88	2.44
(a) Normal speed	3.61	3.24
(b) Fast forward	2.15	1.66
(b) + (a)	0.60	0.51
Prompted recall		
Total	7.33	6.68
(a) Normal speed	8.30	7.77
(b) Fast forward	6.29	5.62
(b) + (a)	0.76	0.72

Source: Bennett 1989

consumers, that could significantly influence the effectiveness with which advertising's informational content is transmitted and received.

ADVERTISING FACTORS AND OLDER CONSUMER RESPONSE

A number of factors relating to the ingredients and style of advertisements can play a part in mediating the effectiveness of advertisements in getting their message across to older consumers. Such factors include the way older people are depicted in advertisements and are used as the mouthpieces for or demonstrators of products or services in advertising. A second set of factors are concerned with production features within advertisements themselves.

Several studies have indicated that the way older role models are depicted in advertisements may have a significant mediating role to play in relation to the informational effectiveness of advertising among older consumers. Festervand and Lumpkin (1985) found in their own survey, along with a review of studies on attitudes toward the portrayal of older people in advertising, that older people usually perceived that advertising represented them inaccurately. Their study suggested that if advertisements continued to depict the older generation in a 'stereotypic manner', older people might form negative attitudes toward and engage in limited boycotting of the sponsoring company and its products.

Advertising, however, is more than a source of purchase-related information to consumers. It is also a means of social communication (Leiss *et al.* 1990) and serves as a 'family album of society' (Belk and Poally 1985: 888). From a socialisation perspective, advertising is important for the internalisation of dominant imagery and ideology because it is the place where culture and symbolism overlap and interact with the economy (Rosow 1974; Williamson 1978; Dickey 1987).

Cues in advertising could provide symbolic models for older consumers' behaviour and affect their self-image as well as wider public attitudes toward them (Swayne and Greco 1987). Thus, the ways in which older people are featured in advertisements also have implications for the social and psychological well-being of members of the mature market.

Smith *et al.* (1984) found that older consumers had certain expectations of advertisements in terms of the way their age-group was depicted, such that negative portrayals of older people in advertisements affected their self-perception in an adverse way. Other studies, however, indicated that older people held a positive attitude toward their portrayal in advertising (Schreiber and Boyd 1980) or were unconcerned with the way they were being stereotyped in advertisements (Langmeyer 1983). In a study commissioned by the US National Council on Ageing, Louis Harris (1975) found that the public generally held negative stereotypes of older people and therefore were not critical of the way older people were portrayed in advertising.

The effectiveness of advertising among older consumers may also depend upon other aspects of commercial message production. Research on attention has further suggested that older people experience greater difficulty with selective attention to messages. What this means is that they may have greater problems than do younger people with attending selectively to certain elements of an advertisement to the exclusion of other elements (Layton 1975). Hoyer, Rebok and Sved (1979) showed, for example, that irrelevant contextual information can significantly slow down the speed and accuracy with which older adults can solve problems.

Zaltman, Rajendra and Rohit (1978) noted that traditional consumer communication efforts may not be effective for older consumers. Among the features that may be particularly important is that the advertising should contain an information-oriented approach which explicitly points out a product's benefits. More peripheral production techniques designed for aesthetic rather than informational appeal may be less effective with this market segment. When communication of brand benefits is the prime advertising objective, a purely informational appeal is likely to be most effective with older consumers (Cole and Houston 1987). This view is consistent with other psychological literature suggesting that older people have difficulty processing target information, especially when it is presented in the context of other irrelevant information (e.g. Rabbitt 1965). Nonetheless, it may be possible to enhance an advertising message's effectiveness still further if music is integrated in a supportive way with the informational component of the message (Gorn *et al.* 1991).

Advertising has a number of purposes which range from increasing brand awareness to eventual brand purchase by the consumer. In between these two responses lie a number of other processes which include the encoding and retention of what the advertising message has to say about a product. Another feature connected with the advertising itself is the way commercial messages are scheduled. The informational effectiveness of advertisements can be measured in terms of the extent to which consumers can remember having seen particular advertisements or are able to recollect specific details about the advertised products. These cognitive responses can be affected by the amount of exposure to an advertisement that consumers have received. This has led some advertising researchers to investigate the significance for advertising impact of the extent to which commercial messages are repeated.

While older consumers have exhibited preferences for information-oriented advertising, research in marketing (Cole and Houston 1987) and gerontology (Perlmutter 1978, 1979) has indicated that older people may experience difficulty in processing information from certain forms of presentation. This may be especially true in the case of information that is rapidly paced, as in broadcast advertising (e.g. Stephens 1982).

Learning is known to be affected by the repetition of to-be-learned material. The impact of repetition on learning can depend on a number of other factors, however. An optimal level of repetition is very important. Insufficient exposure of advertisement to a potential consumer market may produce inadequate learning and retention of product-related information, while over-exposure may cause consumers to switch off and lose interest in it (Zajonc 1968, 1970).

The effectiveness of repetition may depend upon the way it is scheduled. Memory for to-be-remembered material is influenced by whether the material is repeatedly presented according to a 'massed' or 'distributed' schedule. On this matter, there is mixed evidence concerning which of the two methods of presentation is the better (Maccoby and Sheffield 1961; Underwood and Ekstrand 1967; Rothkopf 1968). In a study that used television content, evidence did emerge to show that spacing out repetitions of the same information may prove more effective at enhancing audience memory for that content than having the same message repeated over and over with only small gaps in between each presentation (Coldevin 1975).

In research conducted among young and older consumers on their ability to recall and recognise television advertisements, Stephens and Warrens (1984) reported that presenting an advertisement six times during the course of a movie produced better memory for it than presenting it four times or only twice. This effect occurred equally among consumers aged 54 and over or under 36.

One general piece of advice that has been offered to advertisers who aim their commercials at the mature market is to keep the message simple, explicit and familiar in terms of settings and spokespersons. Careful thought also needs to be given to how best to utilise visual elements of an advertisement to provide memorable features which will stick in the mind and remind older consumers about the advertised product (Schewe 1989).

CONSUMER FACTORS AND THE EFFECTIVENESS OF ADVERTISING

Researchers working with older people have considered the possibility that older adults may have greater difficulty retaining information than do young adults. The evidence regarding this issue is mixed. A few studies have suggested that the ability of older adults to retain information immediately after it has been presented remains relatively unimpaired in older adults (Craik 1968; Raymond 1971), whereas other studies have suggested that there may be a modest decline in short-term memory with age (Arenburgh 1976; Hasher and Zacks 1979; Horn, Donaldson and Engstrom 1981; Parkinson and Percy 1980; Rabinowitz, Craik and Aukerman 1982). This discrepancy between findings may be explained in terms of differences in the way that short-term memory capacity has been measured (Salthouse 1980). Regardless of measurement, however, it seems clear that older adults experience only a modest decline, if any, in short-term memory capacity. This means that when exposed to an advertising message, there is no reason why older consumers should not be expected to process its information just after exposure to the same extent as younger consumers.

Given findings such as these, a number of researchers have suggested that it is not so much reduced memory capacity that impairs the older adult as it is the slowing down of central nervous activity. The possibility that slower central nervous activity contributes to a generalised decline in the rate of cognitive processing has received some support to date and remains a viable explanation for many of the older consumers' difficulties (Andders, Fozard and Lillyquist 1972; Birren 1965, 1974; Cerella, Poon and Fozard 1981; Salthouse 1980). The implication of this finding in the context of advertising is that the older consumer may experience greater difficulty in coping with large quantities of information presented in advertising when exposure duration is brief than do younger consumers.

Memory strategies

Different researchers at different times have implicated encoding and retrieval activities in their attempts to identify sources for the older consumers' memory deficit (Craik 1977; Smith 1980). The central issue has been whether older people are simply unable to take in large amounts of information effectively because they lack the processing capacity to do so, or whether taking in the information is less of a problem than retrieving it from memory once it has been learned, because memory retrieval mechanisms deteriorate with increased age.

With regard to encoding strategies, older adults often fail to encode items semantically. This tendency can contribute to the older consumer's poorer performance on recall and recognition tests compared with the performance of younger adults who spontaneously use deep encoding strategies. Findings from several studies suggest that older people's failure to use semantic encoding is due to a production deficiency. When given specific encoding instructions, these investigations find no age differences in free recall, cued recall, or recognition (White, cited in Craik 1977; Craik and Simon 1980; Cerella, Paulshock and Poon 1982). However, a second set of studies has reported that orienting tasks designed to equalise encoding do not always reduce the size of age differences in recall and recognition (Cole 1983; Eysenck 1974; Simon *et al.* 1982). This line of evidence suggests that processing deficiencies are also involved in the older person's encoding failures. Although results in the area are mixed, findings do appear to depend to some extent on whether recognition, cued recall, or free recall is used to measure memory performance. Processing deficiencies are often found when recognition is used as the dependent variable, whereas both processing and production deficiencies have been found with recall as the dependent variable.[1]

Memory for newly presented information can be enhanced if the individual is given an opportunity to rehearse it, perhaps through repetitive presentation or through uninterrupted repetition of the content in their own mind. Memory capacity can also be improved by using certain strategies for organising information so that maximum use is made of available memory capacity. There is evidence from studies of older consumers that the rate of rehearsal and the use of elaborative rehearsal appears to decline with age (Salthouse 1980; Waugh and Barr 1980). This effect can be offset by giving the person specific instructions about how to rehearse incoming information (Sanders *et al.* 1980; Schmitt, Murphy and Saunders 1981). Similarly, older consumers tend not to use organisational strategies for storing incoming information unless instructed to do so (Craik 1977; Eysenck 1974; Hultsch 1974; Perlmutter 1978). This tendency remains even when the stimulus information is quite amenable to organisation. In fact, very often, stimulus materials with the most potential for organisation produce the greatest differences between young and older adults (Craik 1968; Heron and Craik 1964; Kausler and Puckett 1979).

Finally, older people may fail to use efficient retrieval strategies to guide access to previously stored information. So although older consumers may have paid full attention to an advertisement and logged it in their memory, they may be unable effectively to recall what they saw or heard. Several studies provide evidence for the existence of production deficiencies in the use of cues to direct information retrieval. When cues are provided by the experimenter to guide memory search, age differences are greatly reduced and frequently eliminated altogether (Hultsch 1975; Smith 1977). An additional set of studies, however, fails to confirm the ability of cues to equate recall in older and younger people (Drachman and Leavitt 1972; Mueller, Rankin and Carlomusto 1979). As before, methodological differences seem to be responsible for the disparity in results. It appears that the type and timing of the retrieval cue influence the degree to which cues will reduce age differences in recall (Rabinowitz *et al.* 1982; Smith 1977).

Information quality

Relatively large amounts of information can be expected to provide particular problems for older consumers. Since they tend to use fewer processing strategies

1 In general, recognition measures provide better information than recall measures about encoding deficiencies. Recall tasks do not provide external cues to aid memory search, so one cannot attribute any observed age differences to encoding deficiencies alone. Retrieval deficiencies may also be responsible.

and process information at slower speeds, older consumers may be less able to process amounts of consumer-related information which would pose few problems for younger consumers. Psychologists have noted that as the pressure that is placed upon memory by the presentation of large amounts of information increases, the ability of older adults to deal effectively with that information deteriorates far more rapidly than it would among younger people (Inglis 1959; Talland 1965; Wright 1981). This finding has been found to apply not only in the contrived learning conditions typical of laboratory studies of cognitive information processing, but also within real-life consumer contexts. Older consumers have been found to exhibit a narrower range of product preference judgements than younger consumers. In other words, older consumers may evaluate products along fewer dimensions than middle-aged or young adults (Capon, Kuhn and Gurucharri 1981). This has been explained in terms of a deteriorating ability with age of consumers to hold many different kinds of information at once about a particular product.

Information format

Older adults are affected by the manner in which information is presented. This point applies to the modality of presentation of information and to the way the information is organised. There are important marketing implications here for the impact of particular advertising production techniques and for the choice of communication medium through which to advertise. It was found over 25 years ago that presenting information in a picture format would not aid information recall for older adults as it did for young adults. This finding was originally explained in terms of the observation that visual memory declines more steeply with age than verbal memory (Winograd and Simon 1980). Other investigations have failed to support this assumption and have shown that visual presentations can enhance information recall among older people as well as among younger people (Park and Puglisi 1985; Winograd, Smith and Simon 1982). Even so, younger people seem to benefit more from picture support material than do older people (Taub 1975, 1979; Taub and Kline 1976, 1978).

Questions regarding older people's sensitivity to different modes of presentation has also addressed print versus television formats. Although younger adults seem to benefit when information is presented in a television format, older adults do not react in the same manner. In fact, older adults consistently remember less information than their younger counterparts whether print or television formats are used (Cavanaugh 1983, 1984; Cole 1983).

Similar results have been found in studies examining older people's sensitivity to the way information is organised. Evidence relating to this issue has been gathered by researchers investigating age differences in memory for passages of prose. Even when grammatically well-constructed passages of prose are used, in which information is clearly set out, older people often fail to remember as much content as do younger people (Dixon *et al.* 1982; Spilich 1983). Although thematic organisation of content can be deployed to organise the information in a written passage, this only benefits older people when their attention is explicitly drawn to this organisational feature (Meyer and Rice 1981).

Finally, order of presentation affects the ability of older people to remember items that have just been presented to them. These effects are found among all age-groups however. One particularly powerful phenomenon is the recency effect, whereby the most recently presented items in a sequence are the best remembered. This type of effect occurs to the same extent among older people as it does among younger people (Hagen and Stanovich 1977; Lorsbach and Simpson 1984).

Response format

Research with older people has documented the importance of response formats in influencing performance levels. A good deal of attention has been focused on differences between asking consumers to recall advertising content as compared with inviting them to recognise material to which they have previously been exposed. Recall formats are likely to be more difficult for older adults because the ability effectively to retrieve things from memory deteriorates with age. Thus, when memory for newly presented information is tested using unprompted or minimally prompted recall techniques, older people generally perform less well than do younger people. When the retrieval problem is circumvented by using a more generously prompted test of memory, such as recognition, age differences in memory performance are usually much reduced and sometimes disappear altogether.

Most of the controversy in this area has involved the question of whether or not recognition formats can totally eliminate the age differences in performance that are commonly found in studies that use recall formats. Although early studies found that age differences could be eliminated if recognition formats were used (Schonfield and Robertson 1966), later work found that age differences remained even when recognition formats were used. Evidence of age differences in recognition has been obtained using a wide variety of stimulus materials including nonsense syllables (Gordon and Clark 1974a), words (Erber 1974, 1978; Fozard and Waugh 1969; Gordon and Clark 1974a; Harkins, Chapman and Eisdorfer 1979; Rankin and Kaulser 1979), sentences (Fullerton and Smith 1980), and prose passages (Gordon and Clark 1974b). The contradiction between the earlier and later findings appears to be the result of differences in the way in which recognition was measured between studies. Less stringent measures that were developed by simply counting the number of correct responses tended to produce significantly smaller age differences than stricter recognition measures that corrected for guessing (White and Cunningham 1982).

HOW SIGNIFICANT IS ADVERTISING FOR THE MATURE MARKET?

Older people can be discerning consumers. Earlier chapters indicated that this was not only a growing consumer market segment but one populated by individuals who like to survey available choices in different product and service ranges, utilising a variety of different information sources before making a purchase decision. Advertising is one important source of consumer information and members of the mature market may be influenced in their product purchase choices by advertising.

The impact of advertising can depend upon a number of factors which reside within commercial messages themselves and within consumers. The strength of a commercial message's influence may depend upon its perceived credibility and how much it is liked. If consumers develop unfavourable attitudes towards advertising itself, its commercial impact could be reduced. Older consumers may often exhibit negative opinions about advertising, and may be ill-disposed towards specific advertisements on the basis of their approach to selling to this market segment. The credibility of advertising to the mature market may be enhanced if it uses spokespersons with whom older consumers can identify or whom they are likely to respect. Older consumers do not welcome reminders of their age, but do prefer advertisements in which the advice or sales pitch is presented by someone nearer to rather than more distant from their own age-group.

The ultimate impact of advertising in terms of gross product sales or market share also depends upon its information getting across to the consumers effectively in the first place. Older consumers may exhibit deterioration in certain cognitive abilities which mediate the processing of information from advertising. The main problem can be that older consumers may gradually lose the mental capacity to process, either simultaneously or in rapid sequence, a large or varied amount of product-related information. Whereas young consumers may find advertisements with a great deal of rapid-fire on-screen visual activity, sound effects and verbal information enjoyable and are able to switch quickly between information streams presented in different modalities, older consumers may be distracted from the core commercial message by such production effects.

These issues of representation, attitude and cognitive information processing in the context of advertising to older consumers need to be borne in mind by marketers in designing promotional and marketing campaigns aimed at the mature market. Older consumers are active consumers, but often respond to advertising messages in qualitatively different ways from younger consumers. Finding the appropriate style of communication and optimal volume of information is crucial to the production of effective advertising for this market.

7 The future and the older consumer

A variety of indicators show that older consumers represent a market of growing size and significance for marketers. Key determinants of future demographic patterns, such as changes of life expectancy with improved diet and medical care, and continued growth in the financial status of older people, will mean that the mature market will account for an even larger share of commodity consumption in the decades ahead.

The growth of affluence across the mature market will certainly not be universal. In the first 20 years of the twenty-first century the number of people aged 60 or over throughout the world is expected to increase from 600 million to over 1000 million (WHO 1989). This increase is expected to be much more marked in Third World countries than in developed regions such as Europe and North America. This is due mainly to significant improvements in infant mortality rates in the last 30 years. However, the infant mortality factor may be offset to some extent by the rise in certain diseases such as AIDS.

The mature market has been demonstrated as comprising a heterogeneous group of people. It is certainly not the case that population numbers and an accompanying change in consumption capacity will automatically rise across this consumer segment as a whole. In the United Kingdom, for example, population changes are expected to vary between age-bands within this broad age-group. Up to the middle of the next century, there will be steady increases in numbers of people aged 65+, 75+ and 85+. The majority of these will be women, but the proportion of women may fall slightly during the twenty-first century. The young end of the mature market (50–65 years) may exhibit less of an increase and may even decline during the same period, as a function of a cohort of smaller families emerging during the last years of the twentieth century.

Life expectancy

The next century holds the prospect of increased life expectancy. Environment and lifestyle will together have a significant impact on longevity (McKeown 1979). Medical science will also have an important role to play in increasing the quality of life of older people. One of the key factors underpinning the buoyancy of this broad age-group in the context of mass consumerism, apart from their affluence, is their fitness to enjoy and continue to participate in certain activities.

One school of thought is that life expectancy *per se* does not matter as much as whether people will remain youthful and fit longer, or whether the growth in numbers of people in this age-group will mean more people suffering from chronic disease. The optimistic view is that there will be increased possibilities for postponing serious and debilitating health problems associated with older age (Fries and Crapo 1981). Contrasting opinions have been put forward by others, however (Isaacs *et al*. 1972; Manton 1982). One pessimistic view is that as life expectancy increases, so too will chronic disease and disability (Stout and Crawford 1988). As people live longer, it does not necessarily follow that they experience lower risk of chronic disease, but that the severity of any symptoms can be kept more effectively under control by improved medical treatment (Manton 1982). If the process of ageing can be slowed down or the activity level of the ageing population maintained, then the engagement in the consumer market place will be enhanced over a longer period of their life span.

Work and leisure

Working life has changed dramatically during the twentieth century. The physical conditions of work have generally improved for most people, while the numbers of hours worked have declined. Employment legislation is likely to ensure that these trends continue into the next century. Many more women now participate in the workforce on a full-time basis today than in years past. Work is now something to be combined with raising a family and, for increasing numbers of women, is a life-long activity, just as it is for men. Although women have not yet achieved parity with men in respect of many terms of employment or career progression opportunities, they have become an established and accepted part of the workforce.

For all working people, however, regardless of gender, there is a trend towards a shorter working life. In consequence, leisure time has expanded as increased numbers of people leave full-time employment for retirement or semi-retirement at earlier ages. To accommodate and meet the prospects of this shift, a wider range of leisure-oriented activities have become available to older men and women. In some cases, a hobby may become transformed into a new career direction in later life. Indeed, it may become more and more an established pattern that individuals have more than one career in their working lives. One of these careers, for most people the first one, will be tied to an organisation by which they will be employed. The second will be a quite separate career, perhaps taking the form of an extension of their first career, or may represent a complete departure from it. In either case, the second career will often be one in which the individual operates independently of any specific employer and will represent a fresh turn of direction (Handy 1994).

Leisure activities may, of course, represent an end in themselves, rather than a means to another end, such as making money. They can be distinguished in terms of how 'active' they are. One of the most significant developments of the twentieth century has been the emergence and penetration of the mass media, especially television. 'Watching the box' has become a principal leisure-time pursuit for most people (Smythe and Browne 1992).

Even so, the older consumer who is in good health and has money to spend will also explore ways of entertaining and informing themselves through more active pursuits. Travel at home and abroad represents one such popular manifestation of this drive. Enrolment in day-time and evening classes to get qualifications or to learn for its own sake represents another popular pursuit. Older people who have entered a stage of semi-retirement or retirement have much more time on their hands and therefore more opportunity to pursue new interests.

People reaching what some writers have called the 'Third Age' in the next century will have experienced a rapidly changing social and technological environment and their expectations of leisure-time activities will be shaped by these experiences. The extent to which they are able to participate in leisure activities and which ones they have the opportunity to enjoy will depend upon the resources they have available to them. Increasingly, though, individuals will need to take control of their own resources in later life, through careful planning in earlier life, as society or the state plays a diminished role in the provision of pensions and other benefits.

Some projections into the future have indicated that people will experience more changes of job and career in the next century, with the idea of a job for life becoming a thing of the past. While the concept of 'retirement' will remain, a statutory age of retirement may be abolished, with individuals changing jobs a number of times and retiring at a point of their own choosing. One writer has coined the term 'the portfolio world' in which individuals eschew permanent employment with any one organisation for independence. Different skills and areas of knowledge are acquired through varied work experiences with different employers or 'clients' (Handy 1994). Linked to this concept is the idea that education will not be confined to the first 20 years of life, but will become a life-long process. Individuals will 'learn' as they build their personal portfolios, but will also, from time to time, re-enter more formal education and training to enhance their knowledge and skills. Older consumers will represent a key market for life-long learning, and will increasingly be able to engage in this practice as distance learning facilities provide new opportunities to extend their knowledge and exercise their intellect in ways they had been unable to pursue in their earlier life (Laslett 1989).

Understanding the grey market

There is ample evidence that older consumers are active consumers. Indeed, the older consumer has generally been found to obtain much pleasure and enjoyment from shopping (Lumpkin and Greenberg 1982). Shopping can be as much a recreation as a functional or instrumental activity (Lumpkin *et al.* 1985). Even so, there may be disincentives to shop which become increasingly pronounced as consumers grow older.

Older shoppers may be less mobile than younger shoppers and experience greater difficulties both getting to and getting around shopping centres and major stores. While this may not be such an issue for consumers at the younger end of the grey market age spectrum (e.g. under-60s), it becomes increasingly important for those at the older end (Gelwicks 1970; Lumpkin and Hunt 1989). Those less robust members of the grey market may need somewhere to rest on a long shopping excursion and look to retailers to furnish them with areas where they can relax. Older consumers may also need assistance with packing and carrying their shopping (Lambert 1979). Failing eyesight means they have problems coping with packaging with small print and unclear price tags (Shoemaker 1978; Sciglimpaglia and Schaninger 1981).

Despite these needs, many older consumers, especially at the younger end of the segment, are alienated by special marketing devices aimed at their age-group which make a point of emphasising their age. Younger 'older' consumers in their early 50s often do not classify themselves as old, and find brands promoted with age-related labels, such as 'senior citizens' objectionable (Underhill and Cadwell 1983; Tepper 1994). Marketers are therefore advised to take note of these differences among the older consumer segment. Older consumers, aged 65 and over, seem less concerned by age-related labelling, having somehow come to terms with their age status, and finding no stigma attached to being labelled as 'old' (Tepper 1994).

Communication research is vital to marketing practitioners interested in reaching the mature market. Information about the changing demographic profile of this market, and the involvement of its members in various activities is important, but is not sufficient to provide the depth of understanding needed to communicate with effect to older consumers. Members of this consumer segment have distinctive social values, self-perceptions, and attitudes to media representations of their age-group (see Loudon and Della Bitta 1993). They have their own expectations of products and services, and their own approach to shopping. While knowing about the size, composition and affluence of this market can provide some marketing leads in respect of reaching the mature market, it is important to understand the various factors which could influence older consumers' reception, evaluation and reaction to marketing messages and other devices.

The heterogeneity of the grey market

The grey market does not comprise a single homogeneous mass of consumers. Covering an age span as wide as the younger age-groups put together, this consumer 'category' can be differentiated and divided up according to a number of other demographic, financial, behavioural and attitudinal factors.

Distinctions have been drawn between stages in the consumer life cycle which differentiate among older consumers on such criteria as their marital status, whether they still have dependent children living with them, whether the head of the household is retired, and whether one partner has outlived another. Each of these different categories of older person is associated with distinct patterns of consumer behaviour. Individuals in a pre-retirement stage will exhibit an emphasis upon saving for retirement, securing their home, and possibly ensuring that their children successfully complete their education and become gainfully employed. Older consumers who have retired will have more time for leisure, but will also become more concerned with medical care and products designed to protect good health. The extra time older people may gain through retirement, and the disposable income released through paying off the mortgage or no longer having financially dependent children, places them in the market for a range of leisure activities and related product purchases (Stampfl 1978).

Wealth and health are key defining factors which may vary significantly among members of the grey market, but tend to be correlated with age. Younger members of this consumer category tend to be better off than their older counterparts, as a function of occupational pensions and a wider range of savings and investments. They also tend to be fitter and stronger, as a function of a better diet and the prevalence of values which promote healthy lifestyles.

Even within the same age range, however, it is possible to find a variety of different consumer sub-types defined by their psychological character and styles of consumer behaviour. Members of the grey market may exhibit a wide range of values, motives, interests and activity preferences which shape their general lifestyle orientations (Day *et al.* 1987; Gollub and Javitz 1989) and influence specific product preferences (Lumpkin and Caballero 1985).

Marketing to the grey market

Understanding the psychology of the older consumer is of primary significance. Marketers are concerned about promoting products and services, creating the best image possible for them, and persuading consumers to purchase advertised brands over other similar commodities. To achieve these objectives, marketers must have a thorough knowledge of communication processes and the target markets at which their promotional campaigns and messages are aimed. If the benefits of a product cannot be communicated effectively, the likelihood of consumer purchase is likely to remain unchanged or, in the face of increased marketplace competition, will become diminished for under-sold products. If the product is advertised in such a way as to offend consumers, product purchase may potentially be reduced.

The content of the message and the nature of the appeal to particular consumers represent critical variables. In the context of marketing to older consumers, if advertising creates the wrong impression, challenges core values, or presents inappropriate behaviour or negative images of older consumers, its impact may be seriously impaired (Kubey 1980).

Understanding the psychology of older consumers means knowing what are their core needs and interests, and having an accurate awareness of how this age-group perceives itself. Stereotypes of old people and growing old tend to carry predominantly negative connotations. Older consumers identify with such images less and less. Advertising messages which play on these stereotypes are unlikely to be successful. There are many inaccurate beliefs and misconceptions about the ageing process and how it affects people beyond a certain chronological age. The stereotyped notions about physical and mental deterioration do not apply equally across older consumers as a group, nor do they occur at the same stage in later life for all individuals (Wisenblitt 1989). The mature market contains increasing numbers of people who are physically active and mentally still capable of high levels of cognitive performance.

The decline in social or psychological functioning has been attributed as much to social and environmental conditions and expectations of older people as to an inevitable physical and mental deterioration that accompanies old age. The traditional images of older people can act like a straitjacket, confining their movement and defining a fairly narrow degree of latitude within which they may behave. Improved medical and material conditions may allow people to live longer and potentially to be active for longer periods, but the extent to which older people may strive to achieve their potential may be restricted by negative social stereotypes and limited expectations of what they can or ought to do with their time in later life (Birren and Schroots 1984). Stereotypes about older people's inability to change their ways should gradually become eroded as the concept of life-long learning becomes established and later life is seen increasingly as a significant proportion of the total life-span in which individuals may face new challenges and strive for new goals.

It is essential that media depictions of later life and consumer marketing's communications to older consumers reflect these activity trends and offer more positive images of the mature market to consumers who are a part of that market. The life satisfaction of older people may depend in part on their consumption of appropriate and beneficial products and services which enhance their lives in various ways. More important, the range of consumer opportunities that are deemed appropriate for the mature market and the style in which these commodities are advertised should convey messages which positively enhance older consumers' self-images and perceptions of their self-worth. According to some writers, marketing strategies that incorporate enhanced life satisfaction as a criterion for purchasing specific products and services will be able to approach the mature market more effectively (Sherman and Cooper 1988).

There is more to understanding the older consumer even than just knowing about their needs. There has been a growing recognition, in the past decade, that the over-50s are increasingly developing a new self-image. Some commentators on consumer market developments have drawn a distinction between the 'new age elderly' and the more traditional elderly stereotypes (see Schiffman and Kanuk 1991). A more youthful, healthier, and more affluent generation of older consumer is emerging which has a different outlook on life and different view of themselves from their earlier counterparts. Their new outlook is characterised by regarding age as a state of mind as much as a physical condition, perceiving themselves to be younger than they really are, and by being motivated to pursue lifestyles and activities which would formerly have been exclusively associated with younger generations.

This generally more youthful and more confident outlook of the new age older consumer also has implications for consumer decision-making. This new breed of older consumer is more willing to experiment with new products and services. They are also selective and alert consumers, whose knowledge and experience gives them the confidence to know when a product or service offers good or poor value. But while they retain some of the cautiousness customarily associated with their generation, their more positive outlook and healthier financial position means that they display a much wider range of interests than any previous generation of their age-group and are much more prepared to pursue these interests.

Retailing to the grey market

Those who interface with older consumers at the points of purchase can also learn important lessons from a better understanding of consumer psychology at this end of the age spectrum. Retailers are placing more emphasis on fast checkout, credit and having a wide variety of products. The older consumer goes to the marketplace in search of many things: product information, exercise and social interaction being among them (Lumpkin 1985). Many recent retail trends, however, have brought changes to the retail situation which do not meet the needs of older consumers or their preferred styles of customer service. Older consumers may not want to be rushed around a retail outlet, run up credit, or serve themselves all the time.

Evidence has emerged that some older consumers welcome the availability of home delivery services – even when placing purchase orders on site. Alternatively, the placement of orders remotely by telephone, or other electronic means, is an option which will also prove to be more convenient than finding transportation to and from a retail outlet (Lumpkin and Hunt 1989).

Older consumers may find certain packaging difficult to open and the labelling difficult to read (Erickson 1990). Such problems may lead some older consumers to choose products on the basis of easy-to-open packaging instead of preferred contents and to avoid brands about which they are uncertain. Older consumers like to pick and choose and are hungry for product-related information to help them reach decisions over product purchases. Where that information is not readily available either because package labels are unclear or difficult to read and understand, or because sales personnel provide a more stylised and less personalised service, older consumers will become less satisfied with retail service.

The introduction of new technologies has represented a part of the process of modernisation. While not wishing to argue against such progress where it produces increased efficiencies for retailers and consumers, there have been early indications that older consumers are more anxious about and less comfortable with such developments as scanner-equipped grocery stores, electronic funds transfer, automated teller machines, and telephone ordering schemes (Gilly and Zeithaml 1985). This does not apply to all older consumers and one can expect each succeeding older cohort to have become more experienced with these retail technologies. The important point is that retail personnel will need to be aware of these problems when dealing with older consumers and consider whether there are any steps that can be taken to smooth the transition to a new technological era for consumers who have been socialised into a different style of shopping.

Knowing what appeals to older consumers about products, how to provide appropriate product-related information on packaging or displays in retail outlets, and adopting a form of customer service older consumers expect can do much to enhance their satisfaction and, in turn, their loyalty and repeat spending (Hunter 1987; Silvenis 1979). Many suggestions have been made about how to assist older shoppers and some have been implemented in areas such as packaging design, signage, discounts and customer service (Lambert 1979; Schewe 1985; Wilson 1991). However, this market has not been served in other, more significant ways such as specialty stores offering comfortable and appealing retail environments, which offer opportunities for the older shopper to relax and enjoy the shopping experience.

Older consumers comprise a market segment growing in size and affluence and consequently in their capacity to consume. It is not only the growth of purchasing power among this age-group that underpins the significance of this segment of the population for marketers. Improved diet and medical treatment have meant that people are living longer and enjoy higher levels of fitness and health throughout their autumn years. Thus, they are physically as well as financially equipped to be more active despite their years. Compounded with these important developments is the changing image that older consumers have of themselves. They are no longer as constrained as they once were by a negative self-image which defines a limited range of role expectations. Older consumers now feel more confident openly to display the values, needs and activity preferences of younger consumers. They have become more confident consumers for whom the cautiousness of experience has now become mixed with a greater willingness to be adventurous and experimental. It has become more essential than ever for marketers to understand these changes in the older consumer market and respond to them if they wish fully to capitalise on the new potential which this market segment now holds.

References

Abdela, L. (1991) *Breaking Through the Glass Ceilings: A Practical Guide to Equality at Work for Women and Men.* Solihull, UK: METRA.

Abrams, M. (1984) In DHSS publication, *Population Pension Costs and Pensioners' Income: A Background Report for the Inquiry into Provision for Retirement.* London: HMSO.

Abrams, M. (1990) 'Inequality among the over 55s', paper presented at an Admap/Campaign Seminar, Gold Amongst the Grey, London, 25 October.

Achenbaum, W.A. (1978) *Old Age in the New Land: The American Experiences Since 1790.* Baltimore and London: Johns Hopkins University Press.

Adams, M. and Groen, R. (1975) 'Media habits and preferences of the elderly', *Journal of Leisure*, 2(2), 25–30.

Ahammer, I.M. (1973) 'Social learning theory as a framework for the study of adult personality development', in P.B. Baltes and K.W. Schaie (eds) *Life-Span Development Psychology: Personality and Socialisation.* New York: Academic Press.

Allan, C.B. (1984) 'Measuring mature markets', *American Demographics*, p. 13.

Allen, J., Davis, D., Keesling, G. and Grazer, W. (1992) 'Segmenting the mature market by characteristics of organisational response to complaint behaviour', in R. P. Leone and V. Kumar (eds) *Enhancing Knowledge Development in Marketing.* AMA Educators' Proceedings. Chicago: American Marketing Association, pp. 72–78.

Andders, T., Fozard, J.L. and Lillyquist, T.D. (1972) 'Effects of age upon retrieval from short-term memory', *Developmental Psychology*, 6, 214–217.

Andreason, A.R. (1984) 'Life status change and changes in consumer preferences and satisfaction', *Journal of Consumer Research*, 11, 784–794.

Ansello, E. (1978) 'Broadcast images: The older woman in television', paper presented at the 31st Annual Scientific Meeting of the Gerontological Society, Dallas.

Arenburgh, D. (1976) 'The effects of input condition on free recall in young and old adults', *Journal of Gerontology*, 31, 551–555.

Aronoff, C. (1974) 'Old age in prime time', *Journal of Communication*, 24, 86–87.

Askham, J., Barry, C., Grundy, D., Hancock, R. and Tinker, A. (1992) *Life After 60.* London: Age Concern Institute of Gerontology

Atchley, R. (1974) *Social Forces and Aging.* Belmont, CA: Wadsworth Publishing.

Bader, J.E. (1980) 'Attitudes toward aging, old age, and old people', *Age Care and Services Review*, 2, 1–14.

Baltes, M.M., Mayr, U., Borchelt, M., Maas, I. and Wilms, H.-U. (1993) 'Everyday competence in old and very old age: An inter-disciplinary perspective', *Ageing and Society*, 13(4), 657–680.

Banks, R. (1990) 'Money management for the mature: Their needs and the services competing to meet them', paper presented at 'Over-55 – Gold Amongst the Grey' conference, London: Admap/Campaign, 25 October.

Barak, B. and Rahtz, D.R. (1989) 'Cognitive age and youthfulness: Demographic and psychographic dimensions', in R.E. Kriner and G.T. Buker (eds) *Advances in Health Care Research*. Silver Springs, MD: American Association for Advances in Health Care Research, pp. 47–51.

Barak, B. and Schiffman, R.G. (1981) 'Cognitive age: A nonchronological age variable', in K.B. Monroe (ed.) *Advances in Consumer Research*, vol. 8. Ann Arbor, MI: Association for Consumer Research, pp. 601–606.

Barak, B. and Stern, B. (1985) 'Fantastic at forty! The new young woman consumer', *Journal of Consumer Marketing*, 2(2), 41–54.

Barnes, N.G. and Peters, M.P. (1982) 'Modes of retail distribution: Views of the elderly', *Akron Business and Economic Review*, 13, 26–31.

Barr, N. and Coulter, F. (1990) 'Social security: solution or problem?' in J. Hills (ed.) *The State of Welfare: The Welfare State in Britain Since 1974*, pp. 274–337. Oxford: Oxford University Press.

Bartos, R. (1980) 'Over 49: The invisible consumer market', *Harvard Business Review*, 58(1), 140–148.

Bearden, W.O. and Mason, J.B. (1979) 'Elderly use of in-store information sources and dimensions of product satisfaction/dissatisfaction', *Journal of Retailing*, 55(1), 79–91.

Beeson, M.F. (1920) 'Intelligence at senescence', *Journal of Applied Psychology*, 4, 219–234.

Bekker, L. and Taylor, C. (1966) 'Attitudes toward the aged in a multi-generational sample', *Journal of Gerontology*, 21, 115–118.

Belk, R.W. and Poally, R.W. (1985) 'Images of ourselves: The good life in twentieth-century advertising', *Journal of Consumer Research*, 11, 887–897.

Bell, J. (1992) 'In search of a discourse on aging: The elderly on television', *Gerontologist*, 32(3), 305–311.

Bennett, B. (1989) 'The neglected majority: Over 55s are left in the cold by most television advertisers', paper presented at Admap/Campaign conference: Over 55s: Gold amongst the Grey. London, 25 October.

Bennett, R. and Eckman, J. (1973) 'Attitudes toward ageing: A critical examination of recent literature and implications for future research', in C. Eisdorfer and P. Lawson (eds) *The Psychology of Adult Development and Ageing*. Washington, DC: American Psychological Association.

Berger, J. (1985) 'The new old: Where the economic action is', *Business Week*, 25 November, 140.

Berkowitz, B. (1953) 'The Wechsler-Bellevue performance of white males past 50', *Journal of Gerontology*, 8, 76–80.

Bernard, M. (1985) *Health Education and Activities for Older People: A Review of Current Practice*. (Working Papers on the Health of Older People, No. 2) Health Education Council in association with the Department of Adult Education, Staffordshire: Keele University.

Bernard, M. and Meade, K. (1993a) 'A third age lifestyle for older women?', in M. Bernard and K. Meade (eds) *Women Come of Age: Perspectives on the Lives of Older Women*. London: Edward Arnold, pp. 146–166.

Bernard, M. and Meade, K. (1993b) *Women Come of Age: Perspectives on the Lives of Older Women*. London: Edward Arnold.

Bernhardt, K. and Kinnear, T. (1976) 'Profiling the senior citizen market', *Proceedings*. Spring Business Conference, American Marketing Association, pp. 449–452.

Bernhardt, L.L. (1981) 'Consumer problems and complaint actions of older Americans: A national view', *Journal of Retailing*, 57(3), 107–125.

Berry, S., Lee, M. and Griffiths, S. (1981) *Report on a Survey of West Indian Pensioners in Nottingham*. [Mimeo] Nottingham, UK: Nottingham Social Services Department.

Beyer, G. and Woods, M. (1963) *Living and Activity Patterns of the Aged* (Research Report No. 6). Ithaca, NY: Cornell University Centre for Housing and Environmental Studies.

Birren, J.E. (1956) 'The significance of age changes in speed of perception and psycho-motor skills', in J.E. Anderson (ed.) *Psychological Aspects of Ageing*. Washington, DC: American Psychological Association, pp. 97–104.

Birren, J.E. (1965) 'Age changes in speed of behaviour', in A.T. Welford and J.E. Birren (eds) *Behaviour, Ageing and the Nervous System*. Springfield, IL: Charles C. Thomas, pp. 191–216.

Birren, J.E. (1974) 'Translation in gerontology: From lab to life: Psychophysiology and speed of response', *American Psychologist*, 29, 808–815.

Birren, J.E. and Schroots, G.F. (1984) 'Steps to an ontogenetic psychology', *Academic Psychology Bulletin*, 6, 177–190.

Bishop, J.M. and Krause, D.R. (1984) 'Depictions of ageing and old age on Saturday morning television', *The Gerontologist*, 24(1), 91–94.

Blau, Z.S. (1973) *Old Age in a Changing Society*. New York: Franklin Watts.

Bogart, L. (1972) *The Age of Television*. New York: Ungar.

Bone, P.F. (1991) 'Identifying mature segments', *Journal of Consumer Marketing*, 8(4), 19–32.

Bone, M., Gregory, J., Gill, B. and Lader, D. (1992) *Retirement and Retirement Plans*. London: HMSO.

Botwinick, J. (1970) 'Learning in children and older adults', in L.R. Goulet and P.P. Baltes (eds) *Life Span Developmental Psychology: Research and Theory*. New York: Academic Press, pp. 257–284.

Bower, R. (1978) *Television and the Public*. New York: Holt, Rinehart and Winston.

Bower, R. (1985) *The Changing Television Audience in America*. New York: Columbia University Press.

Bradshaw, J. and O'Higgins, M. (1984) *Equity, Income Equality and the Life Cycle: An Analysis for 1971, 1976 and 1982*. University of York [mimeo].

Bramlett-Solomon, S. and Wilson, V. (1989) 'Images of elderly in *Life* and *Ebony*, 1978–1987', *Journalism Quarterly*, 66, 185–188.

Brewer, M.B., Dull, V. and Lui, L. (1981) 'Perception of the elderly: Stereotypes as pro-totypes', *Personality and Social Psychology*, 41, 656–670.

Bromley, D.B. (1974) *The Psychology of Human Ageing*. Harmondsworth: Penguin.

Brown, P.B. (1986) 'Last year it was Yuppies – This year it's their parents', *Business Week*, 10 March, p. 74.

Brown, C.W. and Ghiselli, E.E. (1949) 'Age of semiskilled workers in relation to abilities and interests', *Personnel Psychology*, 2, 497–511.

Brubaker, T.H. and Pavers, E.A. (1976) 'The stereotype of "old": A review and alternative approach', *Journal of Gerontology*, 31, 441–447.

Buchholz, M. and Bynum, J.E. (1982) 'Newspaper presentation of America's aged: A content analysis of image and role', *The Gerontologist*, 22, 83–88.

Buck, S. (1990) 'Turning an old problem into a new opportunity', *Admap*, March, 20–22.

Buhler, E. (1961) 'Meaningful living in the mature years', in R. Kleemeier (ed.) *Aging and Leisure*. New York: Oxford University Press.

Burnett, J.J. (1989) 'Retirement vs age: Assessing the efficacy of retirement as a segmentation variable', *Journal of the Academy of Marketing Sciences*, 17(4), 333–343.

Burnett, J.J. (1991) 'Examining the media habits of the affluent elderly', *Journal of Advertising Research*, 31(5), 33–41.

Burnett, J.J. and Wilks, R.E. (1986) 'An appraisal of the senior citizens market', *Journal of Retail Banking*, 7(4), 57–64.

Butler, R.W. (1961) 'Ageism: Another form of bigotry', *The Gerontologist*, 169(9), 243–246.

Bytheway, W. (1986) 'Making way: the disengagement of older workers', in C. Phillipson, M. Bernard and P. Strang (eds) *Dependency and Interdependence in Old Age: Theoretical Perspectives and Policy Alternatives*. London: Croom Helm, pp. 315–326.

Caballero, M., Lumpkin, J. and Madden, C. (1989) 'Using physical attractiveness as an advertising tool: An empirical test of the attraction phenomenon', *Journal of Advertising Research*, 29, 16–22.

Cain, L.D. (1974) 'The growing importance of legal age in determining the status of the elderly', *The Gerontologist*, 14, 167–174.

Campanelli, M. (1991) 'The senior market: rewriting the demographics and definitions', *Sales and Marketing Management*, 143(2), 63–69.

Canestrari, R.E. (1968) 'Age changes in acquisition', in G.A. Talland (ed.) *Human Aging and Behaviour*. New York: Academic Press. pp. 169–188.

Capon, N., Kuhn, D. and Gurucharri, M.C. (1981) 'Consumer information processing strategies in middle and late adulthood', *Journal of Applied Developmental Psychology*, 2, 1–12.

Casatta, M.B., Anderson, P.A. and Skill, T.D. (1980) 'The older adult in daytime serial drama', *Journal of Communication*, 30, 48–49.

Cavanaugh, J. (1983) 'Comprehension and retention of television programmes by 20- and 60-year-olds', *Journal of Gerontology*, 38, 190–196.

Cavanaugh, J. (1984) 'Effect of presentation format on adults' retention of television programmes', *Experimental Ageing Research*, 10(1), 51–53.

Central Statistical Office (1986) *Social Trends 16*. London: HMSO.

Central Statistical Office (1990) *Social Trends*. London: HMSO.

Cerella, J., Paulshock, D. and Poon, L. (1982) 'The effect of semantic processing on memory performance of subjects differing in age', *Educational Gerontology*, 8, 1–7.

Cerella, J., Poon, L.W. and Fozard, J.L. (1981) 'Mental rotation and age reconsidered', *Journal of Gerontology*, 36, 620–624.

Chaffee, S. and Wilson, D. (1975) 'Adult life cycle changes in mass media usage', paper presented at the annual meeting of the Association for Education in Journalism, Ottawa, Canada.

Chain Store Age Executive (1988) 'Ageing Americans give marketing advice', August, p. 80.

Chua, C., Joseph, A.C. and Siew, M.L. (1990) 'The antecedents of cognitive age', in M.E. Goldberg (ed.) *Advances in Consumer Research*, Vol. 17. Ann Arbor, MI: Association for Consumer Research, pp. 880–885.

Coldevin, G. (1975) 'Spaced, massed and summary treatments as review strategies for ITV production', *AV Communication Review*, 23, 289–303.

Cole, C. (1983) 'Elderly consumers' responses to advertising: Processing deficiencies versus production deficiencies', unpublished dissertation, Graduate School of Business, University of Wisconsin, Madison, WI.

Cole, C.A. and Balasubrahmanian, S.K. (1993) 'Age differences in consumers' search for information: Public policy implications', *Journal of Consumer Research*, 20, 157–169.

Cole, C.A. and Gaeth, G.J. (1990) 'Cognitive and age-related differences in the ability to use nutritional information in a complex environment', *Journal of Marketing Research*, 27, 175–184.

Cole, C.A. and Houston, M.J. (1987) 'Encoding and media effects on consumer learning deficiencies in the elderly', *Journal of Marketing Research*, 24, 55–63.

Coleman, P. (1993) 'Adjustment in later life', in J. Bond, P. Coleman and S. Pearce (eds) *Ageing in Society: An Introduction to Social Gerontology*, London: Sage, pp. 97–132.

Comfort, A.J. (1988) *A Good Age*. London: Mitchell Beazley.

Comstock, G., Chaffee, S., Katzman, N., McCombs, M. and Roberts, D. (1978) *Television and Human Behaviour*, New York: Columbia University Press.

Corsini, R.J. and Fassett, K.K. (1953) 'Intelligence and aging', *Journal of Genetic Psychology*, 83, 249–264.

Coupland, N., Coupland, J. and Giles, H. (1991) *Language, Society and the Elderly: Discourse Identity and Ageing*. Oxford, UK: Blackwell.

Cowgill, D.O. and Baulch, N. (1962) 'The use of leisure time by older people', *The Gerontologist*, 2, 47–50.

Cox, H.G. (1990) 'Roles for aged individuals in post-industrial societies', *International Journal of Aging and Human Development*, 30(1), 55–62.

Craik, F.I.M. (1968) 'Short-term memory and the ageing process', in G.A. Talland (ed.) *Human Ageing and Behaviour*. New York: Academic Press, pp. 131–168.

Craik, F.I.M. (1977) 'Age differences in human memory', in J. Birren and W.K. Schaie (eds) *Handbook of the Psychology of Ageing*. New York: Van Nostrand.

Craik, F.I.M. and Byrd, M. (1982) 'Aging and cognitive defects: The role of attentional resources', in F. Craik and S. Trehub (eds) *Aging and Cognitive Processes*. New York: Plenum Press.

Craik, F.I.M. and Simon, E. (1980) 'Age differences in memory: The roles of attention and depth of processing', in L. Poon, J. Fozard, L. Cermak, D. Arenberg and L. Thomson (eds) *New Directions in Memory and Aging*. Hillsdale, NJ: Lawrence Erlbaum Associates, pp. 95–112.

Cribier, F. (1981) 'Changing retirement patterns of the seventies: the example of a generation of Parisien salaried workers', *Ageing and Society*, 1, 51–73.

Cumming, E. and Henry, W. (1961) *Growing Old: The Process of Disengagement*. New York: Basic Books.

Cunningham, W.R. (1975) 'Factorial invariance: A methodological issue in the study of psychological development', *Experimental Ageing Research*, 8, 61–65.

Dail, P.W. (1988) 'Prime-time television portrayals of older adults in the context of family life', *The Gerontologist*, 28(5), 700–706.

Danowski, W. (1975) 'Informational ageing: Interpersonal and mass communication patterns in a retirement community', paper presented at the 28th Annual Scientific meeting of the Gerontological Society, Louisville, KY.

Davies, L.J. (1977) 'Attitudes toward ageing as shown by humour', *The Gerontologist*, 17, 220–226.

Davies, B. and Ward, S. (1991) *Women and Personal Pensions*. EOC Research Series, London: HMSO.

Davis, B. and French, W.A. (1989) 'Exploring advertising usage segments among the aged', *Journal of Advertising Research*, 29, 22–29.

Davis, D. (1980) 'Alternative predictors of consumer search propensities in the service sector', *Proceedings*. American Marketing Association, 160–163.

Davis, R.H. (1971) 'Television and the older adult', *Journal of Broadcasting*, 15, 153–159.

Davis, R.H. (1980) *Television and the Ageing Audience*. Los Angeles: University of Southern California.

Davis, R.H. and Davis, J.A. (1985) *TV's Image of the Elderly: A Practical Guide for Change*. Lexington, MA: Lexington Books.

Davis, R.H. and Edwards, A.E. (1975) *Television: A Therapeutic Toll for the Aged*. Los Angeles: University of Southern California.

Davis, R.H., Edwards, A.E., Bartel, D.J. and Martin, D. (1976) 'Assessing television viewing behaviour of older adults', *Journal of Broadcasting*, 20, 69–76.

Davis, R. H. and Kubey, R. W. (1982) 'Growing old on television and with television', in D. Pearl, L. Bouthilet and J. Lazar (eds) *Television and Behaviour: Ten Years of Scientific Progress and Implications for the Eighties*. Rockville, MD: National Institute of Mental Health.

Davis, R.H. and Westbrook, G.J. (1985) 'Television in the lives of the elderly: Attitudes and opinions', *Journal of Broadcasting and Electronic Media*, 29, 209–214.

Davis-Smith, J. (1992) *Volunteering: Widening Horizons in the Third Age*. (Research Paper No. 7, The Carnegie Enquiry into the Third Age). Dunfermline, UK: Carnegie UK Trust.

Dawson, A. and Evans, G. (1987) 'Pensioners' incomes and expenditure 1970–1985', *Employment Gazette*, May, 243–252.

Day, A.T. (1991) *Remarkable Survivors: Insights into Successful Aging Among Women*. Washington, DC: Urban Institute Press.

Day, A.T. and Day, L.H. (1993) 'Living arrangements and "successful" aging among ever-married American white women, 27–87 years of age', *Ageing and Society*, 13(3), 365–387.

Day, E., Davis, B., Dove, R. and French, W. (1987) 'Reaching the senior citizen markets', *Journal of Advertising Research*, 27(6), 23–30.

Day, K. and Cowie, E. (1990) 'Trends in viewing and listening', in *Annual Review of BBC Broadcasting Research Findings*. London: British Broadcasting Corporation and John Libbey, pp. 5–21.

De Grazia, G. (1961) 'The uses of time', in R.W. Kleemeier (ed.) *Aging and Leisure*. New York: Oxford University Press, pp. 113–153.

Demos, V. and Jacke, A. (1981) 'When you care enough: An analysis of attitudes toward aging in humorous birthday cards', *The Gerontologist*, 21, 209–215.

Department of Employment (1988) *Family Expenditure Survey*. London: HMSO.

Dex, S. (1985) *The Sexual Divisions of Work*. Brighton: Wheatsheaf Books.

DHSS (1985) *Reform of Social Security*. Cmnd 9517. London: HMSO.

Dickey, J. (1987) 'Women for sale: The construction of advertising images', in K. Davies *et al.* (eds) *Out of Focus: Writings on Women and the Media*. London: Women's Press.

Dimmick, J.W., McCain, T.A. and Bolton, W.T. (1979) 'Media use and the life span', *American Behavioural Scientist*, 23, 7–31.

Dixon, R.A., Simon, E., Novak, C. and Hultsch, D. (1982) 'Text recall in adulthood as a function of level of initiation, input, modality, and delay interval', *Journal of Gerontology*, 37, 358–364.

Dodge, R. (1958) 'Selling the older consumer', *Journal of Retailing*, 36 (Summer), 73–81.

Dominick, J. and Rauch, G. (1971) 'The image of women in network TV commercials', *Journal of Broadcasting*, 15, 41–47.

Donahue, W., Orbach, H.L. and Pollak, G. (1960) 'Retirement: the emerging social pattern', in C. Tibbetts (ed.) *Handbook of Social Gerontology*. Chicago: The University of Chicago Press, pp. 330–406.

Doob, A.N., and MacDonald, G.E. (1979) 'Television viewing and fear of victimization: Is the relationship causal?', *Journal of Personality and Social Psychology*, 37(1), 170–179.

Doolittle, J.C. (1979) 'News media use by older adults', *Journalism Quarterly*, 56, 311–317, 345.

Douthill, R.A. and Fedyk, J.M. (1988) 'The influence of children on family life cycle behaviour: Theory and application', *Journal of Consumer Affairs*, 22, 220–248.

Douthill, R.A. and Fedyk, J.M. (1990) 'Family composition, parental time and market goods: Life cycle trade-offs', *Journal of Consumer Affairs*, 24, 110–133.

Dowd, J. (1980) *Stratification Amongst the Aged*, Monterey, CA: Brooks-Cole.

Dowd, J., Sisson, R. and Kern, D. (1981) 'Socialisation to violence among the aged', *Journal of Gerontology*, 36(3), 350–361.

Downing, M. (1974) 'Heroine of the daytime serial', *Journal of Communication*, 24, 130–139.

Drachman, D. and Leavitt, J. (1972) 'Memory impairment in the aged: storage versus retrieval deficit', *Journal of Experimental Psychology*, 93, 302–308.

Durand, R.M., Klemmack, D.L., Roff, L.L. and Taylor, J.L. (1980) 'Communicating with the elderly: Reach of television and magazines', *Psychological Reports*, 46, 1235–1242.

Dwight, M. and Urman, H. (1985) 'Affluent elderly as a unique market segment', *Marketing News*, 16 August.

Eckstein, J. (ed.) (1992) *Cultural Trends 1992. 16. Books, Libraries and Reading*. London: HMSO.

Ekert-Jaffe, O. (1989) 'Viellessement et consommation: Quelques résultats tirés des enquêtes françaises sur les budgets des ménages', *Population*, 44, 561–579.

Elliott, J. (1984) 'The daytime television drama portrayal of older adults', *The Gerontologist*, 24, 628–633.

Elwell, T. and Mattbie-Crannel, A.D. (1981) 'The impact of role loss upon coping resources and life satisfaction of the elderly', *Journal of Gerontology*, 36(2), 223–232.

England, P., Kuha, A. and Gardiner, T. (1981) 'The ages of men and women in magazine advertisements', *Journalism Quarterly*, 58, 468–471.

Erber, J.T. (1974) 'Age differences in recognition memory', *Journal of Gerontology*, 29, 177–181.

Erber, J.T. (1978) 'Age differences in a controlled lab recognition task', *Experimental Aging Research*, 4, 195–205.

Erikson, E. (1950) *Childhood and Society*, New York: W.W. Norton.

Erickson, G. (1990) 'Packaging for older consumers', *Packaging*, 35(13), 24–28.

Estes, C.L., Swan, J.S. and Gerard, L.E. (1982) 'Dominant and competing paradigms in gerontology', *Ageing and Society*, 2, 151–164.

Evandrou, M. and Victor, C. (1989) 'Differentiation in later life: Social class and housing tenure cleavages', in B. Bytheway (ed.) *Becoming and Being Old: Sociological Approaches to Later Life*. London: Sage, pp. 104–120.

Eysenck, M.W. (1974) 'Age differences in incidental learning', *Developmental Psychology*, 10, 936–941.

Falk, L.W., Bisogai, C.A. and Sobal, J. (1996) 'Food choice processes of older adults: A qualitative investigation', *Journal of Nutrition Education*, 28(5), 257–265.

Falkingham, J. and Victor, C. (1991) 'The myth of the Woopie: Incomes, the elderly and targeting welfare', *Ageing and Society*, 11(4), 471–493.

Fazio, R.H. (1989) 'On the power and functionality of attitudes: The role of attitude accessibility', in A.R. Pratkanis, S.J. Breckler and A.G. Greenwald (eds) *Attitude Structure and Function*. Hillsdale, NJ: Lawrence Erlbaum Associates, pp. 153–179.

Feather, N. (1975) *Values in Education and Society*, New York: Free Press.

Featherstone, M. (1982) 'The body in consumer culture', *Theory, Culture and Society*, 1, 18–33.

Featherstone, M. and Hepworth, M. (1993) 'Images of Ageing', in J. Bond, P. Coleman and S. Pearce (eds) *Ageing in Society: An Introduction to Social Gerontology*. London: Sage, pp. 304–332.

Festervand, T.A. and Lumpkin, J.R. (1985) 'Response of elderly consumers to their portrayal by advertisers', *Current Issues and Research in Advertising*, 1, 203–226.

Fischer, D.H. (1978) *Growing Old in America*. New York: Oxford University Press.

Foulds, G.A. and Rave, J.C. (1948) 'Normal changes in the mental abilities of adults as age advances', *Journal of Mental Science*, 94, 133–142.

Fouts, G.T. (1989) 'Television use by the elderly', *Canadian Psychology*, 30(3), 568–577.

Fouts, G.T. and Abraham, R. (1986) 'Television program preferences of older viewers', paper presented at the American Association for the Advancement of Science (Pacific Division) Vancouver, BC.

Fouts, G.T. and Abraham, R. (1988) 'Television viewing and viewer motivations in the elderly', paper presented at the Western Psychological Association, San Francisco, CA.

Fox, M., Roscoe, A.M. and Feigenbaum, A. (1984) 'A longitudinal analysis of consumer behaviour in the elderly population', in T.C. Kinnear (ed.) *Advances in Consumer Research*. Vol. II. Association for Consumer Research, Provo, UT, pp. 563–568.

Fozard, J.L. and Waugh, N.C. (1969) 'Proactive inhibition of prompted items', *Psychonomic Science*, 17, 67–68.

Francher, J.S. (1973) 'It's the Pepsi generation: Accelerated aging and the television commercial', *International Journal of Aging and Human Development*, 41, 245–255.

French, W.A. and Crask, M.R. (1977) 'The credibility of media advertising for the elderly', in B.A. Greenberg and D.N. Bollinger (eds) *Contemporary Marketing Thought*. Chicago, IL: American Marketing Association.

French, W.A. and Fox, R. (1985) 'Segmenting the senior citizen market', *Journal of Consumer Marketing*, 2(1), 61–74.

Freysinger, V.J. (1993) 'The community, programme and opportunities – Population diversity', in J.R. Kelly (ed.) *Activity and Aging – Staying Involved in Later Life*. Newbury Park, CA: Sage, pp. 211–230.

Fries, J.F. and Crapo, L.M. (1981) *Vitality and Ageing: Implications of the Rectangular Curve*. San Francisco, CA: W.H. Freeman & Co.

Fullerton, A.M. and Smith, A.D. (1980) 'Age related differences in the use of redundancy', *Journal of Gerontology*, 35, 729–735.

Furse, D., Punj, G. and Stewart, D. (1984) 'A typology of individual search strategies among purchasers of new automobiles', *Journal of Consumer Research*, 10, 417–431.

Gaeth, G.J. and Heath, T.B. (1987) 'The cognitive processing of misleading advertising in young and old adults: Assessment and training', *Journal of Consumer Research*, 14, 43–54.

Gantz, W., Gartenberg, H.M. and Rainbow, C.K. (1980) 'Approaching invisibility: The portrayal of the elderly in magazine advertisements', *Journal of Communication*, 30(1), 56–80.

Garfield, S. and Belk, L. (1952) 'Age vocabulary level and mental improvement', *Journal of Consulting Psychology*, 16, 395–398.

Gelb, B.D. (1978) 'Exploring the gray market segment', *MSU Business Topics*, 26, 41–46.

Gelb, B.D. (1982) 'Discovering the 65+ consumer', *Business Horizons*, May–June, p. 42.

Gelwicks, A. (1970) *Older Americans and Transportation: A Crisis in Mobility.* Washington, DC: US Government Printing Office.

Gerbner, G., Gross, L., Morgan, M. and Signorielli, N. (1980a) 'The mainstreaming of America: Violence Profile No. 11', *Journal of Communication*, 30, 10–29.

Gerbner, G., Gross, L., Morgan, M. and Signorielli, N. (1980b) 'Aging with television: Images on television drama and conceptions of social reality', *Journal of Communication*, 30, 37–47.

Gilbert, J.T. (1935) 'Mental efficiency in senescence', *Archives of Psychology*, 27(188), 1–60.

Giles, H. and Coupland, N. (1991) *Language: Contexts and Consequences*. Buckingham, UK: Open University Press.

Giles, H., Coupland, N. and Wiemann, J.M. (1992) '"Talk is cheap . . . " but "my word is my bond": Beliefs about talk', in K. Bolton and H. Kwok (eds) *Sociolinguistics Today: Eastern and Western Perspectives*. London: Routledge, pp. 218–243.

Gilly, M.C. and Enis, B.M. (1982) 'Recycling the family life cycle: A proposal for redefinition', in A.A. Mitchell (ed.) *Advances in Consumer Research*, Vol. 9. Ann Arbor, MI: Association for Consumer Research, pp. 271–276.

Gilly, M.C. and Zeithaml, V.A. (1985) 'The elderly consumer and adoption of technologies', *Journal of Consumer Research*, 12, 353–357.

Glick, I.O. and Levy, S. J. (1962) *Living with Television*, Chicago: Aldine.

Glynn, S.M. and Muth, D.K. (1979) 'Text learning capabilities of older adults', *Educational Gerontology: An International Quarterly*, 4, 253–269.

Gollub, J. and Javitz, H. (1989) 'Six ways to age', *American Demographics*, 11, 28–57.

Goodhead, V. (1991) 'Marketing to mature adults requires a state of being', *Marketing News*, 9 December, p. 10.

Goodman, R.I. (1990) 'Television news viewing by older adults', *Journalism Quarterly* 67(1), 137–141.

Gordon, S. and Clark, C.W. (1974a) 'Adult age differences in word and nonsense syllable recognition memory and response criterion', *Journal of Gerontology*, 29, 659–665.

Gordon, S. and Clark, C.W. (1974b) 'Application of signal detection theory to prose recall and recognition in elderly and young adults', *Journal of Gerontology*, 29, 64–72.

Gorn, G.J., Goldberg, M.E., Chattopadhuy, A. and Litvak, D. (1991) 'Music and information in commercials: Their effect with an elderly sample', *Journal of Advertising Research*, 5, 23–41.

Graebner, W. (1980) *A History of Retirement: The Meaning and Function of an American Institution, 1885–1978*. New Haven and London: Yale University Press.

Graney, M.J. and Graney. E.E. (1974) 'Communications activity substitutions in aging', *Journal of Communication*, 24, 88–96.

Greco, A.J. (1984) 'Overlooked senior citizen market lends itself well to a segmentation approach', *Marketing News*, 27 April, p. 7.

Greco, A.J. (1988) 'The elderly as communicators: Perceptions of advertising practitioners', *Journal of Advertising Research*, 28, 39–46.

Greco, A.J. (1989) 'Representation of the elderly in advertising: crisis or inconsequence?', *Journal of Consumer Marketing*, 6(1), 37–44.

Greenberg, B.S., Korzenny, F. and Atkin, C.K. (1979) 'The portrayal of the aging trends on commercial television', *Research on Aging*, 1, 319–334.

Gronhaug, K. and Rostvig, L. (1978) 'Target groups and advertising messages', *Journal of Advertising Research*, 18(2), 23–28.

Grundy, E. (1991) 'Age related change in later life', in M. Murphy and J. Hobcraft (eds) *Population Research in Britain*. London: Population Investigation Committee, pp. 133–156.

Guillemard, A.M. (1986) 'Social policy and ageing in France', in C. Phillipson and A. Walker (eds) *Ageing and Social Policy: A Critical Assessment*. London: Gower, pp. 263–279.

Gunter, B. and Furnham, A. (1992) *Consumer Profiles: An Introduction to Psychographics*. London: Routledge.

Gunter, B., Sancho-Aldridge, J. and Winstone, P. (1994) *Television: The Public's View – 1993*. London: John Libbey.

Haber, C. (1983) *Beyond Sixty-Five: The Dilemma of Old Age in America's Past*. Cambridge, UK: Cambridge University Press.

Hagen, J.W. and Stanovich, K.E. (1977) 'Memory: Strategies of acquisition', in R.V. Kail and J.W. Hagen (eds) *Perspectives on the Development of Memory and Cognition*. Hillsdale, NJ: Lawrence Erlbaum Associates.

Haley, R.I. (1968) 'Benefit segmentation: A decision-oriented research tool', *Journal of Marketing*, 32, 30–35.

Haley, R.I. (1984a) 'Benefit segments: Backwards and forwards', *Journal of Advertising Research*, 24, 19–24.

Haley, R.I. (1984b) 'Benefit segmentation – 20 years later', *Journal of Consumer Marketing*, 1, 5–13.

Hamilton, D. R. and Trolier, T. K. (1986) 'Stereotypes and stereotyping: An overview of the cognitive approach', in J.F. Dovidio and S.L. Gaertner (eds) *Prejudice, Discrimination and Racism*. Orlando, FL: Academic Press, pp. 127–163.

Handy, C. (1977) 'Monitoring consumer satisfaction with food products', in H.K. Hunt (ed.) *Conceptualisation and Measurement of Consumer Satisfaction and Dissatisfaction*. Cambridge, MA: Marketing Science Institute, pp. 215–239.

Handy, C. (1990) *The Age of Unreason*. London: Arrow.

Handy, C. (1994) *The Empty Raincoat: Making Sense of the Future*. London: Hutchinson.

Hansard (1990) Written Answers, Cols. 307–310, 25 July.

Hanson, P. (1987) 'Psychographic and lifestyle perspectives on the senior market', paper presented at the Marketing to Senior Segment: The Health and Lifestyles of America's Aging Population conference, Louisville, KY: 16 April.

Harkins, S., Chapman, R. and Eisdorfer, C. (1979) 'Memory loss and response bias in senescence', *Journal of Gerontology*, 34, 66–72.

Harris, A. and Feinberg, J. (1977) 'Television aging: Is what you see what you get?', *Gerontologist*, 17, 464–468.

Harris, L. and Associates (1975) *The Myth and Reality of Ageing in America*. New York: National Council on Ageing.

Hartley, J. T. and Walsh, D.A. (1980) 'The effect of monetary incentive on amount and rate of free recall in older and younger adults', *Journal of Gerontology*, 35, 899–905.

Hartley, J.T., Harker, J.D. and Walsh, D.A. (1980) 'Contemporary issues and new directions in adults' development and learning', in L.W. Poon (ed.) *Ageing in the 1980s*. Washington, DC: American Psychological Association, pp. 239–252.

Hasher, L. and Zacks, R.T. (1979) 'Automatic and effortful processes in memory', *Journal of Experimental Psychology: General*, 108, 356–358.

Havighurst, R. (1963) 'Successful ageing', in R.H. Williams, C. Tibbitts and W. Donahue (eds) *Process of Ageing*, Chicago: University of Chicago Press, vol. 1., pp. 311–315.

Heatherton, T. and Fouts, G. (1985) 'Television and the older viewer: Effects of changes in visual and auditory systems', paper presented at the International Communication Association, Honolulu, HI.

Heckhausen, J., Dixon, R.A. and Baltes, P.B. (1989) 'Gains and losses in development throughout adulthood as perceived by different adult age groups', *Developmental Psychology*, 25, 109–121.

Hendricks, J., Knox, V.J., Gekoski, W.L. and Dyne, K.J. (1988) 'Perceived cognitive ability of young and old targets', *Canadian Journal of Gerontology*, 7, 192–203.

Hendricks, J. and Hendricks, J. (1976) 'Concepts of time and temporal construction among the aged, with implications for research', in J. Gubrium (ed.) *Time, Roles and Self in Old Age*. New York: Human Sciences.

Hendricks, J. and Hendricks, J. (1981) *Ageing in Mass Society: Myths and Realities*. Cambridge, MA: Winthrop.

Hepworth, M. and Featherstone, M. (1982) *Surviving Middle Age*. Oxford, UK: Blackwell.

Heron, A. and Craik, F.I.M. (1964) 'Age differences in cumulative learning of meaningful and meaningless material', *Scandinavian Journal of Psychology*, 5(4), 209–217.

Hess, B.B. (1974) 'Stereotypes of the aged', *Journal of Communication*, 24, 76–85.

Hickey, T., Hickey, L. and Kalish, R.A. (1968) 'Children's perceptions of the elderly', *Journal of Genetic Psychology*, 112, 227–235.

Hill, R.L. and Rodgers, R.H. (1964) 'The developmental approach', in H.T. Christenson (ed.) *Handbook of Marriage and the Family*. Chicago: Rand McNally, pp. 171–211.

Hirsch, P. (1980) 'The "scary world" of the nonviewer and other anomalies: A reanalysis of Gerbner et al. findings of cultivation analysis, Part I', *Communication Research*, 7, 403–456.

Hoar, J. (1961) 'A study of free-time activities of 200 aged persons', *Sociology and Social Research*, 45, 157–163.

Hockey, J. and James, A. (1993) *Age Barriers at Work*. Solihull, UK: Metropolitan Authorities Recruitment Association.

Homer, P.M. (1990) 'The mediating role of attitude toward the ad: Some additional evidence', *Journal of Marketing Research*, 27, 78–86.

Hopf, H.L. and Bedwell, R.T. Jr (1969) 'Characteristics and program preferences of television listeners in Columbus, Ohio, April, 1959', in L.W. Lichty and J.M. Riply (eds) *American Broadcasting, Introduction and Analysis: Readings*. Madison, WI: College of Printing and Typing, pp. 102–131.

Horn, J.L. (1967) 'Intelligence: why it grows; why it declines', *Transaction*, 5, 23–51.

Horn, J.L. (1970) 'Organisation of data on lifespan development of human abilities', in L. R. Goulet and P. B. Baltes (eds) *Life Span Developmental Psychology: Research and Theory*. New York: Academic Press, pp. 423–466.

Horn, J.L. (1975) 'Psychometric studies of ageing and intelligence', in S. Gershon and A. Raskin (eds) *Ageing: Genesis and Treatment of Psychological Disorders in the Elderly*, vol. 2. New York: Raven Press, pp. 19–34.

Horn, J.L. (1978) 'Human ability systems', in P.B. Baltes (ed.) *Life Span Development and Behaviour*, New York: Academic Press, pp. 211–256.

Horn, J.L. and Cattell, R.B. (1966) 'Age differences in primary mental ability factors', *Journal of Gerontology*, 21, 210–220.

Horn, J.L. and Cattell, R.B. (1967) 'Age differences in fluid and crystallised intelligence', *Acta Psychologia*, 26(2), 107–129.

Horn, J.L. and Donaldson, G. (1976) 'On the myth of intellectual decline in adulthood', *American Psychologist*, 31, 701–709.

Horn, J.L. and Donaldson, G. (1980) 'Cognitive development in adulthood', in O.G. Brim and J. Kagan (eds) *Constancy and Change in Human Development*, Cambridge, MA: Harvard University Press, pp. 445–529.

Horn, J.L., Donaldson, G. and Engstrom, R. (1981) 'Apprehension, memory and fluid intelligence decline in adulthood', *Research on Ageing*, 3, 33–44.

Howard, J.A. (1967) 'Consumer interests of the elderly', hearing before the Subcommittee on Consumer Interests of the Elderly of the special Committee on Ageing. United States Senate, 90th Congress, 1st session. 17–18 January, Washington DC: US Government Printing Office, p. 128.

Howell, R. J. (1955) 'Sex differences and educational influences on a mental deterioration scale', *Journal of Gerontology*, 10, 190–193.

Hoyer, W.J., Rebok, G.W. and Sved, S.M. (1979) 'Effects of varying irrelevant information on adult age differences in problem solving', *Journal of Gerontology*, 34(4), 553–560.

Huddleston, P.H., Ford, I.M. and Bickle, M.C. (1993) 'Demographic and lifestyle characteristics as predictors of fashion opinion leadership among mature consumers', *Clothing & Textiles Research Journal*, 11(4), 26–31.

Hughes, M. (1980) 'The fruits of cultivation analysis: A re-examination of the effects of television watching on fear of victimization, alienation, and the approval of violence', *Public Opinion Quarterly*, 44, 287–302.

Hulicka, I.M. and Rust, L.D. (1964) 'Age related retention deficit as a function of learning', *Journal of the American Geriatrics Society*, 12, 1061–1065.

Hulicka, I.M. and Weiss, R. (1965) 'Age differences in retention as a function of learning', *Journal of Consulting Psychology*, 29, 125–129.

Hulicka, I.M., Sterns, H. and Grossman, J.L. (1967) 'Age group comparisons or paired-associate learning as a function of priced and self-priced association and response times', *Journal of Gerontology*, 22, 274–280.

Hulicka, I.M. and Grossman, J.L. (1967) 'Age group comparisons for the use of mediators in paired-associate learning', *Journal of Gerontology*, 22, 46–51.

Hultsch, D.F. (1974) 'Learning how to learn in adulthood', *Journal of Gerontology*, 29, 302–308.

Hultsch, D.F. (1975) 'Adults' age differences in retrieval: Trace-dependent and cue-dependent forgetting', *Development Psychology*, 11, 197–201.

Hummert, M.L. (1990) 'Multiple stereotypes of elderly and young adults: A comparison of structure and evaluations', *Psychology and Aging*, 5, 182–193.

Hummert, M.L., Garstka, T.A., Bonneson, J.L. and Strahm, S. (1994) 'Stereotypes of the elderly held by young, middle-aged and elderly adults', *Journal of Gerontology: Psychological Sciences*, 49, 240–249.

Hunter, B.T. (1987) 'Making food labels readable', *Consumers' Research Magazine*, 70(12), 8.

Inglis, J. (1959) 'Learning, retention and conceptual usage in elderly patients with memory disorder', *Journal of Abnormal and Social Psychology*, 59, 210–215.

Isaacs, B., Livingstone, M. and Neville, Y. (1972) *Survival of the Unfittest*. London: Routledge & Kegan Paul.

Jacobson, D. (1974) 'Rejection of the retiree role: A study of female industrial workers in their 50s', *Human Relations*, 27, 477–491.

Janis, I. and Mann, L. (1977) *Decision Making*. New York: Free Press.

Jantz, R.K., Seefeldt, C., Galper, A. and Serock, K. (1976) *Children's Attitudes toward the Elderly: Report to the American Association of Retired Persons and the National Retired Teachers Association*. College Park, MD: University of Maryland Press.

Jerrome, D. (1993a) 'Intimacy and sexuality amongst older women', in M. Bernard and K. Meade (eds) *Women Come of Age: Perspectives on the Lives of Older Women*. London: Edward Arnold, pp. 85–105.

Jerrome, D. (1993b) 'Intimate relationships', in J. Bond, P. Coleman and S. Peace (eds) *Ageing in Society – An Introduction to Social Gerontology*, 2nd edn. London: Sage, pp. 226–254.

John, D.R. and Cole, C.A. (1986) 'Age differences in information processing: Understanding deficits in young and elderly consumers', *Journal of Consumer Research*, 13, 297–315.

Johnson, L.K. (1973) 'Changes in Memory as a Function of Age', unpublished doctoral dissertation, Psychology Department, University of Southern California, Los Angeles, CA.

Johnson, P. (1990) 'Economic trends in population – last 25 years, next 10 years', *Admap*, March, 14–17.

Johnson, P. and Falkingham, J. (1992) *Ageing and Economic Welfare*. London: Sage.

Jones, H.E. (1955) 'Age changes in mental abilities', in R.M. Elliott, G. Lindzey and K. MacCorquedale (eds) *Studies in Human Development*, New York: Appleton-Century-Crofts.

Jones, H.E. (1956) 'Problems of aging in perceptual and intellectual functions', in J.E. Anderson (ed.) *Psychological Aspects of Ageing*, Washington, DC: American Psychological Association, pp. 135–139.

Jones, H.E. and Conrad, H.S. (1933) 'The growth and decline of intelligence: A study of homogeneous groups between the ages of ten and sixty', *Genetic Psychology Monographs*, 13(3), 223–298.

Kahle, L.R. (ed.) (1983) *Social Values and Social Change: Adaptation to Life in America*. New York: Praeger.

Kahle, L.R., Beatty, S.E. and Homer, P. (1986) 'Alternative measurement approaches to consumer values: The List of Values (LOV) and Values and Life Style (VALS)', *Journal of Consumer Research*, 13, 405–409.

Kaiser, S.B. and Chandler, J.L. (1985) 'Older consumers' use of media for fashion information', *Journal of Broadcasting and Electronic Media*, 29, 201–207.

Kaplan, M. (1979) *Leisure: Lifestyle and Lifespan – Perspectives for Gerontology*. Philadelphia, PA: W.B. Saunders.

Kasten, R.E. (1978) 'Evaluation and fitting of amplification for the aging population', in M.A. Henock (ed.) *Aural Rehabilitation for the Elderly*. Baltimore: Grune and Stratton, pp. 78–94.

Kastenbaum, R. (1974) 'On death and dying', *Journal of Geriatric Psychiatry*, 7, 94–107.

Kausler, D.H. and Klein, D.M. (1978) 'Age differences in processing relevant versus irrelevant stimuli in multiple item recognition learning', *Journal of Gerontology*, 33, 87–93.

Kausler, D.H. and Puckett, J.M. (1979) 'Effects of word frequency on adult age differences in word memory span', *Experimental Aging Research*, 5, 161–169.

Kausler, D.H. and Puckett, J.M. (1980) 'Frequency judgements and correlated cognitive abilities in young and elderly adults', *Journal of Gerontology*, 35, 376–382.

Keane, J. (1985) Address at Florida Atlantic University, Boca Raton, Florida, 5 April.

Keitz, S.M. and Gounard, B.R. (1976) 'Age differences in adults' free recall of pictorial and word stimuli', *Educational Gerontology*, 1, 237–241.

Kelly, J.R. (1990) 'Leisure and aging: A second agenda', *Society and Leisure*, 13(1), 145–167.

Kelly, J.R., Steinkamp, M. and Kelly, J. (1986) 'Later life leisure: How they play in Peona', *The Gerontologist*, 26, 531–537.

Kelly, M.E. (1992) 'Discounters grow wiser to seniors' spending potential', *Discount Store News*, 18 May, 113–114.

Key Note (1995) *Broadcasting in the UK: 1995 Market Report*. London: Chartered Institute of Marketing.

Kiel, G. and Layton, R. (1981) 'Dimensions of consumer information seeking behaviour', *Journal of Marketing Research*, 18(2), 233–239.

Kinnear, T.C., Taylor, J.R. and Sadrudin, A.A. (1972) 'Socioeconomic and personality characteristics as they relate to ecologically-constructive purchasing behaviour', *Proceedings of the Third Annual Conference of the Association for Consumer Research*, pp. 34–60.

Kinsbourne, M. (1974) 'Cognitive deficit and the ageing brain: A behavioural analysis', *International Journal of Aging and Human Development*, 5, 41–49.

Klippel, R.E. and Sweeney, T.W. (1974) 'The use of information sources by the aged consumer', *The Gerontologist*, 14, 2, 163–166.

Klock, S.J. and Traylor, M.B. (1983) 'Older and younger models in advertising to older consumers: An advertising effectiveness experiment', *Akron Business and Economic Review*, 14(4), 48–52.

Knauer, V. (1988) 'The aging alienated consumer', in *The Aging Consumer*, Occasional Papers in Gerontology, No. 8. Ann Arbor, MI: Institute of Gerontology. Quoted in David Loudon and Albert J. Della Bitta, *Consumer Behaviour*, 3rd edn. New York: McGraw-Hill, p. 228.

Knopf, O. (1932) *The Art of Being a Woman*. London: Rider and Co.

Koeske, R.D. and Srivastava, R. (1977) 'The sources and handling of consumer complaints among the elderly', in R.L. Day (ed.) *Consumer Satisfaction, Dissatisfaction and Complaining Behaviour*. Bloomington: Indiana University, School of Business, pp. 139–143.

Kogan, N. (1979) 'Beliefs, attitudes, and stereotypes about old people', *Research in Ageing*, 1, 12–36.

Koponen, A. (1986) 'Personality characteristics of purchasers', *Journal of Advertising Research*, 1, 6–12.

Korzenny, F. and Neuendorf, K. (1980) 'Television viewing and self-concept of the elderly', *Journal of Communication*, 30, 71–80.

Kubey, R. (1978) 'Mood states and television viewing in adults', paper presented at the 31st annual meeting of the Gerontological Society, Dallas, TX.

Kubey, R. (1980) 'Television and ageing: past, present and future', *Gerontologist*, 20, 16–35.

Kuypers, J.A. and Bengtson, V.L. (1973) 'Competence and social breakdown', *Human Development*, 16(2), 37–49.

Kvasnicka, B., Beymer, B. and Perloff, R. (1982) 'Portrayals of the elderly in magazine advertisements', *Journalism Quarterly*, 59, 656–658.

Laczko, F. and Philipson, C. (1991) *Changing Work and Retirement*. Buckingham: Open University Press.

La Forge, M.C. (1989) 'Learned helplessness as an explanation of elderly consumer complaint behaviour', *Journal of Business Ethics*, 8(5) 359–366.

Lambert, J., Laslett, P. and Clary, H. (1984) *The Image of the Elderly on TV*. Cambridge: Cambridge University of the Third Age.

Lambert, Z.V. (1979) 'An investigation of older consumer's unmet needs and wants at the retail level', *Journal of Retailing*, 55(4), 35–57.

Langmeyer, L. (1983) 'Age role portrayals in magazine advertisements: A content analysis', in J.H. Summary et al. (eds) *Marketing: Theories and Concepts for an Era of Change*. Carbondale; IL: Southern Marketing Association.

Laslett, P. (1989) *A Fresh Map of Life*. London: Weidenfeld & Nicholson.

Laurence, M.W. (1967) 'Memory loss with age: A test of two strategies for its retardation', *Psychonomic Science*, 9(4), 209–210.

Laurence, M.W. and Trotter, M. (1971) 'Effect of acoustic factors and list organization in multi-trial free-recall learning of college-age and elderly adults', *Developmental Psychology*, 5, 202–210.

Layton, B. (1975) 'Perceptual noise and aging', *Psychological Bulletin*, 82, 875–884.

Lazer, W. (1986) 'Dimensions of the mature market', *Journal of Consumer marketing*, 3(3), 23–34.

Lazer, W. and Shaw, E.H. (1987) 'How older Americans spend their money', *American Demographics*, 9, 36–41.

Leiss, W., Kline, S. and Jhally, S. (1990) *Social Communication in Advertising*, 2nd edn. Scarborough, Ontario: Nelson.

Lemon, B.W., Bengston, V. and Peterson, J. (1972) 'An exploration of the activity theory of ageing: Activity types and life satisfaction among in-movers to a retirement community', *Journal of Gerontology*, 27(4), 511–523.

Lepisto, L.R. (1989) 'The effect of cognitive age and sex on consumer well-being', paper given at conference on the Elderly Consumer, University of Florida, March.

Levinson, R.M. (1973) 'From Olive Oyl to Sweet Polly Purebread: Sex role stereotypes and televised cartoons', *Journal of Popular Culture*, 9, 561–572.

Lexchin, J. (1990) 'The portrayal of the elderly in drug advertisements: A factor in inappropriate presentation', *Canadian Journal of Ageing*, 9(3), 296–303.

Liggett, J. (1974) *The Human Face*. London: Constable.

Linden, F. (1986) 'The $800 billion market', *American Demographics*, February, 20–22.

Lippman, W. (1922) *Public Opinion*. New York: Macmillan.

Longino, C.F. (1988) 'The comfortably retired and the pension elite', *American Demographics*, 10(6), 22–24.

Longino, C.F. and Crown, W.H. (1991) 'Older Americans: Rich or poor? *American Demographics*, 12(8), 48–52.

Lorsbach, T. and Simpson, G. (1984) 'Age differences in the rate of processing in short-term memory', *Journal of Gerontology*, 39, 315–321.

Loudon, D.L. and Della Bitta, A.J. (1993) *Consumer Behaviour*, 4th edn. New York: McGraw-Hill.

Loughan, C. (1977) 'Movies and senescence: A new naturalism', *The Gerontologist*, 17, 79–84.

Lumpkin, J.R. (1985) 'Shopping orientation segmentation of the elderly consumer', *Journal of the Academy of Marketing Science*, 13(2), 271–289.

Lumpkin, J.R. and Caballero, M. (1985) 'Locus of control and information sources of the elderly', in *Proceedings*, Southern Marketing Association.

Lumpkin, J.R. and Darden, W.R. (1982) 'Relating television preference viewing to shopping orientations, life styles and demographics: The examination of perceptual and preference dimensions of television programming', *Journal of Advertising*, 11(4), 60–67.

Lumpkin, J.R. and Festervand, T.A. (1987) 'Purchase information sources of the elderly', *Journal of Advertising Research*, 27(6), 31–43.

Lumpkin, J.R. and Greenberg, B.A. (1982) 'Apparel shopping patterns of the elderly consumer', *Journal of Retailing*, 58(4), 68–89.

Lumpkin, J.R., Greenberg, B.A. and Goldstucker, J.L. (1985) 'Marketplace needs of the elderly: Determinant attributes and store choice', *Journal of Retailing*, 61(2), 75–105.

Lumpkin, J.R. and Hunt, J.B. (1989) 'Mobility as an influence on retail package behaviour of the elderly: testing conventional wisdom', *Journal of the Academy of Marketing Science*, 17(1), 1–12.

Lutsky, N.S. (1980) 'Attitudes toward old age and elderly persons', in C. Eisendorfer (ed.) *Annual Review of Gerontology and Geriatrics*, vol. 1. New York: Springer, pp. 287–336.

McCleod, P.B. and Ellis, J.R. (1982) 'Housing consumption over the family life cycle: An empirical analysis', *Urban Studies*, 19, 177–185.

MacCoby, N. and Sheffield, F.D. (1961) 'Combining practice with demonstration in teaching complex sequences: Summary and interpretations', in A.A. Lumsdaine (ed.) *Student Response in Programmed Instruction: A Symposium*. Washington, DC: National Academy of Sciences National Research Council.

MacFarlane, A. (1986) *Marriage and Love in England: Modes of Reproduction 1300–1840*. Oxford, UK: Blackwell.

McGoldrick, A. and Cooper, C. (1989) *Early Retirement*. Aldershot, UK: Gower.

Machin, C.R. (1976) 'A transgenerational comparison: The elderly fashion consumer', *Advances in Consumer Research*, 3, 453–456.

Macht, M. and Buschke, H. (1984) 'Speed of recall in aging', *Journal of Gerontology*, 39, 439–443.

McKeown, T. (1979) *The Role of Medicine and Dream: Mirage or Nemesis?* Oxford, UK: Basil Blackwell.

McTavish, D.G. (1971) 'Perceptions of old people: A review of research methodologies and findings', *The Gerontologist*, 11, 90–101.

Madden, D.J. (1985) 'Age related slowing in the retrieval of information from long-term memory', *Journal of Gerontology*, 40, 208–210.

Manton, K.G. (1982) 'Changing concepts of morbidity and mortality in the elderly population', *Milbank Memorial Fund Quarterly/Health and Society*, 60, 183–244.

Mares, M. and Cantor, J. (1992) 'Elderly viewers' responses to televised portrayals of old age: Empathy and mood management versus social comparison', *Communication Research*, 19, 459–478.

Marketing News (1988) 'Survey: Age is not good indicator of consumer need', 21 November.

Markides, K.S. and Bolt, J.S. (1984) 'Changes in subjective age among the elderly: A longitudinal analysis', *The Gerontologist*, 15, 184–186.

Marmor, M. (1977) 'The eye and vision in the elderly', *Geriatrics*, 32, 63–67.

Marshall, V. (1987) *Ageing in Canada: Social Perspectives*. Don Mills: Fitzhenny and Whiteside.

Martin, C.R. (1979) 'A transgenerational comparison: The elderly fashion consumer', *Proceedings*. Association for Consumer Research, 453–456.

Martin, J. and Roberts, C. (1984) *Women and Employment: A Lifetime Perspective*. London: HMSO.

Maslow, A. H. (1954) *Motivation and Personality*, New York: Harper & Row.

Mason, J. B. (1987) 'A bed of roses: Women, marriage and inequality in later life', in P. Allat, T. Keil, A. Brynon and B. Bytheway (eds) *Women and the Life Cycle*. London: Macmillan, pp. 90–106.

Mason, J.B. and Bearden, W.O. (1978a) 'Profiling the shopping behaviour of elderly consumers', *The Gerontologist*, 18(5), 454–461.

Mason, J.B. and Bearden, W.O. (1978b) 'Elderly shopping behaviour and marketplace perceptions', *Proceedings*. Southern Marketing Association, 290–293.

Mason, J.B. and Hunt, S. (1973) 'An exploratory behavioural and socio-economic profile of consumer action about dissatisfaction with selected household appliances', *Journal of Consumer Affairs*, Winter, 121–127.

Mason, S.E. and Smith, A. (1977) 'Imagery in the aged', *Experimental Aging Research*, 3, 17–32.

Mauss, M. (1954) *The Gift*, Glencoe, NY: Free Press.

Meadow, H.L., Cosmas, S.C. and Plotkin, A. (1981) 'The elderly consumer research: past, present and future', in K.B. Monroe (ed.) *Advances in Consumer Research*, vol. VIII. Ann Arbor, MI: Association for Consumer Research.

Media Decisions (1977) 'Don't overlook the $200 billion 55-plus market', October, 59–61.

Mertz, R.J. (1970) 'Analysis of the portrayal of older Americans in commercial television programming', paper presented at the International Communication Association conference, Minneapolis.

Meyer, B. and Rice, E.G. (1981) 'Information recalled from prose by young, middle and old age readers', *Experimental Ageing Research*, 7, 253–268.

Meyersohn, R. (1961) 'A critical examination of commercial entertainment', in R.K. Kleemeier (ed.) *Ageing and Leisure*. New York: Oxford University Press, pp. 243–272.

Meyersohn, R. (1969) 'An examination of commercial entertainment', in R.W. Kellmeier (ed.) *Ageing and Leisure*. New York: Oxford University Press, pp. 268–279.

Michman, R., Hocking, R.T. and Harris, L. (1979) 'New product adoption behaviour patterns of senior citizens for cold remedies', *Proceedings*. Southern Marketing Association, 309–311.

Midwinter, E. (1991) *Out of Focus: Old Age, the Press and Broadcasting*. London: Centre for Policy on Ageing.

Miller, C. (1991) 'Misconception, fear stall advance into mature market', *Marketing News*, 9 December, p. 11.

Milliman, R.E. and Erffmeyer, R.C. (1990) 'Improving advertising aimed at seniors', *Journal of Advertising Research*, 29(6), 31–36.

Mitchell, A. (1983) *The Nine American Lifestyles*. New York: Warner.

Moenster, P.A. (1972) 'Learning and memory in relation to age', *Journal of Gerontology*, 27, 361–363.

Morris, J., Schneider, D. and Macey, S. (1995) 'A survey of older Americans to determine frequency and motivations for eating fast food', *Journal of Nutrition for the Elderly*, 15(1), 1–12.

Moschis, G.P. (1987) *Consumer Socialisation: A Life Cycle Perspective*. Lexington, MA: Lexington Books.

Moschis, G.P. (1991) 'Marketing to older adults: An overview and assessment of present knowledge and practice', *Journal of Consumer Marketing*, 8(4), 33–41.

Moschis, G.P., Mathier, A. and Smith, R.B. (1993) 'Older consumers' orientations toward age-based marketing stimuli', *Journal of the Academy of Marketing Science*, 21(3), 195–205.

Moss, M. and Lawton, M.P. (1982) 'Time budgets of older people: A window on four lifestyles', *Journal of Gerontology*, 37, (1), 115–123.

Mueller, J., Rankin, J. and Carlomusto, M. (1979) 'Adult age differences in free recall as a function of basis of organisation and method of presentation', *Journal of Gerontology*, 34, 375–380.

Mueller, J. and Ross, M. (1984) 'Uniqueness of the self-concept across the life span', *Bulletin of the Psychonomic Society*, 22, 83–86.

Mueller, J., Wonderlich, S. and Dugan, K. (1986) 'Self-referent processing of age-specific material', *Psychology and Aging*, 1, 293–299.

Mundorf, N. and Brownell, W. (1990) 'Media preferences of older and younger adults', *Gerontologist*, 30(5), 685–692.

Murphy, P. and Staples, W. (1979) 'A modernized family life cycle', *Journal of Consumer Research*, 6, 12–22.

Musgrove, P. (1982) *US Household Consumption, Income and Demographic Changes: 1975–2025*. Washington, DC: Resources for the Future.

National Council on Ageing (1975) *The Myths and Realities of Ageing*. Washington, DC: National Council on Ageing.

Neugarten, B.L. and Associates (1964) *Personality in Middle and Late Life*. New York: Atheron Press.

Northcott, H.C. (1975) 'Too young, too old – age in the world of television', *Gerontologist*, 15, 184–186.

Norton, D. (1992) 'Social provision for older people in Europe – in education and leisure', in L. Davies (ed.) *The Coming of Age in Europe – Older People in the European Community*. London: Age Concern England, pp. 38–62.

Novak, T.P. and MacEvoy, B. (1990) 'On comparing alternative segmentation schemes: The List of Values (LOV) and Values and Lifestyles (VALS)', *Journal of Consumer Research*, 17, 105–109.

Office for National Statistics (1996) *Key Data*. London: HMSO.

Ordy, J., Brizzee, K. and Johnson, H. (1982) 'Cellular alterations in visual pathways and the limbic system: Implications for vision and short-term memory', in R. Sekular, D. Kline and K. Dismukes (eds) *Ageing and Human Visual Functions*. New York: Alan R. Liss, pp. 79–114.

Ostman, R.E. and Jeffers, D. (1983) 'Life stage and motives for television use', *International Journal of Ageing and Human Development*, 17(4), 315–322.

Ostman, R.E. and Scheibe, C.L. (1984) 'Characters in American network television commercials as indicators of ageism and sexism', paper presented at the meeting of the International Communication Association, San Francisco, May.

Ostroff, J. (1989) 'An ageing market', *American Demographics*, May, p. 26.

O'Toole, J. (1981) *The Trouble with Advertising*. New York: Chelsea House.

Owens, W.A. (1966) 'Age and mental ability: A second follow-up', *Journal of Educational Psychology*, 57, 311–325.

Owsler, C., Sekular, R. and Boldt, C. (1981) 'Ageing and low-contrast vision: Face perception', *Investigative Ophthalmology and Visual Science*, 21, 362–365.

Oyer, H., Kapur, Y. and Deal, C. (1976) 'Hearing disorders in the ageing: Effects upon communication', in H. Oyer and E. Oyer (eds) *Ageing and Communication*. Baltimore: University Park Press, pp. 175–186.

Page, S., Olivas, R., Driver, J. and Driver, R. (1981) 'Children's attitudes towards the elderly and ageing', *Educational Gerontology*, 7, 43–47.

Palmore, E. (1965) 'Differences in the retirement patterns of men and women', *The Gerontologist*, 5, 4–8.

Palmore, E. (1977) 'Facts on ageing: A short quiz', *The Gerontologist*, 17, 315–320.

Palmore, E. (1982) 'Attitudes toward the aged – what we know and need to know', *Research on Ageing*, 4, 333–348.

Park, D.C. and Puglisi, T.J. (1985) 'Older adults' memory for the colour of pictures and words', *Journal of Gerontology*, 40, 198–204.

Park, D. L., Puglisi, T.J. and Soracool, M. (1983) 'Memory for pictures, words and spatial location in older adults: Evidence for pictorial superiority', *Journal of Gerontology*, 38, 582–588.

Parker, E. and Paisley, W. (1966) *Patterns of Adult Information Seeking*. Stanford, CA: Stanford University, Institute for Communication Research.

Parker, S. (1980) *Older Workers and Retirement*. London: HMSO.

Parkinson, S.R. and Percy, A, (1980) 'Ageing, digit span and the stimulus suffix effect', *Journal of Gerontology*, 35, 736–742.

Passuth, P.M. and Cook, F.L. (1985) 'Effects of television viewing on knowledge and attitudes about older adults: A critical re-examination', *The Gerontologist*, 25(1), 69–77.

Perlman, D., Gerson, A. and Spinner, B. (1978) 'Loneliness among senior citizens: An empirical report', *Essence*, 2(4), 239–248.

Perlmutter, M. (1978) 'What is memory ageing the ageing of?', *Developmental Psychology*, 14, 330–345.

Perlmutter, M. (1979) 'Age differences in adults' free recall, cued recall and recognition', *Journal of Gerontology*, 34(4), 533–539.

Peterson, M. (1973) 'The visibility and image of old people on television', *Journalism Quarterly*, 50, 569–573.

Petre, P. (1986) 'Marketers mine for gold in the old', *Fortune*, 31 March, 70–78.

Petroshius, S. and Crocker, K. (1989) 'An empirical analysis of spokesperson characteristics on advertisement and product evaluations', *Journal of the Academy of Marketing Science*, 17, 217–225.

Pfaff, M. and Blivice, S. (1977) 'Socio-economic correlates of consumer and citizen dissatisfaction and activism', in R.L. Day (ed.) *Consumer Satisfaction, Dissatisfaction and Complaining Behaviour*. Bloomington, IN: Indiana University, School of Business, pp. 115–123.

Phillips, L.W. and Sternthal, B. (1977) 'Age differences in information processing: A perspective on the aged consumer', *Journal of Marketing Research*, 14(4), 444–457.

Phillipson, C. (1982) *Capitalism and the Construction of Old Age*. London: Macmillan.

Pol, L.G., May, M.G. and Hartranft, F.R. (1992) 'Eight stages of ageing', *American Demographics*, 14(8), 54–57.

Pommer, M.D., Berkowitz, E.N. and Walton, J.R. (1980) 'UPC scanning: An assessment of shopper response to technological changes', *Journal of Retailing*, 56(2), 25–44.

Poon, L.W. and Walsh-Sweeney, L. (1981) 'Effects of bizarre and interacting imagery on learning and retrieval of the aged', *Experimental Aging Research*, 7, 65–70.

Rabbitt, P.M. (1965) 'Age and time for choice between stimuli and between responses', *Journal of Gerontology*, 19(3), 307–312.

Rabinowitz, J., Craik, F.I.M. and Aukerman, B. (1982) 'A processing resource account for age differences in recall', *Canadian Journal of Psychology*, 36, 325–344.

Raglan, Lord. (1972) *Retirement Choice*, 2.

Rahtz, D.R., Sirgy, M.J. and Kosenko, R. (1988) 'Using demographics and psychographic dimensions to discriminate between mature heavy and light television users: An exploratory analysis', in K.B. Bahn (ed.) *Developments in Marketing Science – Volume XI*. Blacksburg, VA: Academy of Marketing Science, pp. 2–7.

Rahtz, D.R., Sirgy, M.J. and Meadow, H.L. (1989) 'The elderly audience: Correlates of television orientation', *Journal of Advertising*, 18(3), 9–20.

Rankin, J.L. and Kausler, D.H. (1979) 'Adult age differences in false recognition', *Journal of Gerontology*, 34, 58–65.

Raymond, B.J. (1971) 'Free recall among the aged', *Psychological Reports*, 29, 179–182.

Real, M.R., Anderson, N. and Harrington, M. (1980) 'Television access for older adults', *Journal of Communication*, 30, 74–76.

Reed, H.B. and Reitan, R.M. (1963) 'Changes in psychological test performance associated with the normal ageing process', *Journal of Gerontology*, 18, 271–274.

Reichard, S., Livson, F. and Peterson, P.G. (1962) *Ageing and Personality*. New York: John Wiley.

Reid, L.N., Teel, J.E. and Vanden Burgh, B.C. (1980) 'Perceived risk and interest in risk reducing information of the elderly', *Proceedings*. Southern Marketing Association, Charleston, SC.

Reinecke, J.A. (1975) 'Supermarkets, shopping centres and the senior shopper', *Marquette Business Review*, 19, 106.

Riche, M.F. (1986) 'Retirement's lifestyle pioneers', *American Demographics*, 8, 42–56.

Riche, M.F. (1989) 'Psychographics for the 1990s', *American Demographics*, 11, 24–26, 30–31, 53–54.

Richman, J. (1977) 'The foolishness and wisdom of age: Attitudes towards the elderly as reflected in jokes', *The Gerontologist*, 17, 210–219.

Ripley, J.M. and Buell, S.D. (1954) 'Characteristics of the television audience in Columbus and Franklin County, Ohio', unpublished paper, University of Ohio.

Robinson, J.D. and Skill, T. (1993) 'The invisible generation: Portrayals of the elderly on television', paper presented at the annual meeting of the Speech Communication Association.

Robinson, J.D. and Skill, T. (1995) 'Media usage patterns and portrayals of the elderly', in J.F. Nussbaum and J. Coupland (eds) *Handbook of Communication and Ageing Research*. Matwah, NJ: Lawrence Erlbaum Associates, pp. 359–391.

Robinson, J.P. (1981) 'Television and leisure time: A new scenario', *Journal of Communication*, 31, (1), 120–130.

Roebuck, J. and Slaughter, J. (1979) 'Ladies and pensioners: Stereotypes and public policy affecting old women in England, 1880–1940', *Journal of Social History*, 13, 105–114.

Rokeach, M. (1973) *The Open and Closed Mind*. New York: Basic Books.

Rose, A.M. and Peterson, W.H. (1965) *Old People and Their Social World*, Philadelphia: F.A. Davis.

Rosencrantz, H. and McNevin, T. (1969) 'A factor analysis of attitudes toward the aged', *The Gerontologist*, 9, 55–59.

Rosow, I. (1974) *Socialization to Old Age*. Berkeley, CA: University of California Press.

Ross, I. (1982) 'Information processing and the older consumers' marketing and public policy implications', in A. Mitchell (ed.) *Advances in Consumer Research – Vol IX*. Ann Arbor, MI: Association for Consumer Research.

Rotfield, H.J., Reid, L.N. and Wilcox, G.B. (1982) 'Effect of age of models in print ads on evaluation of product and sponsor', *Journalism Quarterly*, 59, (3), 374–381.

Rothbaum, F. (1983) 'Ageing and age stereotypes', *Social Cognition*, 2, 171–184.

Rothkopf, E.A. (1968) 'Textual constraint as a function of repeated inspection', *Journal of Educational Psychology*, 1, 20–25.

Rowe, E.J. and Schnore, M.M. (1971) 'Item concreteness and reported strategies in paired-associate learning as a function of age', *Journal of Gerontology*, 24, 470–475.

Rubin, A.M. (1982) 'Directions in television ageing research', *Journal of Broadcasting*, 26, 537–551.

Rubin, A.M. (1983) 'Television uses and gratifications: The determinants of viewing patterns and motivations', *Journal of Communication*, 34, 67–77.

Rubin, A.M. and Rubin, R.B. (1981) 'Age, context and television use', *Journal of Broadcasting*, 25, 1–13.

Rubin, A.M. and Rubin, R.B. (1982a) 'Contextual age and television use', *Human Communication Research*, 8, 228–244.

Rubin, A.M. and Rubin, R.B. (1982b) 'Older persons' TV viewing patterns and motivations', *Communication Research*, 9, 287–313.

Ryan, E.B. (1992) 'Beliefs about memory changes across the adult life span', *Journal of Gerontology: Psychological Sciences*, 47, 42–46.

Ryan, E.B. and Cole, R.L. (1990) 'Evaluative perceptions of interpersonal communication with elders', in H. Giles, N. Coupland and J. Weiman (eds) *Health, Communication and the Elderly*. Manchester, UK: Manchester University Press, pp. 172–190.

Ryan, E.B., Kwong See, S., Meneer, W.B., and Travato, D. (1992) 'Age-based perceptions of language performance among younger and older adults', *Communication Research*, 19, 311–331.

Salisbury, P. (1981) 'Older adults as older readers: Newspaper readership after age 65', *Newspaper Research Journal*, 3(1), 38.

Salthouse, T.A. (1980) 'Age and memory: Strategies for localising the loss', in L.W. Poon, J.L. Fozard, L.S. Cermak, D. Arenberg and L.W. Thompson (eds) *New Directions in Memory and Ageing*, Hillsdale, NJ: Lawrence Erlbaum Associates, pp. 47–66.

Salthouse, T.A. and Somberg, B.L. (1982) 'Skilled performance: Effects of adult age and experience on elementary processes', *Journal of Experimental Psychology: General*, 3, 176–207.

Samli, A.C. (1967) 'The elusive senior citizen market', *Dimensions*, 7–16.

Sanders, R., Murphy, M., Schmitt, F. and Walsh, D.A. (1980) 'Age differences in free recall rehearsal strategies', *Journal of Gerontology*, 35, 550–558.

Schalinske, T.F. (1968) 'The role of television in the life of the aged person', unpublished doctoral dissertation. Ohio State University, Columbus, Ohio.

Schaninger, C.M. and Danko, W.D. (1993) 'A conceptual and empirical comparison of alternative household life cycle models', *Journal of Consumer Research*, 19, 580–594.

Schaninger, C. and Sciglimpaglia, D. (1981) 'The influence of cognitive personality traits and demographics on consumer information acquisition', *Journal of Consumer Research*, 8, 208–216.

Schewe, C.D. (1985) 'Gray America goes to market', *Business*, 35(2), 3–9.

Schewe, C.D. (1989) 'Effective communication without ageing population', *Business Horizons*, 32(1), 19–25.

Schewe, C.D. (1990) 'Get in position for the older market', *American Demographics*, 12, 38–41.

Schewe, C.D. and Balazs, A.L. (1990) 'Playing the part', *American Demographics*, 12(4), 24–30.

Schiffman, L.G. (1971) 'Sources of information for the elderly', *Journal of Advertising Research*, 11(5), 33–37.

Schiffman, L.G. and Kanuck, L.L. (1991) *Consumer Behaviour*. Englewood Cliffs, NJ: Prentice-Hall.

Schiffman, L.G. and Sherman, E. (1991) 'Values orientations of new-age elderly: The coming of an ageless market', *Journal of Business Research*, 22(2), 187–194.

Schindler, R.M. and Holbrook, M.B. (1993) 'Critical periods in the development of men's and women's tastes in personal appearance. Special Issue: The pursuit of beauty', *Psychology and Marketing*, 10(6), 549–564.

Schmidt, D.F. and Boland, S.M. (1986) 'The structure of impressions of older adults: evidence for multiple stereotypes', *Psychology and Aging*, 1, 255–260.

Schmitt, F.A., Murphy, M.D. and Saunders, R.E. (1981) 'Training older adult free recall rehearsal strategies', *Journal of Gerontology*, 36, 329–337.

Schneider, K.C. and Schneider, S.B. (1979) 'Trends in sex roles in television commercials', *Journal of Marketing*, 43, 79–84.

Schonfield, D. and Robertson, B.A. (1966) 'Memory storage and ageing', *Canadian Journal of Psychology*, 20(2), 228–236.

Schramm, W. (1969) 'Ageing and mass communication', in M.W. Roley, J.W. Riley and M.E. Johnson (eds) *Ageing and Society, Vol. 2. Ageing and the Professions*. New York: Russell Sage Foundation, pp. 352–375.

Schramm, W. and White, D. (1949) 'Age, education, economic status: Factors in newspaper reading', *Journalism Quarterly*, 26, 149–159.

Schreiber, E.S. (1979) 'The effects of sex and age on the perceptions of TV characters: An inter-age comparison', *Journal of Broadcasting*, 23, 81–93.

Schreiber, E.S. and Boyd, D.A. (1980) 'How the elderly perceive television commercials', *Journal of Communication*, 30, 61–70.

Schuller, T. and Bostyn, A.M. (1992) *Learning: Education, Training and Information in the Third Age* (Research Paper No. 3) Dunfermline, UK: The Carnegie Enquiry into the Third Age, Carnegie UK Trust.

Sciglimpaglia, D. and Schaninger, C.M. (1981) 'Demographic correlates of consumer acquisition of nutritional package ingredients and unit price information', *Proceedings*. American Marketing Association, 193–196.

Scott, P. and Johnson, P. (1988) *The Economic Consequences of Population Aging in Advanced Societies*. CEPR discussion paper, 263, July, London: CEPR.

Seltzer, M.M. and Atchley, R.C. (1976) 'The concept of old: Changing attitudes and stereotypes', in B.D. Bell (ed.) *Contemporary Social Gerontology*, Springfield, IL: Charles C. Thomas, pp. 203–209.

Serow, W.J. (1984) 'The impact of population changes on consumption', in G. Steinman (ed.) *Economic Consequences of Population Change*. Berlin: Springer-Verlag, pp. 168–178.

Sherman, E.M. and Brittan, M.R. (1973) 'Contemporary food gatherers: A study of food shopping habits of an elderly urban population', *The Gerontologist*, 13 (Autumn), 358–363.

Sherman, E.M. and Cooper, P. (1988) 'Life satisfaction: The missing focus of marketing to seniors', *Journal of Health Care Marketing*, 8(1), 69–71.

Sherman, E., Schiffman, R.G. and Dillon, W.R. (1988) 'Age/gender judgements and quality of life differences', in *Marketing: A Return to the Broader Dimensions*. Chicago: American Marketing Association, pp. 319–320.

Shoemaker, R.W. (1978) 'Consumer decisions on package size', *Proceedings*. American Marketing Association, 152–157.

Shorter, E. (1983) *A History of Women's Bodies*. London: Allen Lane.

Siegel, J.S. and Davidson, M. (1984) 'Demographic and socioeconomic aspects of ageing in the United States', *Current Population Reports*, Series p-23, No. 138, Bureau of the Census, August.

Signorielli, N. (1982) 'Marital status in television drama: A case of reduced options', *Journal of Broadcasting*, 26(2), 585–597.

Silvenis, S. (1979) 'Packaging for the elderly', *Modern Packaging*, 52 (October), 38–39.

Simmons Market Research Bureau (1991) *The 1990 Study of Media and Markets*. New York: Author.

Simon, E., Dixon, R., Nowak, C. and Hultsch, D. (1982) 'Orienting task effects on text recall in adulthood', *Journal of Gerontology*, 37, 575–580.

Simmons, L. (1945) *The Role of the Aged in Primitive Society*, New Haven, CT: Yale University Press.

Smith, A.D. (1977) 'Adult age differences in cued recall', *Developmental Psychology*, 13, 326–331.

Smith, A.D. (1980) 'Age differences in encoding, storage and retrieval', in L.W. Poon, J.L. Fozard, L.S. Cermak, D. Arenberg and L.W. Thompson (eds) *New Directions in Memory and Ageing*, Hillsdale, NJ: Lawrence Erlbaum Associates, pp. 23–45.

Smith, D.M. (1979) 'The portrayal of elders in magazine cartoons', *The Gerontologist*, 19, 408–412.

Smith, R.B. and Moschis, G.P. (1984) 'Consumer socialisation of the elderly: An exploratory study', in T. Kinnear (ed.) *Advances in Consumer Research*, II. Provo, UT: Association for Consumer Research.

Smith, R.B., Moschis, G.P. and Moore, R.L. (1982) 'Some advertising effects on the elderly consumer', in J. Summey, B. Bergiel and C. Anderson (eds) *A Spectrum of Contemporary Marketing Ideas*. Carbondale, IL: Southern Marketing Association.

Smith, R.B., Moschis, G.P. and Moore, R.L. (1984) 'Effects of advertising on the elderly consumer: An investigation of social breakdown theory', in R. Belk *et al.* (eds) *Educators' Proceedings*. Chicago: American Marketing Association.

Smith, R.B., Moschis, G.P. and Moore, R.L. (1985) 'Some advertising influences on the elderly consumer: Implications for theoretical considerations', in J. Leigh and C. Marton (eds) *Current Issues and Research in Advertising*. Ann Arbor, MI: Graduate School of Business Administration, University of Michigan, pp. 187–201.

Smythe, M. and Browne, F. (1992) *General Household Survey 1990*. London: HMSO.

Sorce, P., Tyler, P.R. and Loomis, L.M. (1989) 'Lifestyles of older Americans', *Journal of Consumer Marketing*, 6, 53–63.

Spilich, G. (1983) 'Lifespan components of text processing: Structural and procedural differences', *Journal of Verbal Learning and Verbal Behaviour*, 22(2), 231–244.

Spring, J. (1991) 'Seven days of play', *American Demographics*, 15(3), 50–55.

Stampfl, R.W. (1978) 'The consumer life cycle', *Journal of Consumer Affairs*, 12, 214–215.

Stayman, D.M. and Aaker, D.A. (1988) 'Are all the effects of ad-induced feelings mediated by Aad?', *Journal of Consumer Research*, 15, 368–373.

Steiner, A. (1963) *The People Look at Television: A Study of Audience Attitudes*. New York: Knopf.

Stephens, N. (1982) 'The effectiveness of time-compressed advertisements with older adults', *Journal of Advertising*, 1, 38–47.

Stephens, N. and Warrens, R. (1984) 'Advertising frequency requirements for older adults', *Journal of Advertising Research*, 23, 23–32.

Sternthal, B., Phillips, L.W. and Dholakia, R. (1978) 'The persuasive effects of source credibility: A situational analysis', *Public Opinion Quarterly*, 42(3), 286–314.

Stoddard, K.M. (1983) *Saints and Shrews: Women and Ageing in American Popular Film*. London: Greenwood Press.

Stone, L. (1977) 'Walking over Grandma', *The New York Review of Books*, 24, 12 May, 26–29.

Stout, R.W. and Crawford, V. (1988) 'Active life expectancy and terminal dependency: Trends in long-term geriatric care of 33 years', *The Lancet*, I, 281–283.

Strang, R.A., Harris, B.F. and Hermandez, A.L. (1979) 'Consumer trial of generic products in supermarkets: An empirical study', *Proceedings*. American Marketing Association, 386–388.

Strutton, D.H. and Lumpkin, J.R. (1992) 'Information sources used by elderly health care product adopters', *Journal of Advertising Research*, 32(4), 20–30.

Sturges, J. (1990) 'Old habits die hardest', *Marketing Week*, 20 April, 32–36.

Swank, C. (1979) 'Media uses and gratifications: Need salience and source dependence in a sample of the elderly', *American Behavioural Scientist*, 23, 95–117.

Swartz, T. and Stephens, N. (1984) 'Information search for services: The maturity segment', in T. Kinnear (ed.) *Advances in Consumer Research*, vol. II. Provo, UT: Association for Consumer Research.

Swayne, L.E. and Greco, A.J. (1987) 'The portrayal of older Americans in television commercials', *Journal of Advertising*, 16 (1), 47–54.

Talland, G.A. (1965) 'Imitation of response and reaction true in ageing and with brain damage', in A.T. Welford and J.E. Birren (eds) *Behaviour, Ageing and the Nervous System*. Springfield, IL: Charles L. Thomas, pp. 526–561.

Tamke, S.S. (1978) 'Human values and ageing: The perspective of the Victorian nursery', in S.F. Spicker, K.M. Woodward and D.D. Van Tessel (eds) *Ageing and the Elderly: Humanistic Perspectives in Gerontology*. Atlantic Islands, NJ: Humanities Press.

Tan, A. (1979) 'Why TV is missed: A functional analysis', *Journal of Broadcasting*, 21(3), 371–380.

Taub, H.A. (1974) 'Coding for short-term memory as a function of age', *Journal of Genetic Psychology*, 125(1), 309–314.

Taub, H.A. (1975) 'Mode of presentation, age and short-term memory', *Journal of Gerontology*, 30, 56–59.

Taub, H.A. (1979) 'Comprehension and memory of prose by young and old adults', *Experimental Ageing Research*, 5, 3–13.

Taub, H.A. and Kline, G.E. (1976) 'Modality effects in memory in the aged', *Educational Gerontology*, 1, 53–60.

Taub, H.A. and Kline, G.E. (1978) 'Recall of prose as a function of age and presentation modality', *Journal of Gerontology*, 33, 725–730.

Taylor, R. and Ford, G. (1983) 'Inequalities in old age', *Ageing and Society*, 3(2). 183–208.

Tepper, K. (1994) 'The role of labelling processes in elderly consumers' responses to age segmentation cues', *Journal of Consumer Research*, 20(4), 503–519.

Thomas, K. (1976) 'Age and authority in early modern England', *Proceedings of the British Academy*, 62, 205–248.

Titmuss, R.M. (1955) 'Pension systems and population change', *Political Quarterly*, 26, 152–166.

Tokarski, W. (1993) 'Later life activity from European perspectives', in J.R. Kelly (ed.) *Activity and Ageing – Staging Involved in Later Life*. Newbury Park, CA: Sage, pp. 60–67.

Tongren, H.N. (1988) 'Determinant behaviour characteristics of older consumers', *Journal of Consumer Affairs*, 22(1), 136–157.

Towle, J.G. and Martin, C.R. (1976) 'The elderly consumer: One segment or many?', in B. Anderson (ed.) *Advances in Consumer Research*, Vol. 3. Atlanta, GA: Association for Consumer Research, pp. 463–468.

Treat, N.J., Poon, L.W. and Fozard, J.L. (1981) 'Age, imagery and practice in paired-associate learning', *Experimental Aging Research*, 7, 337–342.

Treat, N.J. and Reese, H.W. (1976) 'Age, pacing and imagery in paired-associate learning', *Developmental Psychology*, 12, 119–124.

Tuchman, J. and Lorge, I. (1953a) 'Attitudes toward old people', *Journal of Social Psychology*, 37, 249–260.

Tuchman, J. and Lorge, I. (1953b) 'When ageing begins and stereotypes about ageing', *Journal of Gerontology*, 8, 489–492.

Tuchman, J. and Lorge, I. (1958) 'Attitude toward ageing of individuals with experience with the aged', *Journal of Genetic Psychology*, 92, 199–204.

TV Dimensions '86 (1986) New York: Buying Time Services.

Uhl, K., Andrus, R. and Paulson, L. (1970) 'How are laggards different? An empirical study', *Journal of Marketing Research*, 7(1), 51–54.

Underhill, L. and Cadwell, F. (1983) 'What age do you feel? Age perception study', *Journal of Consumer Marketing*, 1, 19–21.

Underwood, B.J. and Ekstrand, B.R. (1967) 'Response term integration', *Journal of Verbal Learning and Verbal Behaviour*, 6, 432–438.

Universal Almanac (1991) Harrisburg, VA: The Banta Co.

Ursic, A.C., Ursic, M.L. and Ursic, V.L. (1986) 'A longitudinal study of the use of the elderly in magazine advertising', *Journal of Consumer Research*, 13(1), 131–133.

US Bureau of the Census (1982) 'Preliminary projections of the population of the United States: 1982 to 2050', *Current Population Reports*, series p-25, no. 922. November.

US Bureau of the Census (1984) 'Projections of the population of the United States by age, sex and race: 1983 to 2050', *Current Population Reports*, series p-25, no. 952. Washington, DC: US Government Printing Office.

US Bureau of the Census (1987) 'Projection of the population of the United States by age, sex, and race: 1983–2080', *Current Population Reports*, series p-25, no. 955. Washington, DC: US Government Printing Office.

Valle, K.A. and Lawther, K. (1979) 'Interpersonal trust and attribution of responsibility: Determinants of elderly consumers complaining', in Proceedings of the Division 23 program of the 1978 American Psychological Association meeting, 64–67.

Van Auken, S., Barry, T.E. and Anderson, R.L. (1993) 'Toward the internal validation of cognitive age measures in advertising research', *Journal of Advertising Research*, 33(3), 82–84.

Vernhage, F. (1965) 'Intelligence and age in a Dutch sample', *Human Development*, 8, 238–245.

Veroff, J., Douvan, E. and Kulka, R.A. (1981) *The Inner American*. New York: Basic Books.

Victor, C.R. (1985) 'Welfare benefits and the elderly', in A. Butler (ed.) *Ageing: Recent Advances and Creative Responses*. London: Croom Helm.

Victor, C.R. (1994) *Old Age in Modern Society: Textbook of Social Gerontology*, 2nd edn. London: Chapman & Hall.

Vishvabharanthy, G. and Rink, D.R. (1984) 'The elderly: Neglected business opportunities', *Journal of Consumer Marketing*, 1(4), 35–46.

Walker, A. (1980) 'The social creation of poverty and dependency in old age', *Journal of Social Policy*, 9, 49–75.

Walker, A. (1989) 'The social division of early retirement', in M. Jeffrys (ed.) *Growing Old in the Twentieth Century*. London: Routledge, pp. 73–92.

Walker, A. (1993) 'Poverty and inequality in old age', in J. Bond, P. Coleman and S. Peace (eds) *Ageing in Society: An Introduction to Social Gerontology*. London: Sage, pp. 280–303.

Wall, M., Dickey, L.E. and Talarzyk, W.W. (1977) 'Predicting and profiling consumer satisfaction and propensity to complain', in R.L. Day (ed.) *Consumer Satisfaction, Dissatisfaction and Complaining Behaviour*. Bloomington: Indiana University School of Business.

Ward, T. (1980) Out of sight . . . out of focus. *New Age*, no. 9.

Waugh, N.C. and Barr, R.A. (1980) 'Memory and mental tempo', in L.W. Poon, J.L. Fozard, L.S. Cermak, D. Arenberg and L.W. Thompson (eds) *New Directions in Memory and Aging*. Hillsdale, NJ: Lawrence Erlbaum Associates.

Wechsler, D. (1958) *Measurement of Adult Intelligence*, 4th edn. Baltimore, MD: The Williams and Wilkins Co.

Weisenberg, T., Rose, A. and McBride, K. (1936) *Adult Intelligence*. New York: The Commonwealth Fund.

Welford, A.T. (1958) *Ageing and Human Skill*. Oxford: Oxford University Press.

Welford, A.T. (1980) 'Memory and age: A perspective view', in L.W. Poon, J.L. Fozard, L.S. Cermak, D. Arenberg and L.W. Thompson (eds) *New Directions in Memory and Ageing*. Hillsdale, NJ: Lawrence Erlbaum Associates, pp. 1–17.

Wells, W. and Gubar, G. (1966) 'Life cycle concept in marketing research', *Journal of Marketing Research*, 3, 355–363.

Wenner, L. (1976) 'Functional analysis of TV viewing for older adults', *Journal of Broadcasting*, 20, 77–88.

Westbrook, R.A. (1977) 'Correlates of post purchase satisfaction with major household appliances', in R.L. Day (ed.) *Consumer Satisfaction, Dissatisfaction and Complaining Behaviour*. Bloomington, IN: Indiana University School of Business, pp. 85–90.

Westbrook, R.A. and Fornell, C. (1979) 'Patterns of information source usage among durable goods buyers', *Journal of Marketing Research*, 16(3), 303–312.

Whitbourne, S.K. and Slevin, A.G. (1978) 'Imagery and sentence retention in elderly and young adults', *Journal of Genetic Psychology*, 133, 287–298.

White, N. and Cunningham, W.R. (1982) 'What is the evidence for retrieval problems in the elderly?', *Experimental Ageing Research*, 8, 169–171.

WHO (1989) *Health of the Elderly, Report of a WHO Expert Committee*, Technical Report series 779. Geneva, Switzerland: World Health Organisation.

Wilkes, R.F. (1992) 'A structural modelling approach to the measurement and meaning of cognitive age', *Journal of Consumer Research*, 19, 292–301.

Wilkie, W.L. (1994) *Consumer Behaviour*. New York: Wiley.

Williams, R. (1986) 'Images of age and generation', paper presented at the British Sociological Association Annual Conference, Loughborough University, UK.

Williamson, J. (1978) *Decoding Advertisements*. London: Marion Boyars.

Willoughby, R.R. (1927) 'Family similarities in mental test abilities with a note on the growth and decline of these abilities', *Genetic Psychology Monographs*, 2, 235–277.

Wilson, M. (1991) 'Sixty something', *Chain Store Age Executive*, July, 30–33.

Winograd, E. and Simon, E.W. (1980) 'Visual memory and imagery in the aged', in L.W. Poon, J.L. Fozard, L.S. Cermak, D. Arenberg and L.W. Thompson (eds) *New Directions in Memory and Ageing*. Hillsdale, NJ: Lawrence Erlbaum Associates.

Winograd, E., Smith, A. and Simon, E. (1982) 'Ageing and the picture superiority effect in recall', *Journal of Gerontology*, 37, 70–75.

Wisenblitt, J. (1989) 'The older consumer: Educating the educators', in M.H. Morris (ed.) *Atlantic Marketing Association Proceedings*: volume 5, Orlando, FL, p. 382.

Wober, J.M. (1980) *Television and Old People: Viewing TV and Perceptions of Old People in Real Life and on Television*. London: Independent Broadcasting Authority, Research Report.

Wober, J.M. (1984) *Television and the Ages of Man*. London: Independent Broadcasting Authority, Research Paper.

Wober, J.M. and Gunter, B. (1982) 'Impressions of old people on TV and in real life', *British Journal of Social Psychology*, 21, 335–336.

Wolfe, D.B. (1990) *Serving an Ageless Market*. New York: McGraw-Hill.

Woods, R. (ed.) (1994) *Leisure Futures*, vol.1. London: Henley Centre.

Wright, R.E. (1981) 'Ageing, divided attention and processing capacity', *Journal of Gerontology*, 36, 605–614.

Young, M. and Schuller, T. (1991) *Life After Work – The Arrival of the Ageless Society*. London: Harper Collins.

Zajonc, R.B. (1968) 'The attitudinal effects of media exposure', *Journal of Personality and Social Psychology*, 9 (Monograph Supplement 2), Part 2, 1–27.

Zajonc, R.B. (1970) 'Brain wash: Familiarity breeds comfort', *Psychology Today*, 3, 32–62.

Zaltman, G., Rajendra, K.S. and Rohit, D. (1978) 'Perceptions of unfair marketing practices: Consumerism implications', in H.K. Hunt (ed.) *Advances in Consumer Research*, vol. 5, Ann Arbor, MI: Association for Consumer Research, pp. 247–253.

Zhou, N. and Chen, M. (1992) 'Marginal life after 49: A preliminary study of the portrayal of older people in Canadian consumer magazine advertising', *International Journal of Advertising*, 11, 343–354.

Zimmer, X. and Chappell, N.L. (1996) 'Distinguishing the spending preferences of seniors', *Canadian Journal of Ageing*, 15(1), 65–83.

Name index

Subject index

Lightning Source UK Ltd.
Milton Keynes UK
01 March 2010

150793UK00003B/75/A